Stir Up, O Lord

A Companion to the Collects, Epistles, and
Gospels in the Book of Common Prayer

KEVIN CAREY

Sacristy Press
PO Box 612, Durham, DH1 9HT

www.sacristy.co.uk

First published in 2012 by Sacristy Press, Durham

Sacristy Limited, registered in England & Wales, number 7565667

British Library Cataloguing-in-Publication Data
A catalogue record for the book is available from the British Library

ISBN 978-1-908381-03-3

www.jesus4u.co.uk

For Father George Butterworth

Contents

Foreword
The Very Reverend Michael Sadgrove, Dean of Durham

Anyone who knows Kevin Carey, or has heard him speak in the Church of England's General Synod, will not expect him to be an advocate of comfortable religion. One might think that a book reflecting upon the collects, epistles, and gospels of the Church's year would be a devotional bedside companion.

However, *Stir Up, O Lord* is very different in tone. Indeed the title, drawn of course from the collect for the Sunday before Advent, captures the vigorous, even combative, spirit of Carey's writing. His exposition of the Biblical readings and Prayer Book collects is careful, thorough, and informed by a well-populated theological and cultural hinterland. He is not afraid to take on the texts and argue robustly with them and with the ways in which we have become accustomed to reading them. His spirituality is deeply engaged with the politics and passions of human life. If this book has a programme, it is to see the Anglican spiritual tradition in an adult conversation with what it means to be human in the world, not of the sixteenth or seventeenth centuries, but of today. To accomplish this goal, he brilliantly challenges the easy spirituality that endorses our complacent acceptance of the status quo.

I have the privilege of working in a cathedral where Evensong is sung each day according to the liturgy of the *Book of Common Prayer* (BCP). This great book, which, in its seventeenth century incarnation, celebrates its 350th anniversary in 2012, has formed and shaped the prayers of millions of English-speaking Christians. It is my experience that it continues to do this today, and I am grateful for it, yet we need to understand the historical contexts in which the BCP emerged. Its assumptions take us back to a world that is perhaps more different from ours than we often imagine, and these are implicit not only in the words and phrases of its collects but also in the juxtaposition of the epistles and gospels which they complement and—sometimes—interpret. Carey helps us see this background for what it is, and, where necessary, distance ourselves from it so that we read and pray with integrity as worshippers of our own era.

I implied that this book is not really devotional in character. Perhaps I mean that it is mercifully free of the cloying sentimentality that so often passes for devotional writing. It is in fact profoundly helpful in pointing to a devotion that is serious, critical, catholic, and unafraid of truth-telling. To be devoted to God, to humanity, and to the world in this spirit is precisely the vocation of intelligent, grown-up Christianity. I wholeheartedly commend it and recommend it to every thoughtful Christian.

Michael Sadgrove
Durham Cathedral
Advent, 2011

Preface

The Lectionary of the *Book of Common Prayer* is a product of the theology and politics of its time, not just in the composition of the Collects but in the choice of Epistles and Gospels. These necessarily reflect the issues which most engaged churchmen and statesmen during the period of the sixteenth century after the breach of the Church of England with Rome. The political issues which most occupied the compilers included the nature and seat of authority in Church and state, and the relationship between them, and, entwined with these, the role of the episcopacy. The purely theological, or doctrinal, issues which were of most concern were all dependent upon the recent Protestant Reformation in Europe, and included the relationship between faith and good works, the mechanics of the Eucharist and the atonement, and the efficacy of praying to God through intermediaries such as the Virgin Mary and other saints. Some of the theological politics of the time are reflected in the designation of days so that, for example, Candlemas and Holy Week are absent. Conversely, as it was assumed that the social order was static, there was little concern for social and economic justice, personal responsibility and the limits of personal expression and action. It is also significant that almost all the Collects refer to God as "Almighty" rather than "Loving".

Although Biblical scholarship flowered in the half century before Cranmer and his colleagues set to work, they lacked some information which might have altered their choice of readings: Firstly, they believed that Matthew was the source for Mark rather than an expansion of it; secondly, they assigned all the Epistles to the authors named in their titles; and, thirdly, they tended to think of the Evangelical narratives (the Gospels and Acts) as history rather than theology. The extracts were chosen at precisely the time when there was a radical shift from the late medieval practice of understanding the Bible at many levels to understanding it literally. Indeed, one of the great ironies of the Anglo Saxon Biblical tradition is the practice of praising the *Authorised Version* of the Bible and its associate BCP as great literature while insisting, against the practice of reading such works, that it should be read like a scientific or legal treatise.

Many of the issues which divided medieval Catholicism from Protestant reform now divide worshippers within the Anglican Communion and the Church of England, and it is therefore unwise to assume that all of those who read the AV and the BCP are theologically and temperamentally Protestant, although this is widely and erroneously assumed by many of their adherents. I have tried to describe the differences of outlook between the compilers and theological opinion today with the aim of alerting readers to the understandable but considerable gaps in perception which limit the usefulness of the corpus as a whole: no twenty-first century Lectionary devoted to Sundays and the great Festivals could ignore, for example, Luke's social parables or John's account of Mary Magdalene's encounter with Jesus on Easter morning.

I have tried to keep the duplication to a minimum through cross referencing, but, in a work whose individual commentaries are intended to be self-contained, some repetition is unavoidable, and so I apologise to those brave enough to read my thoughts consecutively. It is not advisable to read these commentaries without a comprehensive Biblical commentary. That which is chosen is largely a matter of personal preference, tradition of witness, and temperament.

With these concerns in mind, it is equally critical that we come to an understanding of how this great work is still relevant in our devotion and broader lives. For many Anglicans it has become part of the backdrop of their devotion and these works contain a wealth of spiritual material that still has great impact some 400 years on. By re-situating these writings within their historical frameworks, and linking their traditional themes with modern ethical and devotional perspectives, we may breathe new life into what many congregations deem passé, enabling them, yet again, to fulfil their primary function of bringing us out of habits of thinking so that we may say, with renewed vigour, "Stir up, we beseech thee, O Lord, the wills of thy faithful people".

Kevin Carey
Hurstpierpoint, West Sussex
The Feast of Saint Luke, 2011

The First Sunday in Advent

Collect   *Almighty God, give us grace that we may cast away . . .*
Epistle   Romans 13.8–14
Gospel   Matthew 21.1–13

Today is the first day of the Church's new year, the day when we begin to follow the life of Jesus from before his birth until his sending of the Holy Spirit at Pentecost. It is the beginning of a season of purple, a time for penitence and preparation, a time when the peace of mind and resolution we need are overwhelmed by contemporary impatience which wants everything celebrated in advance and which, in effect, wants to deny the virtue of delayed gratification.

This is, then, the day for major themes, but sometimes compilers are so deeply conscious of the need to establish surface connections between passages on major days like today that they overlook submerged meanings. Christmas, and therefore its anticipation in advent, was not such an important festival as Easter until the late nineteenth century, but one can hear the writer of the Collect long before then worrying about overindulgence, a theme readily taken up by the ascetic Paul in Romans and echoed in Matthew. Perhaps, too, the compilers thought about the supposed animals in the Christmas stable when they selected Matthew's account of Palm Sunday (with his customary habit of multiplying everything by two, no matter how absurd the outcome), and they might even subconsciously have connected the reference in the Gospel to Jesus as the "Son of David" with our sharp turn towards Bethlehem, the City of David, to which Jesus came "in great humility".

This is the clue to one of the major threads in the three pieces: the Collect contrasts the earthly humility of Jesus with his final coming in "glorious majesty", while the Gospel, noting the prophesy that the Messiah would come in meekness, contrives the bewildering paradox of a king sitting on a donkey, almost as outlandish as a king born in a stable or a saviour crucified.

The most obvious themes are waiting and the emergence from darkness into light. The BCP is less inclined than contemporary lectionaries to countenance periods of waiting for waiting (Sundays before Advent) and its compilers cannot have imagined the phenomenon of Christmas paraphernalia in the shops two months before the Feast of All Saints. In the Collect the waiting is eschatological, contrasting our mortality with our rising to eternal life. In Paul, the waiting is decidedly more visceral, as we live our earthly lives in temptation and fear, and, as usual, Matthew links the two ideas together as the people of Jerusalem wait for their king to make all well, a king who is, theologically, human and divine but who was both earthly king and Messiah to the crowd in Jerusalem.

It is difficult today to fully grasp the true depth of meaning in the metaphors of darkness and light which bring comfort in the middle of Winter, connecting very ordinary concerns with the Incarnation. It is challenging for us to imagine a society powered by candles and oil lamps that might go out at any minute, lights whose intensity was magnified by their scarcity, by the darkness of the hinterland they so feebly pierced. Whereas we think of darkness as the exception, as the environment for sleep but also of villains, for people up until the middle of the nineteenth century darkness was the daily hazard of existence. The Collect calls upon us to cast away the works of darkness and put on the armour of light and Romans says that the night is far spent and the day is close at hand, both comforting, counter-intuitive ideas as we approach the shortest day of the year but a sharp illustration of why Christianity was so keen to absorb the pagan Winter Festival.

That very idea of the pagan is surely behind the message in all three pieces about the desires of the flesh. It is one of those ironies which frequently pushes Christianity to the borders of heresy, that what is quintessentially an incarnational religion lapses into dreadful dualism. There may be very good reasons why Paul abhorred the worldly vices of paganism but surely the author of the Collect was largely surrounded by sober folk whose worst excess was an extra slice of meat on one of the few occasions of the year when it was consumed by poorer folk. One senses here the impulse of incipient Puritanism. On the other hand, the balance is restored by Matthew's attack on the shop keepers, as opposed to the shoppers: another example of a subconscious, highly appropriate message for the season.

The passages are individually and collectively designed to get us kick-started for Advent, to move us forward, to alert us to the need to get ready. However, they lack the counterbalance of calling us to be still, which is a contemporary necessity because of the gargantuan proportions of the contemporary lead-up to Christmas, the time of year when it is most difficult to be alone and to exercise a degree of self-control and delayed gratification. Above all, this is our opportunity to think about the connection between the crib and the Cross so celebrated by medieval carol writers, but lost in the Victorian sentimentalism of the manger.

The Second Sunday in Advent

Collect	*Blessed Lord, who hast caused all holy Scriptures*
	... read, mark, learn and inwardly digest ...
Epistle	Romans 15.4–13
Gospel	Luke 21.25–33

At first glance, the story of salvation is straightforward. Jesus, according to Paul, confirmed the promises of God to the Old Testament leaders, or "fathers", which were also clearly anticipated by the Prophets, particularly Isaiah in such images as the "Rod of Jesse" which is a particularly potent Advent icon. Jesus, as the "Minister of the circumcision of the truth of God", is both the inheritor of the Jewish tradition and the spearhead of the mission to the Gentiles foretold by Isaiah. That message, Luke agrees with Paul (one wonders how often they discussed such matters on their journeys), is extremely urgent because we are about to witness "the second coming", the realisation of the Kingdom, the end of the world as we know it, the "Last Judgment". All of this, says the Collect, echoing Paul, can be discerned through the diligent study (or, in those famous words "read, mark, learn and inwardly digest") of the Scriptures.

Would that it were so simple. The crucial problem in this understanding of the sequence is that we are still here. The letters of Paul and the Synoptic Gospels foretell the passing of our known world within a generation. The signs will be catastrophic, but the actual process will be as simple to discern as the growth cycle of the fig tree: when you see its leaves you know that summer is coming. Equally, when you see these signs and portents you know that the Kingdom is coming. Luke rather spoils this tidiness by ending with the words: ". . . earth will pass away but my words will not pass away." One wonders what use words are outside the context of earth.

The second complication lies in the very core of Paul's Epistle to the Romans which is deeply concerned with the connection between Jewish tradition and the new cult of Christianity, with the terrible friction between modernisers like Paul, who wished to free Gentile Christians from Jewish traditional practices, and conservatives in the Pharisaic tradition who could accept the Resurrection of Jesus but saw it as a manifestation within Judaism. This explains Paul's rather tortuous and often ugly use of the reality and metaphor of circumcision as a metaphor of righteousness: Paul wanted to transfer the tradition of physical circumcision to one of inner dedication. A subsidiary problem here, of which Luke would certainly have been conscious, was the way this metaphor might have struck female Christians who, until the end of the first century, were much more equal with men than they were thereafter.

Just as Paul was dealing with a situation of deep division within the nascent Roman Church, so the *Book of Common Prayer* was forged at a time of serious post-Reformation dislocation, which presents us with our third problem. The Collect implies that there is a simple way of reaching agreement on what Scripture means, a point echoed in the Epistle, and implicitly confirmed in the Gospel. The problem then and now is that this is manifestly not the case, the most egregious example being this very Epistle, which was central to Luther's Reformation challenge, and has been an exegetical and Christological battleground ever since.

This grand narrative, then, presents many problems but the central message of the readings is simple. Our purpose in study and witness is to enliven our hope in eternal life. The Collect, drawing on the Epistle, prays that the "comfort of the Holy Word" might give us hope; and the Epistle goes on to refer to the "God of hope" and wishes that all, filled with joy and peace in believing, should "abound in hope". The Gospel is more concrete, describing "the Son of Man coming in a cloud with power and great glory" for, it says, "your redemption draweth nigh."

The Gospel is peculiarly difficult for us looking from such a distance at what was to be a broken hope. The "Second coming" was pushed ever further into the future; a structured Church became necessary, and hope was re-directed away from Jesus on earth to God in heaven, which, in turn, has led to a dialogue, often of mutual incomprehension, between those who are waiting for the Kingdom and those who believe that "the Kingdom is now". Are we, in other words, living on earth in a kind of celestial ante-room, getting ready to share in the divine presence, or does the idea of "God with us" mean that salvation is with us, is imminent as opposed to anticipated? Whatever the difficulties of this discussion in the Middle Ages, they were greatly complicated by an understanding of Romans which seemed to separate salvation from earthly conduct: if righteousness was somehow predetermined, what was the point of hope?

One of the issues we mentioned last week was how the image of light and dark was much more powerful before gas and electricity. A similar point could be made about the portents in Luke. Most Christians before 1700 were never entirely free of astrology and there was an intense intellectual interest in comets and other heavenly bodies. As children of the

"Enlightenment" we were, until recently, much more sanguine but we seem to be moving into a meteorologically more turbulent age and global news coverage means that we are made immediately aware of storms and volcanic eruptions so that although "tsunami" is now part of our vocabulary we are divided over the causes of climate change.

The Third Sunday in Advent

Collect   *O Lord Jesu Christ, who at thy first coming . . .*
Epistle   1 Corinthians 4.1–5
Gospel   Matthew 11.2–10

People in the sixteenth century were much more concerned than we are today with "degree, priority and place", the belief that society could only cohere if people knew their place and behaved accordingly, a concern reflected repeatedly in Shakespeare's plays. Medieval feudalism had been reinforced in Tudor England by the memory of the disastrous Wars of the Roses and the tendency towards national, absolute monarchy and so today's readings would have had much greater resonance then than they do now.

One of the knottiest issues for all the Evangelists was the relationship between John the Baptist and, according to Luke, his cousin Jesus. Contemporary scholars such as Geza Vermes (*Jesus the Jew*) say that Jesus was one of John's disciples and either broke away because John's message was concerned solely with repentance rather than love, or succeeded John after his arrest. Either way, the changed dynamic between the two is a complex issue, more alive during the time of Jesus than when Matthew was writing.

The central theme of the readings is the primacy of God. Matthew's question in the mouth of John: "art thou he that should come?" is a rhetorical device inviting Jesus' reply. After all, other than his parents, nobody knew more about Jesus than John. Jesus points to what he has said and done rather than making a theological statement, and then, in a note to soften the impact of their changed positions, he blesses those (such as John) who will not be offended in him. Jesus then asks people what they thought they were doing when they went out to see John, a question echoed in Paul's almost obsessive justification of his direct accountability to God without the need for other human agency. No doubt this was partly the result of repeated attacks on him by conservatives who wanted to keep Christianity inside Judaism, but there is also a logistical, geographical explanation; even if Paul had wanted to refer difficult issues back to Jerusalem this would not have been practical in a rapidly growing and evolving church. How accountable "Stewards of the mysteries of God" ought to be is a question which has been with us ever since Paul and it was of particular concern in Tudor times when there was real controversy not only about the role of Ministers in such "mysteries" as the Eucharist, but also a questioning of the validity of bishops. The comparison in the Collect between these Ministers and Stewards and such messengers as John the Baptist is therefore as powerful a claim as the one made by Paul on his own behalf. The issue is especially important to Anglicans who have no settled view on the nature and location of authority within Provinces or the Communion as a whole.

In spite of these rather forbidding and complex themes, the real leitmotif which shines through all three readings is a warning against earthly judgment, a surprisingly "liberal" idea summed up in the anachronistically generous summation of the Collect that: "at thy second coming to judge the world we may be found an acceptable people in thy sight". The Corinthians reading concludes with the equally generous and self-denying: "therefore judge nothing before the time, until the Lord come . . . and then shall every man have praise of God." This last phrase must have raised sharp controversy in the light of Paul's attitude to salvation as understood by Luther and his successors.

The generosity of the first two readings is elaborated by Jesus in reply to John's question. Jesus does not say that he cures the sick or gives sight to the blind in exchange for the statement of a doctrinal position, or even in exchange for an act of penitence. His usual sequence is that faith is a prerequisite and that thanksgiving follows healing. Central to his position is that this good news, or Gospel, is given to the poor. The idea that people were equal in the sight of God regardless of their worldly position was a central pillar of Tudor society.

In a rhetorical figure of enormous colour and power, Matthew asks us all why we are so concerned with the outward manifestations of religion, what do we think it is all for? Do we expect a reed or a man dressed in fine clothes? Of course what we should expect is a prophet. John was the last prophet of the old tradition and, after Jesus who was a prophet of both traditions, Paul was the first prophet of the new tradition. The idea is not that John or "Ministers and Stewards of the mysteries" should anticipate or foretell the future, but that the purpose of John and his successors in Paul and clergy up to this day is to proclaim the Word of God, to bring the good news to the poor.

In an age when every clerical utterance which makes reference to secular social reform is apt to be termed "prophetic", we need to be careful what we mean. In many ways, to speak on behalf of the poor rather than to bring the Gospel to them is being only partially prophetic. Surely the core idea is that we should proclaim the promise of Jesus for all people to all people in as truthful a fashion as we can manage, regardless of the way it might be received and how we might have to suffer for it. John, in prison under the charge of the mercurial Herod, knew all about that.

The Fourth Sunday in Advent

Collect   *O Lord raise up . . . Thy power . . .*
Epistle   Philippians 4.4–7
Gospel   John 1.19–28

In contrast to the secular world which has been thinking of Christmas since its return from Summer holidays, today's Epistle which might, depending on the calendar, be read as late as the day before Christmas, gives the first hint of joys to come. St Paul, in one of his startlingly unusual and brilliant hymns (famously set by Purcell in the *Bell Anthem*) urges us to rejoice. Meanwhile, on Jordan's bank, matters are not so straightforward. John is being quizzed by the clergy who want to know who he is and why he is baptising. His credentials are as important to them as those of Jesus are to us. The natural starting point for any such enquiry was Elijah, the most spectacular of the prophets who ascended into heaven and who, it was widely believed, would appear again as the precursor of the Messiah, and so John was being paid at least a backhanded compliment. Only after Elijah would the Messiah, in the words of the Collect: "raise up [his] power and come among us, and with great might succour us".

Given that there was no mechanism in Judaism for recognising the Messiah when he should come, it is difficult to know whether the clergy, or those who sent them, were pleased or disappointed when they heard John's claim put in the words of Isaiah 40.4. Was he just another holy man, or something special? An ordinary preacher would not threaten the status quo but somebody making broader and deeper claims might destabilise the clerical order, which is precisely the threat for which Jesus was ultimately punished. While Jewish baptism was not uncommon, its practice showed John to be a figure to reckon with. In a culture where water was scarce its cleansing significance was even greater than it is today, a significance heightened by a much more concrete grasp of sin than we experience. The Jewish Law was dense with definitions of sin and liberally sprinkled with cleansing rituals. Some of this very concrete attitude can still be seen in the Collect, which sees sin as a "sore" let and hindrance in running our spiritual race. Today, when personal rites of reconciliation (formerly Confession) are rare, a sense of personal sin has often been replaced by an unfocused uneasiness and perhaps even guilt. It is this very imprecision regarding responsibility which makes Paul's joyful outburst so difficult to take. As a Church we are much better at sadness than joy.

What, then, might these readings for the last Sunday before Christmas have to do with the great event? Firstly, and crucially, the Gospel is very careful with the spiritual genealogy of John and, by implication, the Christ that he foreshadows. The actual genealogies in Luke 3.23–38 and Matthew 1.1–17 serve different theological purposes but they underline the importance of the process: the Messiah had to be properly constituted. Secondly, the Epistle calls upon us to rejoice and, in doing so, to be "careful for nothing" because "the Lord is at hand". Paul meant this to mean that the Philippians should prepare for the end time, for the "last judgment", but we are to understand it as an anticipation of the coming of Jesus. For all its dark overtones, the centre of the Collect also reflects the message of God among us, although the references to power and might fit rather oddly with the image, surely alive in all our minds by now, of a tiny and helpless baby.

For us, at the beginning of the twenty-first century, Paul's words are much more significant than they were in an age which was less affluent and less concerned with Christmas. This is not an age nor a time of moderation, and we might go through half of our life before we meet anyone who is genuinely "careful for nothing". We are not to worry about earthly matters in view of the forthcoming end of the world but, says Paul, we are to make our requests known to God. When secularism is at its most turbulent and treacherous, pretending to serve spiritual ends, it is difficult for us to be moderate, to be indifferent to worldly goods and to pray quietly to God that we may be found worthy of Him at the last.

There is an interesting subconscious link between the texts in the matter of journeys: John quotes Isaiah's words about straightening paths and goes on to talk about Sandals, and the Collect refers to Paul's famous metaphor of the race (1 Corinthians 9.24). Paul himself, by contrast, offers peace which passes all understanding. Whatever races we have all been running in our preparation for Christmas Day, they will soon be over.

Just as Jesus was properly courteous to John last week, here John puts their relationship in context; he baptises with water but Jesus will baptise with the Spirit so that, in the words of the Collect, his: "Bountiful grace and mercy may speedily help and deliver us". The Lord is indeed near at hand.

One final phrase needs to be brought into our consciousness: the peace of God "passeth all understanding". The contrast between what is happening around us and what we are asked to consider could hardly be more stark. In spite of all the material goods which pass before our eyes in the days before Christmas, what we are preparing for is a mystery.

The Nativity of Our Lord
or the Birthday of Christ, Commonly Called Christmas Day (December 25)

Collect	*Almighty God, who hast given us thy only-begotten son . . .*
Epistle	Hebrews 1.1–12
Gospel	John 1.1–14

The beginning of the Gospel of John, one of the best known and loved passages in the whole of Scripture, encapsulates a Christian paradox: that we grasp the historical reality and the salvific significance of the incarnation, while contemplating it as a glorious and wonderful mystery. This beginning links being in time with being out of time because the godly nature of Jesus is timeless, whereas his human nature was in time; in the beginning was the Word and in time it was made flesh. The reading from Hebrews is concerned with the position of Christ when he returned to heaven from earth, exploring the motif of Christ the King.

This leaves the humble Collect with the whole burden of the Christmas message that Jesus was born of "a pure virgin." We may need to anticipate the average churchgoer's sense of disappointment on Christmas morning, head full of stars, mangers and shepherds, when served with this esoteric fare, but there are three factors we might want to explain, however briefly. Firstly, in Reformation England Christmas was not a major Church or civil festival and only became so in the late nineteenth and early twentieth century. Secondly, and related to this, the Victorian carol transformed the common perception from high doctrinal seriousness to cloying sentiment. Thirdly, although the doctrine of the incarnation has never been other than fundamental, there was then a far greater concern with the atonement, as witnessed in the Collect which does not designate us the natural children of God, but only children by adoption as the result of the acknowledged incarnation and implied crucifixion. There was, too, the additional factor of a more astringent theological climate, reacting both against an excessive late medieval Marianism, and a related devotion to angels and saints.

Hebrews, too, is deeply suspicious of angels. When these readings were compiled it was still believed that St Paul wrote this letter, but we now know it to have been written perhaps a century later. This explains its concern with combating the ubiquitous heresy of gnosticism which sought to exalt the spirit at the expense of the physical, casting an odd and unfavourable light on the concept of incarnation. The text hedges its bets in a number of ways, the most prominent of which are the emphasis on the heavenly life of Jesus before the incarnation and after the Resurrection, the emphasis on the transience of all physical things, and the use of grammar which, subconsciously at least, fuses the "persons" of Father and Son.

It would be wrong to dismiss the major theological concerns already mentioned, but how do they accord with contemporary sentiment? Firstly, by contrast with an age which showed little concern for economic or social justice, once we have seen past the sentimentality of the baby, we are inclined to focus on the helpless Jesus as a symbol of all human poverty, injustice and helplessness. Secondly, we are more conscious of the post-Reformation history of Anglicanism, whose wings might be characterised as respectively focused on the incarnation and the atonement, although there has naturally been, Anglicanism being what it is, a third tendency to emphasise and strengthen the links between the two: there is no Crucifixion without incarnation. Thirdly, it would be unrealistic for us to live our Christmas without any reference to the world in which we live. That being so, we are more likely than our Tudor and Stuart forebears to think about the relationship between the incarnation and society.

Paradoxically, what we might be less inclined to think about seriously is the very nature of incarnation. Our world is so materialist that we are often in danger of being driven into dualism, into the heresy of the gnostics; excess generates its own reaction. We might also be less awestruck by the image of light in John, surrounded as we are by artificial light to such an extent that our children may never know complete darkness. We are also less caught up with the imagery in John and Hebrews of a quasi-physical place called heaven.

Nonetheless, these readings, in spite of their apparent misalignment with our times, contain the essence of who we are as Christians and how we should frame ourselves on one of the three most important days of our year. Jesus was born, died for us and rose from the dead, and these earthly events were an infusion of our timeless God into the world. It would be hard on us to linger too long on the second of those three days (although the Christmas tree symbolises the union of light and death), yet Christmas without Good Friday is inconceivable. It must be a source of pain to all Christians that so many people come to church to celebrate this festival but do not stay the course, through Lent to Calvary and Emmaus.

Today it might be easiest, surrounded by the Christmas we have forged for ourselves in the secular world, to focus on the child who came to bring good news to the poor, but unless we see this event within its infinite and mysterious context, we will only have grasped a fraction of its meaning. The sheer wonder of John's two great proclamations, that in the beginning was the Word and that the Word was made flesh and dwelt among us, can only be realised if we consider them together. That is his genius and our rendezvous with mystery.

Saint Stephen's Day
(December 26)

Collect	*Grant, O Lord, that in all our*
	sufferings here upon earth . . .
For The Epistle	Acts 7.55–60
Gospel	Matthew 23.34–39

St Stephen, the first recorded Martyr, has the most meteoric career in the whole of the New Testament. He appears at the beginning of Acts 6, elected as one of seven Deacons to serve at table so that the Apostles might devote their lives to "higher things". He is seized by the religious authorities, proclaims a blistering testimony of Jesus in front of his persecutors which occupies the whole of Chapter 7, and is stoned to death in the sight of Saul for blatant blasphemy.

The distinction between those chosen to bear witness to Christ through serving the poor and those who dedicate their time to prayer would seem to be somewhat stark (some would argue it was the beginning of the Church's decline from Grace), particularly in view of Stephen's testimony which equals any recorded by Luke from the mouth of Peter or other leaders. He unfolds the Jewish sacred tradition, showing how it connects seamlessly with the life and witness of Jesus, and in his particular devotion to the Holy Spirit he is comprehensively and coherently Trinitarian. He is a scholar as well as a waiter.

That tradition from Abel (a somewhat curious figure in this context) to Jesus has its darker side, described by Matthew. Prophets are uncomfortable witnesses of God's Word, and the Jews, so enmeshed in their moral and religious legalism, frequently punished those sent to warn them. In the case of Jesus, that traditional clash between the Word and the Law was compounded by the lack of a mechanism in the tradition to discern the presence of the longed-for Messiah. Thus, Jesus was killed because he would not deny a Messianic claim, and when Stephen set out the same claim and reinforced it by reference to classical Judaism, his fate was sealed.

The passages in Matthew and Acts both underline the gravity of what was at stake and the harshness of the conflict this entailed. The natural conservatism of long observance made it difficult for the Jews to respond to the call for religious transformation proclaimed by Zacharias, Jesus and Stephen, and, as the Collect points out in an elegant encapsulation of Acts, the missing element was a failure to heed the promptings of the

Holy Spirit. The warning is timely when so much of our recent attention has necessarily been concerned in Advent with the purposes of creation, and at Christmas with the mystery of the Incarnation, because it is only through the Spirit that we can be nurtured in our witness through the Church of which Stephen was a founder.

Luke, characteristically, depicts a link between the earthly Stephen and the heaven for which he is shortly bound; a link which is only possible through an intense witness of mind and body, opening a channel through which the power of the Spirit may flow from heaven to earth. This enabling is the fruit of the sending of the Spirit after the Ascension of Jesus and contrasts sharply with the palpable loneliness and hardship of prophets like Zacharias. We, as members of the Church, living in the power of the Spirit, are provided with that very mechanism of recognition which the Jews of the Old Testament, and the contemporaries of Jesus who figure in Matthew's bleak assessment, lacked. This places upon us a responsibility for witness as awesome as the means with which we have been provided.

The Collect draws attention to the idea, exemplified in Stephen, of steadfastness in the face of earthly suffering. Most of us will never have to undergo his ordeal but in times of trouble we should stay faithful for, we are reminded in Matthew, Jesus wants to gather us under his wing "as a hen gathereth her chickens under her wings", but, the passage continues ominously, "ye would not; behold, your house is left unto you desolate."

Other than Stephen's winning combination of humility and eloquence, the quality that stands out, noted in the Collect, is his forgiveness of his persecutors. This is not the healing forgiveness of tranquillity nor the cold, measured forgiveness of the self-righteous, but forgiveness in the terrible moment. It resembles the forgiveness of Jesus on the Cross but is much more dramatic. Crucifixion was such a notoriously slow process that Pilate wondered that Jesus died so quickly (Mark 15.44), but stoning was sharp and short, carrying with it a degree of direct personal contempt which is only vicarious in crucifixion. Stephen looked up to heaven and forgave, which means, in this context, that he was commending his murderers to God, praying that they might join him in heaven: he could not, even in death, stop serving his fellow humans.

How often do we look up to heaven, beyond the text, beyond the prayer, stretching our imagination into areas of risk, or even danger? Stephen took the risk and saw "the Son of Man standing on the right hand of God." After that, the stones could not come soon enough nor hard enough for either party. The Jewish authorities were outraged and frightened; Stephen was exultantly at peace. He had seen his final destination. We do not have that privilege, but the extent to which we can be drawn into the mystery depends upon our openness to the Spirit.

Saint John the Evangelist's Day
(December 27)

Collect	*Merciful Lord, we beseech thee to cast thy bright beams of light . . .*
Epistle	1 John 1.1–10
Gospel	John 21.19–25

Many scholars doubt that one person wrote the five works attributed to "John": the Gospel of St John, the Letters of John 1–3, and the Book of Revelation of St John the Divine. These doubts are based on grammar, style and lexicography, but could one man have laid down his nets at the Sea of Galilee, be well connected with the priestly class in Jerusalem, stand at the foot of the Cross, write Revelation at the turn of the first century, and die in Ephesus c. AD 105? Such speculations do not affect the validity of John's propositions, which the Collect somewhat sententiously refers to as "doctrine"; the Bible is an indivisible corpus regardless of questions of authorship.

The choice of texts indicates a Tudor belief in Johannine authorial coherence: the Collect describes John as an "Apostle and Evangelist", thus accepting his extended lifespan. 1 John uses phrases such as "which we have seen with our eyes", "which was manifested unto us" and "that which we have seen and heard", and John's Gospel recounts a scene from the Last Supper played out after the Resurrection, underscored with a specific witness statement which some might think too pointed to be plausible.

The Collect prays that the light of God may shine upon the Church, perhaps implicitly referring to the turmoil in the Churches of the Book of Revelation and the Letters, yet 1 John is serenity itself. What immediately strikes home is the sharp contrast between the serenity of the Letters and the Gospel on the one hand, and the near hysteria of Revelation on the other.

There is something rather uncomfortable in the conversation between Jesus, Peter and John, an element of something akin to competitiveness. There was a time when this might have been over-emphasised, when the Western Church asserted the Biblical primacy of the Pontificate and, later, when that primacy was contested. However, it is generally agreed now that it would never have occurred to the John of Revelation, writing to the Seven Churches, that there was a centralising authority in Rome in succession to Peter.

John's most telling metaphor (cf. The Nativity of our Lord) is the antithesis between light and darkness which was much stronger before the age of artificial light than it is now. A person living alone might drop a candle and be cast into complete darkness or set his flimsy house on fire. Light was not only a massively powerful metaphor for the good and the glorious, it also contained elements of risk, as do all vital regenerative forces. Loving God without risk seems inconceivable. Echoing Psalm 119.105, the antithesis of the metaphor is driven home in the Letter: "God is light, and in him is no darkness at all." This is contrasted with the conclusion: "if we say we have not sinned, we make him a liar and his word is not in us." What might be said about our post-industrialisation view of light might equally be said about our post-"Enlightenment" view of sin. It is important for us in the depth of winter to imagine a world without light and a world which was much more deeply conscious of sin as a barrier to salvation.

All this having been said, the central point of our remembrance is John the Evangelist, the writer of the fourth Gospel which Burridge (*John*) sums up as "*sui generis*". Biblical criticism today tends to make a less sharp division between this and the Synoptics, but the "high" Christology which it contains is both intense and uniquely imaginative. Burridge writes that what John says about the trinity, the link between earth and heaven wrought by the incarnation, and the Grace of God are, it may be argued, beyond doctrine, because they are sharply concerned with what Jesus said and did, rather than with what it might mean and how the sacred mysteries are effective. It is out of such controversies that this Book was born.

Some have likened John 21 to the last of T.S. Eliot's *Four Quartets*, *Little Gidding*, but there are now many who say that this chapter was an Epilogue written much later than the end of the First Century. Whatever the case, it is certainly much less elegant than all that precedes it. However, what we need to carry with us is the joy, noted in the Letter, within which we look to God as we seek to live in the light made sharper by the shadow of the Cross, at whose foot John stood. If, in the words of the Letter, "we walk in the light, as he is in the light, we have fellowship one with another, and the blood of Jesus Christ his son cleanseth us." The origins of the testimony of John may now appear to be somewhat problematic but the nascent theology could not be clearer. What we must value above all is the metaphysical dimension which John provides as an enriching counterpoint to the narrative of the life and sayings of our saviour. While it might just be possible for sceptics to reduce Our Lord to a holy man who went about saying wise things and doing good, John, from the opening of his Gospel (cf. The Nativity of our Lord) until he lays down his pen in today's Gospel, is equal to St Paul as one of our founding theologians.

The Innocents' Day
(December 28)

Collect   *Almighty God, who out of the mouths*
                    of babes and sucklings . . .
For The Epistle   Revelation 14.1–5
Gospel   Matthew 2.13–18

This is the fourth day of the Octave of Christmas but the first time we have read a Christmas narrative. It begins after the wise men have first met Herod, visited Jesus and then left him, going home without revisiting Herod. In Matthew, the angel appears to Joseph (cf. Luke 1.26 where the angel appears to Mary) and warns him of the threat from Herod. Typical of Matthew, the place of exile is determined by a cryptic and obscure prophetic citation; there are literally scores of prophetic pronouncements about Egypt. The Holy Family remains there until Herod's death, some two years later. Meanwhile Herod, in a direct echo of the fate of the Egyptian first males in Exodus 11, causes all boys under the age of two, not just the first born, to be killed in fulfilment of an obscure saying of Jeremiah.

The events themselves, as they are written, are highly unlikely. The recorded life of Herod shows him perfectly capable of such a cruel deed, but his arbitrary powers were limited, and such a massacre would have been recorded and long resented. The doings of an artisan family, even reported to Herod by visitors, would hardly have triggered a reaction much more fierce than that which met occasional Messianic uprisings. That same obscurity would have made exile both unlikely and unnecessary.

We therefore need to look at Matthew's theological purpose in constructing his narrative. The place to start is his genealogy at the beginning of Chapter 1, which draws a stylised line from Abraham to Joseph (whereas Luke's stylised line begins with Adam and casts doubt on Joseph's parenthood). Primarily, Matthew wants to establish a direct link between the birth of Jesus and the liberation of the Jews from Egypt, and so he invokes memories of Exodus by taking Jesus to Egypt so that he may return from it to Israel. Secondly, he wishes to contrast the sordid and tyrannous nature of earthly kingship with the love and glory of the divine kingship of Jesus. Thirdly, he tries to reinforce the sacred genealogy of Jesus by citing Rachel, possibly the most sympathetic woman in the whole of Genesis, and the mother of Joseph who, again, has strong connections with Egypt. It is best in these circumstances not to be too concerned with the historicity of the narrative, but to read the whole passage, with its mass of internal and possibly subconscious cross-references, as an intricate piece of Christological poetry. It tells us about our liberation from the tyranny of Egypt and, by extension, from the tyranny of sin. It warns of bloodshed which will descend upon the faithful arbitrarily (as it was doing when Matthew wrote). It speaks of exile, experienced by the Jews, by Jesus, and by many of Matthew's contemporaries after the dispersion of the Christian Church, as well as the Jewish Temple cult from Jerusalem in AD 70. Lastly, and critically, it offers a schematic and intricate link between the two Testaments.

This broad interpretation of Matthew explains the apparently eccentric choice of the passage of Revelation for the Epistle. The Lamb, who is Christ, is being followed, "whithersoever He goeth" (including into exile) by the 144,000; clearly a reference to the patriarchs and prophets of old. A new song is sung before the Lamb and also, in an echo of Daniel, before the elders and the four beasts. What spoils this exotic tableau is the reference to the saved as virgins "not defiled by women", a decidedly odd approbation on a feast to celebrate infants.

As for those infants, the Collect somewhat muddies the waters by saying that infants glorify God by their deaths when the reference in Psalm 8.2 clearly states that mouths of babes and sucklings praise the

Lord because he has seen off the enemy, which is certainly not the case in Matthew. It then goes on to use the word "innocence" to mean penitent, as opposed to not yet capable of responsibility.

In spite of the textual eccentricities the central message is clear, but Matthew's story is only a pretext; the Innocents are simply a narrative device for one of Matthew's many discussions of kingship. Christ, the Lamb, is contrasted with Herod the infanticide, and his rich and glorifying heavenly kingdom is contrasted with the den of paranoia which Herod inhabited. In the mouths of the elders in Revelation there is no guile, but Herod says one thing and does something else.

Another theme which has recently come into prominence because of our contemporary condition is the thought of Jesus and his earthly parents as exiles. For the Jews, Egypt was as bad as it got. The whole of the Old Testament is a dialogue between God and His Chosen People, mirrored in the internal dynamics of their faithfulness and unfaithfulness, and in the external contrast between their faithfulness and the idolatry of Egypt. In considering the contrast between host and guest we are perhaps too apt to notice how different exiles are from us instead of imagining how different we are from them. We, after all, no matter how jaundiced, view them from the comfort of our own cultural background, whereas they view us from a standpoint of bewilderment and loss. We resent them, but they resent their exile. This is but one example of how changing circumstances enable us to find different lessons in our sacred texts.

The Sunday after Christmas Day

Collect   *Almighty God, who hast given us*
               thy only-begotten son . . .
Epistle   Galatians 4.1–7
Gospel   Matthew 1.18–25

Matthew's approach to the birth of Jesus is, with the exception of the angel, rather male and down-to-earth, stressing the importance of the paternal line through Joseph in spite of Jesus' being born of the Holy Ghost. Joseph, equally concerned about his family's honour and Mary's reputation, is determined to keep her pregnancy secret until he is told of its origin. In contrast with Mary's role in Luke, Joseph receives the message from the angel in a dream. Matthew, as usual, justifies these events with a quotation from Scripture, Isaiah 7.14, though whether there is any significance in the customary virginity of an unmarried Jewish girl is questionable. Joseph marries Mary and it is interesting to note that Matthew does not rule out the possibility that Jesus had younger siblings.

Paul is not quite so straightforward because of his characteristic clumsiness with analogy. The first sentence of the Epistle serves only to confuse except insofar as it establishes that there is a state of childhood in which we are helpless. Essentially he is saying that the Jews (as representative in some way of humanity) were subject to the Law until they were liberated from it by the birth and death of Jesus to become adopted sons of the Father. As sons, we receive the Holy Spirit and are no longer servants but heirs. The Collect takes up the theme of regeneration and adoption in the Holy Spirit.

Not surprisingly, the key themes in the readings concern parentage. Joseph's mind is put at rest by the Angel, but also indirectly by Matthew's introductory genealogy, which at a critical point involves questionable sexual relations. Examples abound, including Rahab, who was possibly prostitute (1.5), Ruth, a Moabitess (1.6), and Bathsheba (1.6), the mother of Solomon after her marriage to David who had committed adultery with her and then ordered the death of her husband, Uriah the Hittite. A more fundamental and uncomfortable question concerns the doctrine of the "Virgin Birth". Is this an instance of Matthew finding a proof text for events, or is it, conversely, Matthew's misreading of Isaiah which determines the shape of his narrative? As the doctrine is contained in the Creed we must necessarily assent to it, but the question must still be asked, as all statements of doctrine, no matter how hallowed, being humanly formed, are provisional. The oddity of this doctrine is that it tends towards the very dualism that the incarnation denies.

The other issue of parentage which looms large in the Collect and Epistle is our own. The notion of adoption presents us with a theological conundrum. We are all children of God Our Parent but when, in the figure of Adam, we were expelled from Eden, did we lose that parentage as creatures of the creator? Paul asserts that we did, but goes on to say that we have been adopted as a result of the incarnation. The Collect, in line with Reformation theology, situates the adoption in the Crucifixion. The theological understanding of our childhood in God may be put in a simpler form than the theology of adoption; just because we "fell" or turned away from God or, in Paul's terminology, became subject to the Law, it does not mean that we ceased to be God's children. A further issue with the adoption metaphor is that it forces us to ask whether all humanity was adopted as a result of the incarnation, or was this a privilege accorded only to Christians, or even only to some Christians. The first question was hardly addressed by Reformation theologians but the second became critical, particularly to Calvin, who made explicit what had previously been implicit, that only "the elect" were saved by Christ's death.

The Collect, first read on Christmas Day, now falls into its proper context by saying that God sent his son "to take our nature upon him". Whatever the complexities of Matthew's narrative and Paul's generative theology, the fact of the incarnation stands out in monumental relief. As already noted, the essence of this doctrine is that it unites rather than divides the human and divine, a concept so difficult for the early Church that it took some four centuries to crystallise into the "one person, two natures" doctrine of the Council of Chalcedon (AD 451). There were extremists of both sorts asserting that Jesus was not human, or only human, and others, bearing in mind the Grecian deities, who proposed that he was a demigod. The very difficulty of the formulation, its quasi political nature, and its Greek philosophical context, should all warn us of the fragility of our human metaphors for divine mysteries. We are too apt to recite the Creed in much the same way as we recite the multiplication table, but each phrase of it, for all its provisionality, was hard won. One way of looking at the incarnation is that the very difficulty of humanity coming to terms with the Godhead was critically mediated by Jesus, who literally embodied God's self-communication with all mankind. Again, this understanding emphasises the universality of the act rather than particularising it to all or some Christians.

Opinions will differ but we might be comforted by the thought that Jesus was not an only child. In accordance with Chalcedonian thinking we must try to remember the humanity of our Saviour who, like all of us, needed the warmth and security of family love. It is almost too easy to write: our Saviour who, like all of us.

The Circumcision of Christ

(January 1)

Collect	*Almighty God, who madest thy blessed*
	son to be circumcised . . .
Epistle	Romans 4.8–14
Gospel	Luke 2.15–21

Renaissance painting, the English Pastoral, and a certain degree of sentiment have combined to make much more of Luke's shepherds than is justified, thus undermining his main point. At the time of Jesus, shepherds were the lowest of the low. They did not own their flocks, they bore the extreme heat of the day and the cold of the night, and they were often on the move because of the extreme scarcity of grass. (The Carol, for once, is accurate when it says, "On the lonely mountain steep".) Worst of all, their occupation condemned them to an almost permanent state of ritual uncleanliness. They were held in a similar degree of contempt as travelling folk are today (cf. The Second Sunday after Easter). It was these social outcasts who were the first to hear the good news and they were the first to worship an infant scarcely better off than they. Of course, they wanted to share the news (and perhaps enjoy the rare experience of being the centre of attention and being bought food and drink) but the public reaction is beautifully poised in the word "wondered".

Enter Mary, the victim of a Reformation reaction against late medieval Marian excess (cf. The Nativity of our Lord), for the first time in her own right but with no speaking part. By tradition, Luke is supposed to have known Mary, and his sentence, "Mary kept all these things, and pondered them in her heart" (repeated in 2.51), and Simeon's promise at 2.35a (cf. The Presentation of Christ in the Temple), have fixed the character of Mary in spite of contrary evidence, particularly in John (19.26–27) who might be supposed to have known her better. To have so promptly responded to Gabriel and no doubt put up with sceptical jibes about her conception before marriage ("Holy Ghost! Pull the other one!") must surely have required a certain degree of mental toughness.

Luke's account of the circumcision itself is cursory (compared, for instance, with that of his cousin John 1.59–79) but its significance is neatly summed up in the Collect's phrase: "obedient to the law for man." It then turns rather gloomy after briefly praying for the "circumcision of the spirit" (one of Paul's favourites) before praying that "our hearts, and all our members, being mortified from all worldly and carnal lusts, we may in all things obey. . ". In spite of some linguistic decorousness it is difficult to avoid the conclusion that the author, writing on the theme of circumcision, is specifically thinking about sexual lust. It might be useful in this context to bear in mind that the sixteenth century witnessed a sharp tightening of sexual morality. This was in part because one of the more unfortunate consequences of transatlantic exploration was the export from Europe, with devastating effect, of endemically mild diseases such as influenza to the Americas, and the import of endemically mild sexually transmitted diseases—notably syphilis—which did not wreak the same havoc, but certainly shook the culture permanently (in the way, for example, that HIV/AIDS caused panic, though only fleetingly). Given the precariousness of lineage and the vagaries of medicine, the apparently excessive concern with sexual lust over other sins is understandable.

Mercifully, the Collect's theme is not picked up from Paul, who is concerned with one of the central issues of Romans, the relationship between Jewish and gentile Christians. Having received the training it is understandable that his approach is somewhat Pharisaical; he says that because Abraham believed in God before he was circumcised, Abraham is therefore the father of all true believers, whether Jews or gentiles, and not just of the Jews who count him as the father of their race. Time and again Paul makes this point in different ways to try to keep the infant Church united, often getting himself into the most painful linguistic contortions. Put simply, the message of Romans, here and elsewhere, is that what counts is the "righteousness of faith" in Jesus and not circumcision under "the law of man". He concluded, with another quasi-legal argument, that if those who simply observe Jewish Law are the true heirs of Abraham, then faith counts for nothing.

Although the Jews were by no means the only people in the Eastern Mediterranean to practice circumcision, they seem to think they were, and the whole of their Scripture from Abraham onwards contains numerous references to the purity of the circumcised and the impurity of the uncircumcised, but, like all such grand motifs, it is easy to forget its significance and simply concentrate on the thing itself. The account in Genesis (17.1–14) tells of the founding covenant between God and Abram (re-named Abraham) and contains the arresting phrase: "my covenant in your flesh shall be an everlasting covenant." Every male child was physically bound up in that covenant history, literally for life. And "for life" in another way too because God linked the command of circumcision with the fruitfulness of his people. Directly after the circumcision edict, God promises Abraham that his wife Sarai (re-named Sarah) will have a baby (17.15–16).

The Christian and secular calendars run their separate courses, but on this New Year's Day we might leave the last word with the shepherds who, when they heard the good news, "came in haste", "made known abroad the saying which was told them concerning this child", and "returned, glorifying and praising God for all the things that they had heard and seen". We could hardly make better resolutions than to imitate the spontaneity, missionary zeal, and gratitude of those humble shepherds.

The Epiphany
or the Manifestation of Christ to the Gentiles (January 6)

Collect	O God, who by the leading of a star . . .
Epistle	Ephesians 3.1–12
Gospel	Matthew 2.1–12

By one of the quirks of the calendar we read about the Innocents before we reach the Epiphany (cf. The Innocents' Day). Wise men, "Three Kings" according to tradition, probably astrologers, saw something curious in the sky. Their origin is somewhat clouded by Matthew saying they came from the East, but followed a star to the East. It is more plausible that they saw a star from where they were in the East (the gifts suggest the Arabian Peninsular), but the main purpose is to demonstrate the exotic nature of the visitors. Matthew also wants to contrast these venerable men with the wicked Herod. One can see why the news might have troubled him, but why "all Jerusalem"? Part of the answer is that Judaism lacked a mechanism for recognising the Messiah. It preferred, to paraphrase T.S. Eliot, to travel rather than to arrive; it preferred waiting for the Messiah to proclaiming him. As a decent scholar, Herod knew perfectly well where Christ should be born, but the question gives Matthew the opportunity to refer to the prophetic foundation for his narrative (probably Micah 5.2). Herod, behaving like a pantomime baddie, is already plotting to kill the child but the wise men outwit him. They worship Jesus and bring gifts traditionally associated respectively with kingship, priesthood, and burial (Nicholas King: The New Testament).

Before leaving the Christmas narratives we might wish to contrast the mystical and demotic Luke with the down-to-earth and political Matthew. These are the only two accounts we have and, with the exception of the intervention of an angel and the attribution of Mary's conception to the Holy Spirit, they do not overlap. As always, I find Geza Vermes illuminating (*The Nativity*).

This is a very special day for us, as designated in the sub-title of the Feast of "the Manifestation of Christ to the Gentiles". Judaism is not a missionary religion, and so the decision to preach Jesus to the Gentiles (Acts 15) was a remarkable proceeding without which Christianity might have disappeared with the Jerusalem Temple in AD 70. We should not forget, as Paul glories in his self-designation of "Apostle to the Gentiles", that Peter's testimony, following his conversion of Cornelius (Acts 10), was critical.

Paul says he must preach the Mystery of Christ "which in other ages was not made known unto the sons of men", which "from the beginning of the world hath been hid in God", as it is now revealed. Part of that revelation was that the Gentiles should be "fellow heirs" of the Gospel. The formal declaration confirmed Paul's view, but he had long held it and he is always careful to maintain his direct authority from Christ, for it was better to be "less than the least of all saints," than to be accountable to the religious conservatives in Jerusalem (Galatians 1.12). The end point, as the Collect notes, is that we "may after this life have the fruition of thy glorious Godhead".

For us the wise men present a paradox. We have in general lost our faith in wise men, both because of failures following an inflated view of the power of science, and because there is a contemporary aversion to ranking one opinion higher than another. However, we are more openly astrological than at any time since the "Enlightenment". Wise men tend to appear in accounts of different, usually oriental, cultures and perhaps it is part of Matthew's intention to stress the contrast between scruffy Palestine and the opulent East. Tradition has made a good deal of this sparse raw material, and one aspect of it which is particularly attractive today is the multi-ethnic origin of "the kings". Another attractive feature, noted in Matthew, is the domesticity of the scene. The kingly trio, back stage left of the crib, is profoundly misleading. The travellers visit Jesus in his home presumably some time after his birth and before the exile. It is easy, between the crib and the cross, to forget the domestic Jesus who, if we count in both the exile and a three-year mission, spent more than 80% of his life at home. We might also speculate on what

Mary and Joseph did with the gold.

One further aspect of the readings which bears consideration is the juxtaposition of earthly and heavenly powers. Christianity, unlike other major religions, has always had an uneasily equivocal relationship with the secular powers. The early Church was naturally anxious not to alienate the Roman authorities and preached a doctrine of obedience to the state, cited in the sixteenth century by a series of political (some would say Erastian) settlements which put the secular monarch at the head of national churches. The contrast, then, is not so sharp as it might be between earthly and heavenly powers, with the exception of caricature figures like Herod, who just happened to be in the wrong place at the wrong time. Since the eruption of Roman internecine politics into Palestine in the figure of Pompey the Great in 65 BC, the not unfriendly relations between Rome and Palestine (1 Maccabees 8) came to an end and the economically insignificant but strategically important territory suffered the collateral damage of a series of "world wars" which ended with the Emperor Augustus. Herod was not to know that, and his position was made precarious by Augustus' being proclaimed a god. Faced with this degree of complexity, Jesus' visitors were not only wise in following the intimation of his birth but also in leaving, once their mission was accomplished, by another way.

The First Sunday after the Epiphany

Collect   *O Lord, we beseech thee mercifully*
                  to receive the prayers . . .
Epistle   Romans 12.1–5
Gospel   Luke 2.41–52

We are not, says Paul, to think of ourselves more highly than we ought, one of those nice phrases similar to "she is no better than she ought to be". It all boils down to a somewhat overlooked basic question behind the aphorisms: how well ought we to think of ourselves? Having established this point, we can then try to avoid excess. The Collect takes a slightly different angle by referring to our actions rather than to the thoughts generated by our whole, rather complex selves, when it prays that we should "perceive and know" what things we ought to do.

The Gospel is not much help in trying to solve this problem, because it presents us with one of those occasions when the divinity and humanity of Jesus become entangled in the same narrative. Do we not experience a rather uncomfortable feeling that the human Jesus would not have got away with the conduct which the divine Jesus was able to justify? As we can only aspire to behave like Jesus, we are left by the Collect and Epistle with our problem, to which we will have to return in due course.

Luke begins by saying that the parents of Jesus went up to Jerusalem every year for the Passover. This statement is not easy to accept at face value if the Holy Family lived at Nazareth rather than Bethlehem, as this would have involved more than two weeks of expenditure without income. Jesus might, however, have gone up for the Passover with his parents in the year of his coming to manhood. Luke still refers to him as "the child Jesus" and the confusion as to his whereabouts on the return journey arises because, until he was a man, he could travel with either the men or the women. After a day's travel when the two groups came together to eat, they found that Jesus was not there, at which point normal parental panic set in. They forgot that their child was in some way special or, as we might put it, divine. Instead of thinking, "remember the angel that we each saw; he is bound to be under God's protection, let us not worry", they turned about and went to Jerusalem. Having arrived there, they again forgot who their son was, the kind of person they had heard he was destined to be, and so it took three days before the penny dropped and they went to the Temple. Mary rebuked Jesus and he replied, not very graciously, that he must be about his Father's business. Luke said, in a statement of deep discomfort, that they did not understand his reply but, in one of his favourite phrases, Mary stored all of this up in her heart (cf. The Circumcision of Christ) and they went home and we hear nothing of Jesus for almost two decades.

What are we to make of the reaction of his parents? The obvious answer is that Luke had not worked out the status of Jesus with the same theological precision declared some 400 years later at the Council of Chalcedon (451). According to that doctrine, resting on the famous Kenotic phrase of Paul (Philippians 2.5–8), Jesus as a man put his divinity by. Jesus was therefore not supposed to have been more theologically gifted than the any other man. He might have been more gifted than his peers because he was inclined towards religious studies, but Luke definitely leans towards a Jesus in this story who is behaving in a quasidivine way, displaying learning that astonishes his audience. That ambivalence would explain the puzzled parental reaction. They had a special child but were not clear in what way he would be special. Luke, with the benefit of hindsight, could look back at the childhood. All Mary and Joseph knew was that his birth had been highly irregular, but that they had been reassured by divine intervention that it was all for the best. You try to bring up your child properly and when you think that he has misbehaved he claims divine exception!

This story is also important because it underlines Luke's literary device of situating the centre of his two-volume narrative in the Temple until the final critical shift to Rome. What were the elders to make of the learning of this boy? Their puzzlement surely prefigures their reaction to Jesus the man. Here is a figurative foretaste of what is to come.

As all three readings are in some way concerned with "good conduct", we should note their antitheses: the Collect gives us the power to perceive and know but calls upon God to give us "the grace and power to fulfil the same". Paul says that we should not conform to this world, but should be transformed by the renewing of our minds, and the Gospel shows Jesus to be a listener as well as a teacher.

Which leads us back to our initial problem. One way of expressing our sense of self is that we should perform our own kind of Kenosis, that we should recognise that anything we do that has any merit comes not from ourselves but from God, to whom we must offer it back in sacrifice. The good too frequently fall into the trap of attributing what they do to their own virtue, taking credit instead of giving the credit to God. Consequently, contrary to popular fiction, those who do good are in greater danger of falling into sin than those who are obviously wicked.

The Second Sunday after the Epiphany

Collect	*Almighty and everlasting God, who dost govern all things . . .*
Epistle	Romans 12.6–16[b]
Gospel	John 2.1–11

A wedding without wine was a disaster because wine was only drunk on special occasions. The top table were in serious danger of disgrace and Mary, acutely conscious of the impending catastrophe, asked Jesus to help. Notwithstanding his reluctance to perform miracles on request, the answer to His mother was rather harsh, but he soon made up for this by saving the occasion. This is the first miracle in John and it is simple and domestic, without drama or pathos, public but discreet. No doubt word got around that the wonderful replenishment was attributable to Jesus but that the actual deed was done downstairs near the door, rather than upstairs in full view of the guests.

The way in which Jesus bore witness to the Father varied according to time and place. This is a theme which Paul takes up vigorously in the later part of Romans. Clearly there was a good deal of competition within the emergent Church. We can feel from the time of Pentecost that the Holy Spirit was almost viscerally active, but that this caused some friction. All kinds of people were anxious to exercise their newly found gifts, but there was a degree of grandstanding. Paul needed to calm people down. In a passage very similar to 1 Corinthians 12—except that there seems not to be a "problem" of people speaking in tongues—he starts by reminding everybody that their gifts come from God, a message which, given our propensity to show off, cannot be repeated often enough. He then commends individual spiritual gifts, qualifying their use with temperate advice, before going on, in an echo of Ecclesiastes 3, to list a series of virtues and activities, again commending each.

As the messages from the readings are only indirectly connected, and reasonably obvious, it is difficult to find something new or arresting to say, but we might begin by thinking about individual gifts and asking ourselves how much we know about the gifts of our congregation. We know which rotas people are on (sometimes entrapped by tradition and inertia for decades) and we might know what people do or have done for a living, but what else do we know? How have they been visited by the Holy Spirit? How often do we ask people, given a clean sheet, what they would like to do?

As a related issue, what might we prevent people from doing by failing to delegate? In spite of decades of modern management theory there are still far more half-demented, workaholic clergy than comfortable team leaders. There is here a serious issue of trust, for we must not mistrust the gifts which are given by the Spirit to those around us. One reason why we might is the exuberance which Paul is seeking to check. Leadership can be both intoxicating and addictive and so its exercise, as Paul points out, should be temperate. That is, however, not to say that enthusiasm should be dampened; it simply needs to be channelled.

A further thought on gifts is triggered by looking again at the wedding. Nobody in the room except for Mary knew that Jesus had special gifts and she had to be somewhat discreet in the way that she dropped a hint to the waiters. Out of despair or deference, they took the hint and obeyed Jesus' somewhat unlikely request to fill the water pots. From the perspective of the top table, he was nothing special, the son of a builder with a bit of a reputation for Scriptural exegesis in the neighbouring town, and yet he saved the day. We must always be careful to leave ourselves open to the flowering of previously unknown or unseen gifts.

This is, to an extent, a matter of temperament. Some people think that highly gifted people, such as musicians, are relatively rare. The work of Gustavo Dudamel in Caracas (*Orchestral Manoeuvres*), who handed out musical instruments to slum children who have recently recorded Beethoven and Mahler symphonies, is only one more piece of evidence confirming my belief that humanity has been much more richly endowed by the Spirit than most of us know, but that the exercise of arbitrary or simply blinkered power represses a massive variety of talent.

Which brings us, finally, to a consideration of power. It might be argued that the exercise of earthly power is necessary for the maintenance of good order, but that in itself speaks of flawed humanity because in essence power is the opposite of love. Where love creates space, power closes it down. We must therefore always be careful, as Paul notes, to be as temperate as we can in the exercise of power, to keep it to an absolute minimum. Perhaps Jesus' reluctance to exercise His own powers explains His somewhat graceless remark to Mary. The Jews knew a great deal about power, both spiritual and temporal, stemming respectively from their Scriptural studies (Moses, Samuel and Daniel spring to mind) and from the reality of Roman occupation. Jesus was to confront "the powers that be" (an ominously conservative phrase) and Paul himself had been the victim of both religious and civil persecution, but his claim to discuss these issues is greater, because he had also been a persecutor, exercising the kind of power from which he later suffered. We need a considerable degree of social imagination to understand what it is to be subjected if we are to be temperate.

The Third Sunday after the Epiphany

Collect   *Almighty and everlasting God, mercifully*
             look upon our infirmities . . . stretch forth
             thy right hand to help and defend us . . .
Epistle   Romans 12.16^c–21
Gospel   Matthew 8.1–13

Matthew's story of Jesus and the Centurion is dramatic, and yet less so than Luke's (7.1–10), in which the Centurion has such faith in the effectiveness of Jesus that he does not even come himself to ask for a cure for his servant. Rather, he sends Jewish elders to plead on his behalf, although, it must be said, the utter transparency of the Centurion is somewhat compromised by the elders saying that he had built a synagogue, a clear attempt by the occupying power to curry favour with the locals.

Matthew is much less complex and reflects his customary concern with power, politics, and the faithlessness of the Jewish religious authorities. The Centurion wishes his servant to be cured of palsy and asserts that the physical presence of Jesus is not required. This contrasts sharply with miracles performed at the behest of faithful Jews, and Jesus remarks on the faith of the Centurion, the like of which he has not seen. The Centurion explains his attitude to power, and we can see its extent from Acts 21.31 to the end. Yet there is more to it than that. The occupying and supposedly brutal Centurion is an iconic figure contrasted with the supposedly devout Jewish authorities (notably Matthew 27.54). That contrast is underlined by Matthew's customary summation of the punishment for unfaithfulness, the "weeping and gnashing of teeth."

Such stern measures for unfaithfulness are, Paul reminds us, reserved for the Lord. We are to overcome evil with good, and leave any repayment to the Almighty. In one of those flashes of deep pastoral insight, Paul recognises the difficulty of what he preaches when he says, "if it be possible, as much as lieth in you, live peaceably with all men." The Collect, in a memorable phrase, calls upon God to "stretch forth thy right hand". Incidentally, we should not, carried away by the Centurion's faith, forget the lowly leper at the beginning of the Gospel, who worshipped Jesus and expressed a simple faith. The religious authorities are therefore clamped between the leper and the Centurion.

Although the Centurion is very matter-of-fact when he describes how he gives orders and how they are carried out, and although it is easy to be swept along by the way that Jesus effects his acts of power, what makes the Centurion and Jesus in some way similar is that their very great respective authorities are derived from on high. Although slow communications (cf. Paul's wintering in Malta in Acts 28) made delegation inevitable, Roman military hierarchy went from the Centurion right up to the God/Emperor, whereas Jesus says his authority derives from the Father.

The idea of lines of authority would have been second nature to sixteenth century subjects of an almost absolute monarch who, in turn, claimed to derive authority directly from God (and not, therefore, from the Pope or any other ecclesiastic). Perhaps we have greater difficulty, in an age of dispersed and in many respects global power, in grasping the clarity and simplicity of the power model we are being offered here. Taking an example of the economist J.K. Galbraith, if we think about a multinational company, it is not subject to the law of a single country. Rather, it is driven by the need to produce shareholder value. But the shareholders, who are often the pension funds of the company's own employees, have to rely on managers even though they are nominally in control through the board of directors. The whole enterprise is subject to massive internal pressures (such as labour surpluses and shortages) and massive external pressures (such as world prices). It is difficult, says Galbraith, to see who has any power at all. We might better think of the enterprise as operating like an ant colony. For that, and other reasons associated with our suspicion of arbitrary power, we might view the Centurion's self-assurance with some distaste. We believe that authority needs to earn consent rather than simply imposing it. This, however, should not obscure the truth behind what the Gospel tells us. The point is not what the Centurion has, but the value he assigns to it. What he has is nothing compared with what Jesus has. All that has been given to him in his limited sphere is useless in the face of his servant's palsy. The man, in his strength, realises his weakness, just as the leper, in his weakness, recognises his weakness.

Lying behind all the readings is the idea of the precariousness of existence: the Collect talks about "infirmities. . . dangers and necessities", the Epistle refers to "hunger [and] thirst", and the central figure of the Gospel—off-stage like the hero of a classical Greek drama—is the servant taken suddenly and fatally ill. Faced with such worldly vagaries, it is tempting to worship God in the hope of achieving some kind of appeasement, and praying as if some kind of deal can be made. The Centurion sums up the truth, his prayer acting as a counterweight to his subsequent lecture on authority: "Lord, I am not worthy that Thou shouldst come under my roof; but speak the word only and my servant shall be healed." After all power and authority has been put by, after all the propitiation and supplication has been set forth, we are left with this simple prayer, which we should apply to ourselves as we prepare to receive Holy Communion.

The Fourth Sunday after the Epiphany

Collect	*O God, who knowest us to be set in the midst of so many and great dangers . . .*
Epistle	Romans 13.1–7
Gospel	Matthew 8.23–34

After Romans 3.22–24, on which the Reformation turned, the passage of Scripture most quoted in the sixteenth and seventeenth centuries is the opening of Romans 13. From turbulent German "free" cities and petty principalities in the 1520s, to the France of the all powerful Louis XIV at the end of the seventeenth century, the issue was where religious authority lay after, the outright renunciation in the former, or severe dilution in the latter, of Papal authority. In the early 1520s, Luther's Reformation was almost wrecked by populist uprisings in the name of religious freedom, which forced him into the arms of the princes, and the Catholic king of France had to reach and enforce a settlement with the Huguenots. Responding to turmoil, Protestants and Catholics alike turned to Romans 13 to develop the doctrine of the "Divine Right of Kings".

Paul goes much further than Jesus' "render unto Caesar" (Matthew 22.2) by explicitly saying that Christians should obey rulers because "the powers that be are ordained of God. Whosoever therefore resisteth the power resisteth the ordinance of God." Rulers are, regardless of their individual behaviour, intrinsically beneficial: "not a terror to good works, but to the evil" (a difficult claim to sustain in the reign of the Emperor Nero!). The clinching phrase, however, introduces the passage, "let every soul be subject unto the higher powers", and, taken together with, "ye must needs be subject . . . for conscience sake", the civil authorities were assigned with formidable moral and religious authority. Paul probably meant that we should all be subject to God represented by civil powers, but I doubt that he could even have imagined that this would be taken to mean that the Church should be ruled by the civil powers. It is easy to adopt a somewhat superior attitude to this post-Reformation assertion, but Germany and France were split by bloody religious wars in the sixteenth century, succeeded in the seventeenth century by the Thirty Years War in Western Europe (1618–48), and civil war in England (1642-51). It seemed right to many that the civil ruler "beareth not the sword in vain, for he is the minister of God".

Surprisingly, given the climate of the times, the Collect refrains from reference to the civil authorities, and concentrates on the Gospel which puts the discussion of earthly power into context by showing divine power at its most spectacular. The Collect pleads that, due to our own frailty, we cannot stand upright and must call upon God, a clear reference to Peter's attempt to walk on water in a later, related story (Matthew 14.28–31). Even though they had been his followers for some time, his disciples had no faith in Jesus and after he had calmed the storm they asked "what manner of man is this?" One wonders what would have convinced them.

The balance of the Gospel contrasts that power of God with human degradation. There are two men (another instance of Matthew seeing double!) who are so mad that they live naked amongst the tombs, abusing themselves and frightening anybody who comes near. The devils within recognise Jesus and, in being cast out, ask to be sent, via the swine, to a watery doom. The city around seems to have been more worried about the loss of revenue from the drowned pigs than the recovery of the two men, although at the end of Matthew 14 they are more grateful.

Here we have an implied framework: because humanity is capable of being as degraded as those possessed, it needs the civil power, but because we are all capable, like the disciples, of losing our faith, we need the power of God, portrayed in the Gospel in the power of Jesus. This presents us with two issues. The first is the idea of devils. No doubt there are people who are possessed and require a form of exorcism, but a more useful image might be that of the addict who becomes a criminal outcast, serially stealing to find the money for his next fix. The more difficult issue is how we face Paul's political theory in a democratic society. One obvious starting point is the need for us to question our cynicism. Do we really believe that most people in public life are "in it for what they can get out of it"? Does our political partisanship and institutionalised antagonism—uniquely sharp in the United Kingdom in contrast with other equally democratic countries that have a greater tradition of consensus—lead us to be unjust in our assessment of politicians? Is there anything we should or can do to reduce the friction and negativity of the adversarial process? Three further questions might seem less obvious. Firstly, is it true that we foist onto politicians all of the difficult decisions we are not prepared to make ourselves? Secondly, are "they" really all the same? Finally, what responsibility do we have in a democratic society to take personal responsibility, and not be so prepared to leave it to "them"? These are all questions about adopting a proportionate, rational and even respectful view of the power that we give to politicians, and the power we retain. Scepticism is a necessary democratic corrective, but cynicism is un-Christian, because it denies the presence of God in the other.

In these times of deep insecurity we might not wish to accord divine sanction to those who rule us with our consent, but we might reflect on the difficulties they face and pray that they turn to God in their many hours of need.

The Fifth Sunday after the Epiphany

Collect   *O Lord, we beseech thee to keep thy*
              church and household . . .
Epistle   Colossians 3.12–17
Gospel   Matthew 13.24^b–30

One of the important books analysing our state at the beginning of the twenty-first century is Robert Putnam's *Bowling Alone*, which describes the erosion of what we call "social capital", the unseen but vital glue which holds society together. Putnam says that our social mobility and our private cars allow us to spend more and more time with people we like and to avoid people we don't. Before the First World War, people were locked into their own communities with those they liked and disliked, respected and despised, but there was no chance of getting away. You could not even escape through radio, television, or cinema.

So it was at the time of Jesus. People lived in a society where the wheat and tares, however defined, were not, as they are for us, some distant band of teenagers staring from the front page of the weekly paper, they were right there. Not that everybody was satisfied with this live and let live policy. The religious authorities, brought up in a tradition of legalist refinement, used all their intellectual energy to draw distinctions between acceptable and unacceptable behaviour, and this is the point of Jesus' parable. We have to live together, side by side, suspending judgment until the harvest of the Lord which will make a radical split between the wheat and tares, foreshadowing the longer account in Matthew 25.

The Collect recognises the need to rub along together in its use of the terms "Church and household" to describe the collection of those who "lean only upon the hope of Thy heavenly grace". Paul, a tireless striver for unity, urges the Colossians to exercise forgiveness and to live in charity. He goes on to point out how the Church can foster a spirit of unity: "let the word of Christ dwell richly in you in all wisdom, teaching and admonishing one another in Psalms, and hymns, and spiritual songs."

Hymn singing promotes solidarity but it is not enough and, in that context, there are three points that we might consider. The first is simple; the image in the parable fails because tares cannot be turned into wheat. The second is the extent to which our churches, where those who are "gathered", make all kinds of assumptions about those who are not? Paul calls upon the "Elect of God, holy and beloved", but what about the rest?

In the sixteenth century (cf. The Sunday after Christmas Day) this idea was taken by many reformers to mean that only a small number of the virtuous would be saved, and there was a natural temptation to include themselves among that number. To a certain extent that "gathered" tradition has remained a background feature of a Church of England, which is open to all and, by definition, not exclusivist—but this does not necessarily stop us from making it difficult for others to join us. To what extent, as a Church, are we a household which has to live with and love the awkward and the unprepossessing? During discussions where people are described as "mission opportunities", are we not in danger of thinking of them as tares and ourselves as wheat? Notice in Jesus' story how anxious the servants are to get on with the job of rooting out, while their master is content to leave things as they are until the critical moment.

The third point is to consider how we think of that critical moment. I have used the word "radical" in the sense that there seems to be no fudging; we are either wheat or weed. In the sense that a door is either open or shut, there has to be some kind of decision about the kind of people we have been. But is that really so? The parable implies, as does Matthew

25, that the difference in numbers between the wheat and the tares is not very great. So we form a picture of a society which has a fair number of obviously good people and a fair number of obviously bad people, with some in the middle whose cases are too difficult to call.

We need to question this picture because it is based on a very narrow human understanding of what God's love might be like, as it makes it like our kind of love and that is questionable. If we are to console ourselves with the thought in the Collect that we are dependent upon heavenly grace, and defended by the mighty power of God, then we are surely right to expect a rather more lenient time at the harvest than ordinary human justice would mete out. As we were created freely to love God, we need to ask what it is that we have to do in order to cut ourselves off forever from the possibility of being enfolded back into our Creator. We might go further and ask whether, given that we are all creatures of the Creator, any of us was made in such a way that we could take decisions which will cut us off forever from our Creator. In other words, are there any tares at all? In trying to answer that question we are likely to turn to the most obviously wicked occupants of our prisons, but only God knows what hand each of us has been dealt and how we are playing it. Of those who have most, most is expected.

The Sixth Sunday after the Epiphany

Collect	*O God, whose blessed son was manifested that he might destroy the works of the devil . . .*
Epistle	1 John 3.1–8
Gospel	Matthew 24.23–31

Two thousand years of Christianity have challenged our theological imagination to make sense of a doctrine of the Kingdom, which was simple and compact until about the time that the New Testament was completed. Writers like Matthew and Paul were convinced that the arrival of the Kingdom, which involved the end of the physical world and the Last Judgment, was imminent. By the end of the first century, when the author of 1 John was writing, doubts began to creep in and the Church had to adjust to a world without immediate eschatological resolution. As long as basic astronomy was a mystery there was always room for astrological speculation. Oddly, then, at a time when we know more about the workings of the universe than at any time in history, we are just beginning to be uncertain about how long we will survive as a race. From the time of Brahe (1546–1601), Galileo (1564–1642), and Kepler (1571–1630), we became progressively more certain of the age of our planet, and how long it was likely to last before the sun imploded, but in the early 1970s doubts set in. Resulting from human activity, they swung wildly from "nuclear winter" to "global warming". Now we do not know whether we have, through our own excess, tipped the planet critically into irreversible catastrophe, or whether our current unusual weather is a blip that can be corrected or which will correct itself. Our uncertainty has given Matthew's vision new bite.

By the time that Matthew was writing, it is clear that the early Church had taken such a grip on certain theological circles that people thought its claims were worth contesting or subverting. Matthew's false prophets were early gnostics (cf. The Nativity of our Lord) and religious eccentrics who could be challenged on well-worn ground, but our false prophets have proved much more difficult to handle, because they are not external but internal. It is all too easy for us to convince ourselves that our consumption is reasonable: that the school run is unavoidable, that the weekend break on a cheap flight is nugatory, and that "a little (or not such a little) of what you fancy does you good". Whatever the scientific opinion on the status of the planet, we are now at least living in a time of uncertainty directly resulting from unbridled Western consumerism.

In 1 John, half an eye is kept on possible eschatological closure, but the purpose of this passage is to explore the relationship between love and the possible emergence of a different, less dramatic, kind of end time from that portrayed in Paul and the Synoptic Gospels. We are, says 1 John, the sons of God and, in a truly wonderful theological break-through it continues, "it doth not yet appear what we shall be: but we know that, when He shall appear, we shall be like Him; for we shall see Him as He is." In heaven we shall be like God if we try to imitate His love. There is no sin in Jesus who "was manifested to take away our sins; and in Him is no sin." There is the catch. We can only hope to try to imitate Jesus because we are the sinners for whose transgressions He, who was pure, was manifested. The Collect echoes the thought but goes on to introduce the essential ingredient of hope which enables us to go on trying to imitate our Saviour.

The Collect concludes with a reference to the end of time when "he shall appear again with power and great glory", echoing the conclusion of the Gospel which talks of the sounding of the trumpet (Exodus 19). The necessary corollary of 1 John's "it doth not yet appear what we shall be" is that we do not know what will happen when we are born again outside of time and space, but the confidence of those who say we do is quite remarkable.

Matthew's theological statement is one side of the coin, but although it highlights the contrast between sinners and the pure, 1 John has an element of "give". The sixteenth century, forging a theology of atonement out of the ruins of late medieval scholasticism, had no time for the subtleties of Aquinas, but we who think of ourselves as "Catholic and Reformed" probably see less of a potential conflict between our two New Testament readings than the initial compilers. Perhaps it is a matter of temperament, living in the shadow of a crisis as were Matthew and the author of 1 John, and as we are now, whether we opt for the sharp imagery of the Gospel or the gentler speculation of the Epistle. The basic theology, as set out in the Collect, is both reassuring and clear; by the incarnation we have been made the "Sons of God" who may hope to be made "like unto Him".

After a long period of doctrinal disputes over a variety of issues, ranging from the efficacy of vestments to the nature of the Eucharist, argued from different perspectives in a context of assurance, the theology of uncertainty is a welcome restorer of perspective and humility. The very certainty of assertion detracts from a proper sense of the mystery of our childhood in God, and how our hope has been made possible. The attempts of all three readings to penetrate that mystery, and the different emphases and language they choose, serve to underline the point that there is no such thing as a completed theological enterprise.

The Sunday called Septuagesima
or the Third Sunday before Lent

Collect	*O Lord, we beseech thee favourable to hear the prayers of thy people . . .*
Epistle	1 Corinthians 9.24–27
Gospel	Matthew 20.1–16

I am just old enough to remember the days before the Dock Labour Scheme when Liverpool men queued up at the gates in the hope of a day's work, a mode of employment made more visible to us today by similar queues in Iraq which have become the targets of terrorist attacks. Those queues in which men will risk their lives for small reward underline the uncertainty of their livelihood. Matthew's account shows the corrosive competitiveness which can arise from such hardship so that men find it hard to understand that the good of others does no damage to themselves. After all, if the day's work in the vineyard was properly covered by the foreman, favouring people who started working late would not damage the prospect of work for the morrow for those who have arrived early, but it was a hard lesson. Even today in a thriving economy we are apt to see economic and social relations in terms of what we call the "zero sum game", where my gain is your loss and vice versa.

The Lord's "game" does not work that way, of course. Grace is infinite and, as St Paul points out, we are not in a race where only one person can win. If we discipline ourselves in the virtuous life we can all, in the words of the Collect, be mercifully delivered in spite of just punishment for our offences.

Regardless of the avowal of Jesus that he came most particularly to minister to the weak, the poor and to sinners—three groups of people not to be taken coterminally—succeeding generations have found this hard to accept. To its shame, the Christian Church has often sided with the rich and strong against the poor and weak. Even today, many Christians, particularly in the United States, follow the Jewish tradition that earthly wealth is a sign of God's favour and, in a less extreme way, many find it hard to reconcile the "feckless" life with the attainment of eternal happiness. Paul was proud that he did not beat the air but lived his life for a purpose, but he did not, as the Collect does not, make the mistake of counting his chances of eternity as better than those of anyone else. Indeed he is careful to say that his quest for restraint is to ensure that he is in a worthy condition to preach, a prerequisite which cannot be over-emphasised.

All depends, the three readings concur, on God's mercy whose nature is so graphically portrayed in the way the labourers in the vineyard were rewarded. The order in which the labourers were paid is significant. Had those who worked all day been paid first they would no doubt have gone home by the time the latecomers were paid, but the master is very specific with his steward, insisting that the latecomers be paid first in full view of the others. This is a necessary lesson in virtue, that it consists in what it does, and not in a comparison with what others do. We are all too apt to compare ourselves favourably with others and, I suspect, if we were asked we would count ourselves among those who laboured all day.

That self-assessment, of course, ignores the warning of the Collect that we continually rely upon mercy when we fall short. However often we fail to do what we should, we are given another chance until that time when our life ends, when we will be judged according to God's infinite mercy. Those who labour in the heat of the day and those who are only taken on at the eleventh hour have different burdens. Who is to say that the ardour of the labour is any more or less difficult to bear than the frustration of idleness, as the chance of something to take home to the family dwindles. In spite of overwhelming research which shows that most of the unemployed would prefer to work, our society still likes to divide itself between "hard working families" (to use a favourite phrase of governments of both parties) and the "scroungers" characterised in callous journalism.

The further observation of the master, which is relevant, relates back to mercy; it is not for us to decide who is worthy of what. The master has given what he thinks fit to the latecomers without violating his agreement with those who came first. It is useless to use ideas of human "fairness" to measure divine grace but, further, it is not helpful to use conventional ideas of "fairness" to assess the human condition. The great political theorist John Rawls (A Theory of Justice) proposed that in making social rules we should put ourselves behind a "veil of ignorance", not knowing whether we are weak or strong, talented or untalented, strong or weak. Even the unwillingness to work might be regarded as some kind of weakness.

Perhaps the most difficult sentence to digest is the last, that the last should be first and the first last, with the forbidding rider that many are called but few chosen. To take this seriously is not only to grant the special mission of Jesus to the poor and weak, it is also to accept that we might be among the last who, in the fullness of time, are made first. We only have a problem with the idea if we think that we are first and might be demoted to last.

The Sunday called Sexagesima
or the Second Sunday before Lent

Collect   *O Lord God, who seest that we put not*
              our trust in any thing that we do . . .
Epistle   2 Corinthians 11.19–31
Gospel   Luke 8.4–15

Corinth, the capital of the Roman Province of Achaia (Greece), on the main East/West trade route on the isthmus between the mainland and the Morea (Peloponnese), a city of two great ports, was a byword in the first century for loose living, crowned as it was by the Temple of Venus with its 1,000 prostitutes. Everything about it was turbulent, including its Jewish community, swelled by the expulsion from Rome by the Emperor Claudius (AD 49, Acts 18.2). After Rome it was the most important city that Paul visited (Athens was then a backwater university town), which explains why he spent eighteen months there (Acts 18.9–11), but begs the question of why he never returned, even though he spent subsequent time at Ephesus only a four-day sail away. The general view is that 1 Corinthians reduced the opposition to Paul and brought about the reform he required, and that 2 Corinthians, particularly the third part from which the reading is taken, was the final blow to his Judaising opponents.

Some have made a virtue of the varied tone of this Epistle, but at best the style is rhetorical and erratic, no more so than in Chapter 11. Paul attacks his opponents by saying that he is at least equal to them in ordinary matters, but that for Christ he has suffered more than any of them.

Luke's account of the parable of the sower is well fitted to Paul's Corinth. There was plenty of pagan, stony ground where goodness and generosity were trodden under foot. There were countless novel enthusiasms which quickly sprang up and died for want of authenticity and commitment. The thorns of greed were virulent in a market where anything could be sold and bought. The conditions Jesus describes in simple agricultural terms are familiar to us today, for although Christians are not immune to the direct temptations of the devil, nor from sudden and venal enthusiasms, our greatest danger lies in the thorns, the cares of the world that can so easily choke us even if we continue our regular church-going. The earth's requirements can so easily become part of the fabric of our lives, a "given" in our frame of reference. Although we hope to escape the kind of persecution which Paul suffered, we need to examine ourselves scrupulously to see whether we have been infested and (to mix metaphors) are in danger of having the spiritual life choked out of us.

It is tempting to step back from the conflation of Paul's sufferings with the seed that fell on good ground, to say that we will only produce good fruit if we suffer, but there is a strong sense in which that is true. Paul's Christian witness took place at a time of danger and uncertainty. For a second time he lists the dangers he has already experienced (cf. The First Sunday in Lent), there is another shipwreck (on Malta) to come, and, by tradition, martyrdom in Rome. Our Christian witness is, by and large, grounded in a libertarian culture, although we will often quite properly regret the indifference in which Christ is held. Our suffering, then, our mission to produce good fruit depends upon the Word of God working in us so that we bear public witness to it in a diverse world which often refuses to rank one value, ethic or religion above another. There is much talk of "Mission", but the chief mission of our lives should be to bear daily witness to Christ, not leaving it to clerically organised initiatives. There is a risk that we might lose people we suppose to be our friends by defending our values and our commitment to Christ, and it is a danger we often avoid out of politeness (cf. The Fourth Sunday after the Epiphany).

Paul is so anxious to defend Christ that his outbursts are both violent and endearing. The studied and urbane religiosity of the dinner party and the cathedral choir stall are not for him, as he is embarrassingly, affirmatively blunt, and yet he still faces attacks on his sincerity. Only this can explain his explicit list of sacrifices and his insistence at the end of the passage that he is telling the truth. We can only hope that our modesty will not be tested in such extreme circumstances.

We, like the Corinthians, are exposed to endless fashions and enthusiasms which we mistake for substance. Our media could not survive without generating excitement through novelty, and enjoying the sparkling froth of our society is harmless unless we mistake it for the substance of life. If we begin to live for things instead of living with them, we are in danger of idolatry. Again, it isn't the obvious pitfalls which most often pose the danger, but the endemic cynicism and self-consciousness which govern public and social life.

One of the dangers which the Corinthians faced, according to both Luke and Paul, was the introduction of secular tactics into religious disputes. Paul's opponents behaved like adversarial politicians, and it is all too easy for us to follow the same course when discussing the genuinely held differences in the way we bear witness to Christ. The last place in which we should expect to find acrimony is the Church. The whole history of the interaction between Paul and the Corinthians, and the parable of the sower, are a warning to the fractious and the shallow. Our calling demands a high seriousness, an avoidance of faction, and, above all, a willingness to suffer in whatever way God requires, that his Word may live in the world.

The Sunday called Quinquagesima
or the Sunday Next before Lent

Collect	*O Lord, who hast taught us that all our doings without charity are nothing worth . . . that most excellent gift of charity . . .*
Epistle	1 Corinthians 13
Gospel	Luke 18.31–43

"Love" is one of the most abused words in the English language, most frequently confused with desire and not infrequently with lust. It is one of the curiosities of tradition—the triumph of sentiment over meaning—that St Paul's great hymn of love in 1 Corinthians 13 is commonly read at weddings. The thought behind this is simple enough, that because the couple are in love they wish to hear the praise of love. But it does not correspond with "that most excellent gift of charity" cited in the Collect. The love of a marrying couple is voluntary and, although we might never expect it to be easily practised, there is the general expectation that it will be both mutual and rewarding to both parties as givers and takers. The love in all three readings is of a very different kind, given without expectation of reward, and often with the expectation of the opposite. For all its strivings and benefits, married love is, in Paul's words, a childish kind of love. Grown-up love is more exacting.

The ultimate love which constitutes Paul's model is the love of Jesus for each of us, supremely and sublimely expressed in his death on the Cross. The Gospel acts as a Lenten prologue to the events which will culminate in the *Triduum*, but Luke, the most skilful craftsman and most anthropocentric of the evangelists, points up the awesome mystery of Christ's love for us in the simple tale of the blind man. The love which Jesus shows him in curing him of his affliction is contrasted with the rebukes of those who were walking in front of him, telling the man to keep quiet. He will not, and in this brief encounter we are reminded of the denial of Jesus by his followers, and the faith of the repentant thief. The cost of his passion was incalculable to the disciples, for they had still not learned, in spite of countless similar incidents, about the extent of Jesus' love for the poor and weak.

When Paul has faithfully gone through all of the issues raised with him, out of the almost interminable complexities of Romans, this great hymn emerges with crystalline clarity. Paul says that whatever importance may be attached to other matters, love is our ultimate purpose and takes precedence over proclamation, faith, benevolence and even martyrdom. This is a crucial point in Romans, because Chapter 13 is set against a plethora of additional, but secondary, requirements. That point is relevant today in the broader context of our church life, where ritual and doctrinal purity, judgement, the perceived requirements of Scripture, and even hierarchical status, are given priority over love. We should also note that the term "charity" in this context is frequently confused with benevolence when Paul is clear that it takes precedence.

Paul's list of love's positive attributes (*inter alia*), "suffereth long . . . envieth not . . . vaunteth not itself . . . is not easily provoked . . . beareth all things . . . never faileth", corresponds closely with Jesus' prediction of his own suffering and death, "delivered unto the Gentiles, . . . mocked, and spitefully entreated, and spitted on: and they shall scourge him and put him to death."

There are three aspects of love which need further consideration here. Firstly, there is no element of reciprocity in love. We should not love our children and then complain if they do not love us. We love our children so that they may love their children. Love is not a boomerang where something we send out comes back, it goes on and on and on. Secondly, love has nothing to do with liking, and is most eminent when it is bestowed on people we do not like. In this sense—and many parents will recognise this—it is possible and necessary to go on loving a person we do not like. Thirdly, one of the true elements of love is to respect difference. We are now so able to select the people we spend time with that we may be losing the practice of tolerance, which is a necessary prerequisite for love (cf. The Fifth after the Epiphany).

Love is the essence of our faith but, as Timothy Radcliffe points out (*What Is The Point of Being A Christian?*), that does not make us better people, just more exacting aspirants. Jesus sets us an example we cannot hope to replicate, and Paul's demands are scarcely less exacting but, without negating Paul's ranking, we have faith in the saving grace of Jesus, and in the hope of his Resurrection when we shall see him "face to face".

It is tempting to think that the faith of the blind man is being contrasted with the lack of faith of Jesus' followers, but in fairness Luke says that the meaning of the journey to Jerusalem was hidden from them. They could only see "through a glass darkly". We, like Paul, are children of the Resurrection and have no such escape clause. We have before us, in the Gospel, the pattern of the love of Jesus for all of us, and in the Epistle we have its human encoding. Knowing what we know, and loving as we should love, let us never rebuke those who seek Jesus, even if we think (as his followers clearly did) that the man was (selfishly though understandably) seeking a cure. Where they saw selfishness, Jesus saw faith. That is a hard lesson for us, but just as he loved his followers nonetheless, so he loves all of us now.

The First Day of Lent
Commonly Called Ash Wednesday

Collect   *Almighty and everlasting God, who hatest*
                  nothing that thou hast made . . .
For The Epistle   Joel 2.12–17
Gospel   Matthew 6.16–21

The noun "fast" comes from the verb "to hold fast". On Ash Wednesday we are beginning forty days of preparation for Easter, but what kind of a haul should it be? Is fasting an anachronism from a bygone age when, even without Lent, it would have been inevitable from after Christmas until Spring in Northern Europe, before the advent of agricultural surpluses and the reliable means of storing them, or is fasting a contemporary imperative? A good starting point is to imagine what a genuine fast might be like today. It would comprise of a staple diet of grain-based products and water with occasional vegetables and fish; no television, radio or other entertainments; no consumerism. We would be obliged to give all that we saved to the poor and, remembering Matthew, we would have to remain cheerful throughout. A far cry from giving up chocolate!

Perhaps fasting was inevitable until the sixteenth century, but the purpose behind it is to concentrate the mind on higher things and repent material excess, quite different from reversing material excess by dieting for the good of our health and the enhancement of our appearance.

Over time, the terms "repent" and "penance" have become rather mixed up. The first is a "turning again" to God, mentioned in the Collect. The second is one means of showing a change of heart or, rather, of enacting the change without, to cite Matthew, showing it to others. It is easy to see in Joel how the two ideas have fused, so that Lent is a time of turning back to God and doing so in a concrete way through penitence: "turn ye even to me . . . with all your heart, and with fasting". Latterly there has been an attempt by the Church to encourage us to do something positive in Lent to show our change of heart, rather than simply concentrating on self-denial, but it is the latter which is still firm in the popular and even the Christian imagination.

Joel asks us to "rend our hearts". In a phrase well beloved of politicians (particularly those in charge of finance), if it isn't hurting it isn't working, and we might say that of our Lenten observance. If it does not wrench us out of our usual pattern of life then we are not working hard enough. Joel calls for an impressive package of special measures to signify a change of heart, to avert the ultimate catastrophe of God abandoning his chosen people. In our case the special occasion is not self-denial for its own sake, nor even to give us latitude to be generous to others, but to prepare for the Easter solemnities. Fasting is an honourable and joyful offering, says Matthew who rather spoils his message by invoking the actuarial argument by contrasting the corruptibility and vulnerability of earthly compared with heavenly goods. Put crudely, this argument justifies good behaviour on the ground that it somehow accumulates salvific merit; a position which was particularly unpopular at the time of the Reformation, one of the causes of which was the sale of indulgences: Papal promises of eternal life in exchange for a financial contribution to a "good cause". Joel, like many of his predecessor prophets, is deeply suspicious, on God's behalf, of extravagant ritual observance in the place of a genuine penitence where the heart, rather than the garments, was truly rent.

If we genuinely look into our hearts and examine what we have said and done, we might come face to face with a person we do not like very much. There is a strand of self-loathing in penitence which can easily be taken too far, turning a sober self-assessment into a particularly pernicious form of self-indulgence, where people cannot see themselves but only enjoy a caricature. Most of us are neglectful, lazy, and passive rather than actively wicked. We are not deliberately walking away from God or our neighbour, and it is therefore helpful to think of penitence in an active, as well as in a self-denying, mode. This is not a modern attempt to take the pain out of penitence, but rather, we live such opulent lives that doing something will probably be more taxing than giving up something.

Behind our self-analysis there lies one aspect of our existence which the Collect draws out in its phrase, ". . . God, who hatest nothing that thou hast made". Ultimately, we exist so that we can freely love God who is love. Penitence is the act of recognising the wrong choices we have made, and penance might or might not be a good method of ensuring our better judgment. The problem with penance, as Matthew and Joel point out, is that it can be perversely addictive at one level and, at another, it can feel like a process of exact retribution. Getting ready by reaching outwards seems like a much more wholesome approach to Easter.

There has to be some sensible place between the medieval enforced fast and the contemporary fashion for giving up cheese or alcohol in

pursuit of a slimmer waist line, just as there must be some balance between genuine self-denial and the ability to reach outward to others.
What matters is that we are able to engineer a change of heart which
takes us from a passive, self-satisfied spiritual state into a deliberative
preparation for the commemoration of the passion, death, and Resurrection of Our Lord Jesus.

The First Sunday in Lent

Collect	*O Lord, who for our sake didst fast*
	forty days and forty nights: . . .
Epistle	2 Corinthians 6.1–10
Gospel	Matthew 4.1–11

The temptation of Jesus after his forty day fast in the wilderness sharply
raises the issue of his true manhood. Any temptations set before a being
who was solely God would be a farce, because he would know in advance
what was going to happen and it would, in effect, be no temptation at
all. Jesus had set aside his Godhead when he became a man (Philippians
2.15–18, cf. The First Sunday after the Epiphany), and Matthew says that
he was hungry. There might also be in these events an echo of the Lord's
deliberate temptation of Job.

The first temptation, after a period of fasting, was the most direct.
Jesus was invited to perform a supernatural trick of turning stones into
bread to satisfy his own hunger. The second is more outlandish, asking Jesus to demonstrate his total trust in God by risking his life. In
many ways the third temptation was the most difficult, because people
who know themselves to be good must always be tempted to take away
earthly power from the wicked so that good may prevail. Jesus' reply,
that man does not live by bread alone, is straightforward, but his riposte
to the second, that God should not be tempted, again raises the question
of how far Matthew understood the Christology that Paul had set out.
He says that the hungry Jesus was human and also God but, conten-
tiously, he at least implies that Jesus knew himself to be God. The third
reply is along the same lines, but equivocal; saying that the devil should
only worship God at least implies a reversal of the devil's proposal that
Jesus should worship him.

In spite of any misgiving we might have about the theme of fasting and mortification (cf. The First Day of Lent), the three readings are tied together by that theme. Noting the fasting in the Gospel, we are, in the words of the Collect, to imitate Jesus' fast by subduing our flesh to the Spirit. Fasting appears in the Epistle amongst a daunting list of acts of witness. Paul is saying that we must use the resources for good which we have been given to resist the bad. This is the first of Paul's lists of misfortunes in 2 Corinthians (cf. The Sunday called Sexagesima), set out not to glorify himself, but to show how difficult it may be to bear witness to Jesus. When Paul was writing this letter, the position of Christians was doubly dangerous. They might easily be persecuted for being Jews (who had immunity from worshipping the Emperor but who were often targeted as a political scapegoat) or for being Christians (who were not separately immune). We might remember that we only have forty days of hardship to face for Our Lord, whereas many Christians are called upon for much greater sacrifices. There were many Christian martyrs in the twentieth century and there are likely to be as many in the twenty-first. Intolerance leads so easily to persecution, and persecution to execution.

Paul, anticipating the end of the world, says, "behold, now is the accepted time; behold, now is the day of salvation". For Christians in a crisis that is true, but in a paradoxical way we have a much more difficult task. We do not think the end of the world is near, we are not faced with a choice between honouring Jesus or denying him. We experience nothing so thrilling nor so sharp. Instead, we are trying in Lent to prepare for an Easter that comes around every year. We are frequently met with indifference and occasionally we have to decide how far to confront hostility. In the main, our faith is a uniform strand of a uniform, cyclical life of religious and natural seasons. Our task is to realise the sharpness of witness in a world grown dull and we might start with the latter part of Paul's list: "sorrowful, yet always rejoicing; as poor, but making many rich; as having nothing, and yet possessing all things". Put like this, the reality of God's presence in our lives is both vast and immediate, vast in the resources to which Paul refers but immediate in the reality of the incarnation. Now that we have set out on our Lenten observance, we know we can turn to Jesus for comfort, a man who faced the devil alone.

It is unfashionable to think of the devil as a personified phenomenon, but we still need to consider what might divert us from our Lenten purpose. There is the obvious temptation of breaking the "booze and chocolate" ban, but a less obvious, more insidious temptation is to go through the motions without being serious, to see the means as the end, and to forget why we are doing what we are doing. It is not too late to begin, to be honest with ourselves in defining what will provide us with a real challenge. For those who find it easy to fast, read. For those who find it easy to read, fast. For those who find it easy to read and fast, pray. As nobody finds it easy to pray, that line of argument can go no further.

We might also want to reflect in the next few weeks, as we prepare for Easter, that the temptations Jesus faced were scant reward for his forty days of solitary prayer and fasting, but our present comfort and future reward are equally assured, comforting ourselves that at last Easter is on the distant horizon.

The Second Sunday in Lent

Collect	*Almighty God, who seest that we have no power of ourselves to help ourselves . . .*
Epistle	1 Thessalonians 4.1–8
Gospel	Matthew 15.21–28

We know that Jesus was without sin, but did he initially make a mistake when he refused to help the woman of Canaan whose daughter was possessed by an evil spirit, or was he simply testing her? His response is as churlish as hers is deft. She pleaded with him, acknowledging that he was the "Son of David", but he said nothing. His disciples would send her away but, after proclaiming that he was sent to minister to the lost, he still refused, even though she had worshipped him, likening herself to a little dog. She persisted, saying that even dogs were allowed to eat crumbs from the master's table. He praised her faith, relented, and cured her daughter. If he was mistaken, he soon corrected himself. If he was testing her, she passed with flying colours.

It is not sinful to be wrong, and if we concede that Jesus was, it allows us to see him in a different and more human light. The story is heightened in its meaning by the fact that the woman was asking nothing for herself, but only for her daughter, who apparently had no control over what was happening. The Collect takes up the idea of the helplessness of the daughter by pointing out that we can do nothing for ourselves.

It then goes on to draw an antithesis between the body and the soul. Paul, who is always, in theory at least, deeply antagonistic to dualism, fuses the sanctity of the body and our spiritual health, by saying that the one is the vessel which is the home of the other. The evil spirit does not uniquely inhabit the soul nor ravage the body; by doing the first it does the second. We often only know how afflicted we are spiritually when we examine our physical behaviour.

Interestingly, Paul cites the Gentiles as egregiously immoral even though Matthew is clear that the Gentile daughter was blameless. At one level the war between good and evil is almost separate from what we do. The Collect emphasises our powerlessness, and the Gospel portrays Jesus as the channel of God's power to heal. At another level the Epistle is clear that we know the Commandments and we have the means, through God's grace, of making moral decisions. The imagery of the vessel is at the very least subliminally sexual and, typical of Paul, subconsciously specific to the female, who is the vessel, as opposed to the penetrator, in the act of fornication. We need to be clear that such bias is corrected in our understanding. The notion of the female temptress and the male victim is at once glib and hopelessly indicative of a former era.

What might it mean for somebody to be possessed by an evil spirit? It seems to denote the victim's complete inability to take moral decisions. The person is inhabited and paralysed, and the cure is not to reverse the position by making the person sacredly inhabited and paralysed in the opposite extreme by being incapable of making moral decisions. The opposite of being paralysed is being freed to exercise the will. We may all be inhabited by sin which paralyses our moral decision-making, we may frantically lust after another person, but almost always we emerge wounded and exhausted. Following the Collect's general view, we may then recognise our sinfulness and pray for God's forgiveness, but Paul more dramatically speaks of vengeance.

The ideas of human weakness and God's mercy on the one hand and God's vengeance on the other, are very difficult to reconcile. It is as if Paul is wrestling with his traditional Jewish upbringing and his Christological perception. As the Bible is indivisible we are left with the same problem, but we must surely give precedence to the New Covenant over the Old. The Crucifixion and Resurrection, however we understand the "mechanics" of atonement, radically alter the relationship between God and his people. If it does not, there is no point in being a Christian.

At a more mundane level it is easy to see how our bodies can be an obstacle to rather than a channel for the reception of God's Word. An obsession with earthly pleasure—or, in a different way, our fall into addiction—blinds us to the purpose of creation. We were made to love God freely and to thank him for his creation by enjoying it in the way he wishes. We must, however, remember at this point that it is equally sinful to dismiss the physical world, and not least our own bodies, as intrinsically harmful or even wicked.

Because we were created not only as sexual beings but also as sexually competitive, with our urge to perpetuate our race only surpassed by our need to eat regularly, it is easy both to dismiss and to exaggerate the significance of concupiscence which, at the lowest level, trivialises sexual relations, but which at its worst wrecks lives. It is an area of moral life which, without knowing the motives and resources of the people concerned, we are apt to generalise and judge. We might also note that, nested in Paul's customary tirade against sexual sin, there is a reference to fraud. If we paid as much attention to that as to the sex lives of our neighbours, the world would be an unrecognisably better place.

The Third Sunday in Lent

Collect	*We beseech thee, almighty God, look upon the hearty desires of thy humble servants . . .*
Epistle	Ephesians 5.1–14
Gospel	Luke 11.14–28

Last Sunday's themes of fornication and devils are taken up again today, but are given broader treatment. The Collect is more upbeat, speaking of our "hearty desire" to do good and calling on God to stretch forth his right hand of majesty to defend us. We will surely need such assistance in view of Paul's list of our wrongs, which expands from sexual sin to covetousness, idolatry, and loose talk. Luke's reference to a an evil spirit is the starting point for a deeper discussion.

To counter bad behaviour and become worthy of God's kingdom we are, says Paul, to behave like children, to imitate Christ, and to give thanks. We are, after all, the children who have come out of darkness and who live in the Spirit. We have, in Baptism (cf. Easter Day, Anthem, Romans 6.9) risen from the dead whereby Christ gives us light. In Luke's

Gospel the people are not sure whether they can tell the difference between darkness and light. Some think that Jesus casts out devils with the power of the chief devil, Beelzebub, but Jesus reasonably replies that a house divided against itself cannot stand. Turning the argument back on his accusers, he compares their claim to cast out devils on God's behalf with his own claim to do the same. In a typically Lucan turn, the discussion is then seen from a different angle. It does not matter how strong you think you are on your own, as an exorcist or a rich man, you are nothing without God. Then the two sets of ideas are fused in a way that is counter-intuitive both symbolically and theologically. For us, the idea that something that harms us can be fought off by having its own weapons turned against it is familiar in the field of vaccination, and even in moral theology. There is an argument that to know the evil is necessary to combat it, but for Jesus there is no spiritual vaccination, and in his explanation there is a serious warning, particularly for those who think themselves holy. When we reject the devil and try to live a holy life, the cleaner we are (and, even more so, the cleaner we think we are), the more prone we are to re-invasion. Far from being immune from wickedness, those who feel themselves safest are most vulnerable. As the rich man's downfall is great when his defences are overpowered by a richer man, so the fall of a holy person is greater than that of a sinner. Luke then becomes touchingly physical by putting an earthy blessing into the mouth of a woman, to which Jesus replies by exhorting us to hear the Word of God and keep it.

Paul's customary catalogue of misdeeds is enlivened by his antagonism to foolish and vain talk (cf. James 3.1–12) which brings the discussion to an altogether more significant level than his discussion of other vices. Nobody supposes, says Tom Wright in *Simply Christian*, that God minds very much if we call out his name in a moment of anger, frustration or surprise. However, referring to the house of the devils, it is those who put themselves on conversational terms with God that are most likely to fall into vain talk, which consists not so much of bald blasphemy, but in anthropomorphising God. Making "him" seem, paraphrasing Wright again, like us. Wright says, referring to the image of light and dark, that if we are alone in a house at night and are plunged into gloom by a power cut, we grope for matches and use them to find a candle which we light to find a torch, but we don't go out in the morning with a torch to see if the sun has risen. The question arises in this context, referring to our discussion for last week, whether Paul's notion of God's wrath is just such a piece of foolish, anthropomorphic talk.

Just as the tongue can be used for or against Good (cf. James 3.1–12) so it can be used deliberately for or against our neighbour. This is a danger to which the holiest of us must be alive. Sweetness of speech and temper is so rare that we remark upon it, because malice and cynicism are so ubiquitous that they are part of the common currency of our social lives. Paul also counsels against gossip, which frequently leads to our hurting others by accident, which may not be such a bad reflection on our part, but which may do as much damage as the deliberate slur.

We children require the mighty arm of God to defend us from all kinds of wickedness, not all of which is spectacular. There is a sense in the Collect and the Gospel that we not only need to be defended against ourselves, but also our enemy, characterised as the devil, which raises the question of how we can prepare ourselves. As with speech and immoral acts, our enemy is insidious. There is, after all, no such thing as a discovered con-man! We should be careful of paranoia because God's creation is good, but that does not mean that we should not be vigilant. The corollary of careful talk is careful listening. Sometimes evil is traumatically manifested, but most often it proceeds by degrees. It might be a word, or it might just be an inflection. We know from the Nazis that pettiness turned to contempt, then to discrimination, dehumanisation and, finally, slaughter. In a way quite opposite from that which was meant by our own war-time propagandists, careless talk costs lives.

The Fourth Sunday in Lent

Collect   *Grant, we beseech thee, almighty God,*
that we, for our evil deeds . . .
Epistle   Galatians 4.21–31
Gospel   John 6.1–14

One of the central problems of our existence is understanding continuity and change. What makes the senior citizen the same person as the baby born 70 years before? We see the problem in a different guise when a political party in government changes its leader (John Major for Margaret Thatcher, Gordon Brown for Tony Blair) when it wants to appear both new and yet continuous. Paul spent a good deal of his time (cf. The Circumcision of Christ) wrestling with this problem. To what extent was Christianity different from and yet continuous with Judaism? The argument for difference in the life, death, and Resurrection of Jesus was easy enough, but the continuity issue was more problematic because not only had the Jews, directly or indirectly, been responsible for the death of Jesus, but Paul himself, as a Jew, had persecuted his followers. The Rabbi in Paul needed to find the clinching argument in detailed Scriptural exegesis, not in a generalisation. The key for Paul was Abraham, who had been in a relationship with God before he was made the father of the Chosen People through the birth of Isaac. His point is that Isaac was born as part of the "promise", whereas Ishmael was only born "of the flesh" (Genesis 16.1–16). This idea sits uneasily with Paul's view that Christianity is the heir to Abraham by virtue of the fact that he was chosen by God before he acknowledged the Covenant through the act of circumcision. If we value consistency this is a serious disjuncture, but in truth Paul was forging Christian theology throughout his mission in a blacksmith sort of way; the gilding came later. It would be too much to expect otherwise and so we should, having noted the problem, hang on to the main point that he is making: no matter what continuity there may be, the New Covenant is a radical break with the old that has transformed us from slaves into free people. There could be nothing more radical and yet familiar to Jews than a New Covenant. Paul had cracked the continuity/change dilemma and this was a new version of the same thing.

There still remains the vexed question, in all three readings, of who's in and who's out of this New Covenant. In hindsight, John could look back on the miracle of the feeding of the 5,000 as a sign of this New Covenant. What started as a spectacular manifestation of God's power became iconic, first when seen through the prism of the Maundy Thursday institution of the Eucharist, then in the appearance of the Risen Lord at Emmaus, and later in countless gatherings for the breaking of bread. The fish was not forgotten—it became one of the earliest Christian symbols (*Ichthus*) and a counterweight to the meat dominated Jewish tradition.

What matters about the great feast is that there were no entry checks or tickets. Jesus fed those who turned up. No matter there were mockers and pick pockets as well as the devout and the curious. From this we ought to take comfort for, in the words of the Collect, we will be "mercifully relieved" in spite of our "evil deeds". Here is another dilemma that never quite goes away, and to which we have referred previously (cf. The Second and The Third Sunday in Lent). In this wondrous scene—and in many others—Jesus shows no sign of being selective, but is open. If anything, he has a preference for the poor and weak, the wicked and the marginal but, to use an unbiblical, contemporary word, he is relaxed. If what he does at this feast prefigures the Eucharist, then what are we to make of the preconditions for accessing the Eucharist? What kinds of rules are we entitled to make about children, sinners, or even the unbaptised? Does the Eucharist belong to the Church, or does it belong to the human race? After all, John reports that people did not follow Jesus because he was a wonderful theologian or a priestly figure, but because he worked miracles, notably curing disease.

Another way in which the feeding of the 5,000 might resemble the Eucharist is in the bewilderment of the disciples. Jesus asked Philip a simple question, to which he did not receive the reply: "It doesn't matter how many there are, Lord, you can feed them." Rather, he was very matter of fact, estimating the minimum cost of supply. Andrew, Peter's brother, did have an inkling of what might be in Jesus' mind when he mentioned the five loaves and two fishes. What happened when Jesus gave thanks? We don't know, as we only see the result. What happens when the priest consecrates the elements? It is all too easy to recite a theological formula exclusive to a Christian denomination. Arguing about the Eucharist has been a futile and often harmful theological pastime for the past 500 years.

The reaction of the crowd, as articulated by John, is enigmatic. Is the prophet that is supposed to come into the world the Messiah, or just another prophet? In terms of adulation, the response is pretty mild in comparison with the spectacular act which Jesus has just performed. Are we not, too, in danger of taking God's love for granted and are we not, too, in danger of down-grading the magnificence of the deeds of Jesus because we cannot explain them in a way that contemporary atheists would understand? We tend to be somewhat sheepish about miracles, but whatever our view, it is remarkable in the jigsaw that makes up the Gospels that this piece is so prominent in all four.

A final note. The disciples collected the fragments.

The Fifth Sunday in Lent

Collect	*We beseech thee, almighty God, mercifully to look upon thy people . . .*
Epistle	Hebrews 9.11–15
Gospel	John 8.46–59[a]

Imagine a charismatic figure erupting onto the scene claiming to be the fourth person of the Christian Godhead, preaching that there is no after-life but that the Kingdom is now. We would say such things as: there are only three persons in the Trinity of which Jesus was the only-begotten Son; the sacrifice of Jesus was not only full but final in underwriting our eternal life; and, anyway, a woman could not fulfil this role. That gives us some idea of the magnitude of the claim that Jesus was making. He claimed, in the teeth of a fiercely monotheistic religion, to be using our kind of theological language: the second person of the Godhead, co-eternal with the Father, and an underwriter of eternal life. As we have already noted (Fourth Sunday in Advent), Judaism had no mechanism for recognising its long-awaited Messiah, and there had been a series of obvious fakes (cf. Acts 5.36–39). So the reaction of the Jews to Jesus is coherent, not scandalous. It was hard to be told that, in sticking to their old ways, they were "not of God." Their understandable reaction was to accuse Jesus of the unspeakable offence of being a Samaritan (our word "traitor" is not strong enough) and being possessed by the devil (cf. The Third Sunday in Lent). Jesus replied that those who believed in him would not die, a preposterous claim to those Jews who did not believe in the afterlife. He then compounded the scandal by claiming to be greater than Abraham, summing up his claim by saying that the Jew-ish God was his father who honoured him, capping the argument with, "before Abraham was, I am."

After that bravura performance which almost led to Jesus' prema-ture death, Hebrews is somewhat laboured. It takes the theme of the Old and the New Covenant and depicts them in the graphic language of sacrifice. Whereas the Jews had sought to cleanse themselves from sin through offering animal sacrifices, Jesus, the great High Priest, had offered himself as the sacrifice to cleanse ours sins. He is not—the meta-phor lurches awkwardly—a tabernacle made with hands, but made of the Spirit. Viewed on its own this is a radical enough claim, but timing is important. Hebrews (in spite of its designation in the King James Bible) was not written by St Paul, but much later, so the claim by then would

not have been so radical; not least because by then the Jewish tradition
of animal sacrifice had been discontinued (since AD 70 when the Temple
was destroyed). In many ways, Hebrews has the feeling of protesting too
much.

During the past weeks we have been considering the issue of continuity and change, and in the Gospel Jesus puts it at its most acute in
claiming both association with the Father and superiority in himself, not
just through the Father, over Abraham. Being alive to the radicalism, the
impossibility, of these claims, is a fitting preparation for the reception of
the Crucifixion and Resurrection which are no less radical and improb-
able. It is too easy for us to fall into a pious annual cycle without feeling
the freshness and scandal of what Jesus said in this Gospel and then
suffered. The "Church by Law established" is a difficult place in which
to perceive—and from which to proclaim—this sense of utter newness.
When people ask us who we are and why we are, the answers tend to be
measured, even cautious, rather than being alive with affirmation. Are
we not in danger of behaving, like Sir Humphrey, as God's civil service?

On one crucial point, it is important to query the meaning in Hebrews of ". . . the blood of Christ . . . offered himself without spot . . .
to purge your conscience from dead works". Taken literally, this makes
us into God's pawns, an understandable but excessive sixteenth century
Reformation reaction to the supposed emphasis of Aquinas on the efficacy of good works in the salvific process. As the Collect says, it is only
by the goodness of God that we will be "preserved evermore", but that
is not to say that we will either be preserved after a life of failing to heed
our conscience or, much worse, of pretending that we do not have one.
Much of this discussion is unnecessarily confrontational and rhetorical.
There is no strand of Roman Catholic theology which proclaims human
independence of the atonement, and no Evangelical strain of theology
which proclaims that the way we behave is indifferent. Most of us—not
out of a sense of compromise but of necessary mutuality—would now
see the importance of both.

This Sunday, observed in some Christian traditions as "Passion Sunday" or the beginning of "Passiontide", is our last chance to consider these
fundamental theological issues before we are swept up into the events
that lead to Calvary. It is important that at this point we understand not
precisely why Jesus did what he did, nor how that affects who we are,
but that we understand the magnitude of the claim and the promise.
If these are not as radical as Jesus says they are, then the Crucifixion is
preposterously excessive and the Resurrection is incomprehensible. If

we do not take the Godhead of Jesus seriously, as the Jews failed to do, then we end up as they did, puzzled, angry, and in denial.

The Sunday Next before Easter

Collect   *Almighty and everlasting God, who, of thy*
             tender love towards mankind . . .
Epistle   Philippians 2.5–11
Gospel   Matthew 27.1–54

Nobody in the sixteenth century would have considered Matthew's Passion anti-Semitic or, rather, it would have constituted a major foundation stone of their anti-Semitism. (Did the unmatched power and pathos of Bach's *St Matthew Passion* make the Shoah that bit more possible?) All the Evangelists, faced with the bifurcation of Christianity from Judaism and the need to mollify the Romans, not unnaturally blamed the Jews, but only Matthew squarely blames the people as opposed to their leaders. All four use the highly suspect Barabbas device (cf. Geza Vermes, *The Passion*). Matthew's account of the Judas episode, on the other hand, is much more elaborate than the other Gospels (although it makes a somewhat incongruous appearance in Acts (1.15–20), which somewhat mitigates populist guilt. A further complexity, even overlooked by sixteenth century adherents of *sola scriptura*, is that the death of Jesus was prophetically foretold as an act of the Father, in which the Jews, if they had any part at all, only played a mechanistic role. Perhaps the medieval exegesis was slipshod, but more likely it was economically self-interested and it should act as a warning at a time of religious tension between Christians and Muslims. After all, just as we claim a fuller inheritance than the Jews, there are Muslims who say their religion would not have been necessary had it not been for Christianity's fall from its high ideals. We will fall even further if we use religious controversy as a weapon of economic or social oppression.

The language of blame is particularly unhelpful (if it can ever be said to be helpful) in considering both Matthew's attitude towards the Jews and, sequentially, our attitude to our anti-Semitic forebears. What we are required to do is to understand Matthew's meaning and the subsequent meanings attributed to him. Matthew is always concerned to show the kingship of Jesus and to contrast this with earthly powers. In the Passion narrative he has the opportunity to contrast Jesus with all kinds of characters: with the obdurate religious authorities, the treacherous Judas, the obfuscating and ultimately cowardly Pilate; even the thieves in Matthew (unlike Luke) act as foils for King Jesus. Like us, medieval and Reformation interpreters could only see the historical figures as shadows, but they were ever conscious of the Jews, particularly when the ruling classes were deeply in debt to their bankers. What they did to the Jews, successive Christian generations did to other minorities. We may feel less culpable, but it is salutary to add up the millions who have been killed in genocidal mayhem since the end of the Second World War while we have sat on our hands.

Nothing could contrast more with the crude but high claims of Matthew than the subtlety and gentleness of Paul's supremely theologically imaginative association of Jesus with the suffering servant in Isaiah 52.13–53.12. Jesus, who could properly count himself equal with God, suffered himself to be made in our likeness, to be our servant of no reputation. He was obedient, even to death on the Cross, and was therefore exalted. In an age when Godhead, both in Judaism and paganism, was associated with power, this was an amazing claim. Paul is asking people to kneel before a man who has died a criminal's death. The enormity of Paul's claim is even greater if, following contemporary liturgical practice in many Christian traditions, today's Gospel follows the entrance of Jesus into Jerusalem. Its absence (and even the refusal to use the term "Palm Sunday") is the direct result of a Reformation reaction against ritual, which might have been understandable at the time, but which now looks gratuitously perverse (given his primary status, the complete absence of Matthew 26 in what we now call Holy Week is puzzling). Matthew's contrast of the kingly entrance of Jesus and his ignominious death is, admittedly, another strand of anti-Semitic sentiment, but it is also a lesson in our own fickleness, to which, noting the Collect, we can only react with the kind of humility which might protect us from our arrogance towards other religions, races, and cultures.

Which leads us, inevitably, to the difficult issue of how we are to square the uniqueness of our Christian experience, grounded in the Passion and death of Jesus, with his extraordinary humility. Should our response to other religions be formalistic tolerance, an easy condescension or outright hostility? All are evident in our Christian tradition and each has its own dangers, but it is particularly difficult to see how Christians can justify hostility as an element of Christian worship. Better to give thanks for what we enjoy, and endeavour to share it, than to attack others for not equally enjoying it. Here lies the great fault in Judas. It is not that he was not devoted to Jesus; far from it. In many ways he was the archetypal fanatic, too devoted, too anxious for early success, impatient of apostolic dithering and religious disaster. What started as commitment concluded in disdain, and then disaster. Judas thought he understood Jesus better than Jesus understood himself. In spite of history's fascination with the story, not least in our own time, its message has failed to dampen a fiery strand of Christian aggression which makes a nonsense of Paul's hymn to humility, written, let us remember, when Christianity was facing a much greater challenge than it faces today. We are still in grave danger of using Matthew for our own selfish and bitter ends.

Monday before Easter

For The Epistle   Isaiah 63
Gospel   Mark 14

Chopped into pieces, the pronouncements of the prophets sound clear and consistent, but viewed in the round, what stands out is inner turmoil. The multi-authored Book of Isaiah is inevitably volatile, but in this passage even "the Third" Isaiah is deeply troubled. The scenario is always the same. God rescued his Chosen People from slavery in Egypt and almost from the first moment of their liberation, they turned their backs on him. He still loves them, but his prophets proclaim that the only way the people will be brought back to faithfulness is through terrible vengeance. The result is that God's prophets and foreign powers form an uneasy alliance against the people and their secular and religious leaders. Thus, in a remarkably dramatic passage which associates wine with blood, the outsider comes in red, as if from the wine press, where, says Isaiah, he has trodden the grapes alone. That fruitful treading will turn violent, and the blood from it will sprinkle his garments. Yet no sooner is the vengeance pronounced than he looks back to the great love shown by God for his people and, here is the paradox, Isaiah calls on him to look with pity on the unfaithful people, because his sanctuary has been violated by the outsiders he sent.

The Gospel, too, is full of inner conflict but, this being Mark (cf. Saintt Mark's Day), there is a complete absence of heightened language. Chapter 14 opens with the plot against Jesus set in a handful of words. The scene then shifts to the house of Simon the Leper, who is hosting a dinner during which a woman anoints Jesus, causing some dissent, which he dispels by saying she is foreshadowing his burial. There is no evidence that the woman in question was Mary Magdalene (Mark names her at the tomb in 15.47 alongside Mary the mother of Joses), nor is there any evidence that Judas led the dissent, but Mark reports his defection immediately after Jesus' praise of the woman. John 12.1–8, more credibly, names Mary of Bethany as the anointer and, less credibly, specifies Judas as the leading dissenter. Mark is clear about the significance of the woman's act but, over time, this woman and two others were rolled into a composite caricature of a reformed prostitute, unfit to be a leader of the early Church.

The emblematic pitcher of water leads Jesus and his disciples to the upper room, to another domestic scene shot through with external threat. Not only is the first Eucharist performed against a background of treachery, it is at least partly performed in the presence of the traitor. Mark (unlike Matthew) does not specify Judas' exit but, more importantly, the four accounts of the Institution of the Eucharist (Matthew 26.26–29, Mark 14.22–25, Luke 22.15–20, and 1 Corinthians 11.23–26, which is the earliest) are by no means consistent, as Paul Bradshaw points out (*Eucharistic Origins*). The passage from Isaiah anticipates the pattern of this "Last Supper", both domestic and global, sacrificial and treacherous, constituted of the bread of solidarity and the wine of risk. The difference between the two sets of images is that the outcome in Isaiah is always in the balance; there is, contrary to popular sentiment, no closure in prophesy. Its self-referential arguments are always inconclusive, but in Mark's Jesus, acting in the full knowledge of his forthcoming death, we have the assurance of his Resurrection which he promises directly after the image of the scattered sheep, and the sustaining food of his own flesh and blood.

Mark then proceeds to describe the events of the Thursday night and Friday with his usual, unsentimental briskness. The three chief disciples, Peter, James and John fail three times to watch and pray, foreshadowing Peter's three denials. Judas arrives with the religious militia and Jesus is kissed by Judas, arrested, and abandoned by all his friends (including a young man who only appears in Mark and, by tradition, is said to be Mark, who leaves his outer garment in order to escape). Again, cinematographically, Mark interweaves the public trial with the almost domestic fireside denial. Jesus condemns himself as "the Christ, the son of the Blessed" and is mocked by his accusers.

The impending doom in Isaiah and the betrayal, abandonment, trial, and mockery of Jesus seem so cataclysmic that we may wonder how they relate to us, but Isaiah's dilemma is not singular nor traumatic, but familiar and chronic. Jesus was betrayed by a friend and abandoned by the others, tried by defensively pietistic and frightened officials, and mocked by recent admirers of his great works, relieved at his fall from power. Put this way it looks more familiar: unfaithfulness is the natural corollary of free will in imperfect beings; friendships forged over decades can be broken by the most trivial of misunderstandings; officials that are not prudentially defensive are usually hounded out of office; and the phenomenon of the idol set up to be knocked down is so familiar that it is often used to differentiate the reporting of celebrity behaviour from soap opera. One of the most haunting qualities of the Passion narrative, seen best in the stark words of Mark, is its familiarity. There is nothing in it which we do not recognise. There is no role in it, other than that of Jesus, which we could not play. If we look carefully and honestly at these events, it will not be long before we see ourselves; people not only of blood and betrayal, but also of wine and ointment.

Tuesday before Easter

For The Epistle   Isaiah 50.5–11
Gospel   Mark 15.1–39

One of the major differences between the Passion narratives is the depiction of Pilate. In Matthew he is obfuscating and cowardly (cf. The Sunday Next before Easter); in Luke, as we shall see (cf. Thursday before Easter), he is a rounded, even complex figure; in John (cf. Good Friday) his behaviour is sarcastic and theatrical. But in Mark he is a straightforward, pragmatic Roman. Pilate follows the procedure, asks the questions, weighs the weak legal argument (Jesus is prepared to proclaim himself to the religious authorities, but not to Pilate) and the strong political imperative of keeping his fractious subjects quiet, and then makes a sharp, definite decision. One gets the impression that he is not very much bothered either way, and that if the factors were differently weighted he would have made a different decision. The soldiers take Jesus to their barracks for a bit of sadistic fun, which immediately brings to mind our "suffering servant" passage from Isaiah (cf. Isaiah 42.1–4, 49.1–6, 50.4–9, 52.13–53.12). Like Jesus, the figure in Isaiah presents his back for beating, his cheek for plucking, and his face for spitting. The soldiers, well aware of Jesus' claim of kingship, reported uncritically by Pilate in spite of Jesus' silence on the point, set him up as a mock king. Against the background of notorious Jewish antagonism to Roman rule, this piece of political pantomime was important in strengthening the flimsy case for summary execution. Jesus then is led out, assisted in carrying his cross beam by a stranger from Cyrene whose sons, Rufus and Alexander, went on to be adherents of the early Church (Romans 16.13), underlining the effect Jesus had on their father, Simon. Contrary to a plethora of misleading painting (summed up in the hymn "There is a green hill far away"), Jesus was crucified at the Jerusalem rubbish tip. A kind attempt was made to drug him but he refused, and his garments were divided amongst the soldiers (cf. Psalm 22.18). Yet it was their Centurion who recognised him as the Son of God after his death. The kingship theme is reiterated in the superscription. The mocking continues, coupling the religious authorities and the thieves, and there is the curious episode of the cry of Jesus to the Father being mistaken for an appeal to the Prophet Elijah, whose reappearance was supposed by some to be a necessary precursor to the arrival of the Messiah.

We know so much about the Passion of Jesus compared with the rest of his life, but so little of the detail is consistent over all four accounts that it is tempting to try to assemble a consistent, combined narrative. This "historicist" approach has severe theological limitations. What matters in the different accounts is why the Evangelists selected their material. Mark's spare style belies a deep theological purpose set out in 1.1: "the beginning of the Gospel of Jesus Christ, the Son of God", the very words used by the Centurion in the last verse concerning Jesus' life as a human like us. This uncomplicated approach, so different from the dialogues between Jesus and the Jews in John, allows Mark to lay out his material in a series of sharp observations, giving the story a dramatic momentum which moves with inevitable assurance to its climax.

The cry of Jesus, "My God, My God, why hast Thou forsaken me?" has been the subject of deep controversy. This was epitomised in Albert Schweitzer's thesis (*The Search for The Historical Jesus*) that Jesus the man, voluntarily deprived of his godly foreknowledge, thought that his mission had failed, but as almost every detail of this account refers to Old Testament sources, it would seem unfair not to apply the same criterion here. The call upon God in moments of despair is a common feature of the prophesies of Isaiah and Jeremiah, which form the material out of which the Passion narratives are wrought, and so it is natural for Jesus to cite the opening verse of Psalm 22. The reward of the "suffering servant" in Isaiah for his humility and patience pre-figures the Resurrection, which is the definitive answer to Schweitzer.

The complaint of Jesus serves the important function of reminding us that Jesus was a human being who suffered all the humiliation and pain which Mark describes. His unfathomable purity and flawless obedience may tempt us to see the Passion narratives as a series of symbolic, scripturally derived tableaux, rather than as a series of cynical, sadistic, humiliating, excruciatingly painful events, combining the worst mental and physical cruelty that man could devise. This real man, who preached a Gospel of repentance and humility was killed because his very goodness was a goad to those who knew they should do better. In a way that was inevitable from the start, the confrontation between a loving Jesus and a hating world was bound to end this way, but just as our shortcomings are real, so was the pain he felt for us. On the other hand, the reality of Jesus' suffering has been brought home by the last century's shared catastrophes, which led to the idea that Jesus is always to be found among the suffering who can take comfort from his presence with them. He not only suffers for us, but with us.

Another form of distancing is to think that only a highly specific section of the human race, at a given place and time, caused the death of our Saviour. As we are indivisible in creation and all equally flawed, we must all bear our guilt. In a sense which it is not easy to impart with the necessary impact, we are all still hammering in the nails.

Wednesday before Easter

Epistle   Hebrews 9.16–28
Gospel   Luke 22

The exigencies of sequencing the different accounts of the Passion separates Luke 22 from its natural partner (1 Corinthians 11; cf. Thursday before Easter), but it allows us to consider the institution of the Holy Eucharist in the light of Hebrews' elaborate Christology. Just as the First Covenant was sealed with animal blood (Exodus 12.21–22, Numbers 19.5–6, Leviticus 1–7), all things that are sacred must be sprinkled with blood, and without it there is no remission. The Temple, made with hands where, for the Jews, Tom Wright says (*Simply Christian*), heaven met earth, is replaced by heaven meeting in earth in the incarnation. Whereas things of the Law could be cleansed with animal blood, heavenly things require a High Priest sent from heaven. Thus, the priest and the victim become fused because Jesus sacrificed himself for sin.

This Christology of priest and victim as the initiator of the New Covenant might apply equally to the Institution of the Eucharist and penal substitution in the death of Jesus. The Reformation saw a radical shift from emphasis on the former to the centrality of the latter, which might explain the way the readings have been chosen and yoked, allowing us only to infer a Eucharistic dimension in Hebrews, which is explicit in tomorrow's Epistle. Like most dichotomies, this one is false, born, as most are, out of a tactical need for differentiation; in this case between Reformers and Catholics. This is still a cause of tension between the traditions, in spite of the recognition that the Eucharist and Crucifixion are symbiotic and that to debate their respective "mechanics", which occupied so much theological energy in the sixteenth century, is to call their mysterious nature into question.

As many Christian traditions choose today to think about the betrayal of Jesus, there is one final question we must consider: how credible is the whole Judas episode? Jesus, as he declares at his arrest, spoke openly in the Temple; he was a public figure. In the cramped environment of Jerusalem he would have been easy to find. Luke says that the authorities were frightened to make a move, "for fear of the people", but what difference did Judas make? One answer, cited by the evangelists themselves, is that Scripture had to be fulfilled (cf. Zechariah 11.12–13). The very inevitability of the events might explain why Luke has Judas, the instrument, not the initiator, present at the Eucharist. There follows a discussion of the name of the betrayer, significantly entwined with "strife among them" over whom was the greatest. This leads to a dialogue on service and humility which will be rewarded with the heavenly life, featuring a moving address to Peter, looking beyond his denial: ". . . when thou art converted, strengthen thy brethren." Only Luke completes this episode by saying that Jesus "looked upon Peter" after his third denial.

Luke's account of Jesus' prayer on the Mount of Olives is short but dramatic, showing Jesus supported by an angel and sweating drops of blood. These two circumstances (verses 22.43–44) are now thought by most scholars to be a non-Lucan interpolation. After the prayer, in a nice Lucan touch, Jesus finds the disciples sleeping "for sorrow." Judas effects the arrest of Jesus, who is then blindfolded, beaten, and mocked, in the "softening up" process before the trial. In Luke (cf. Rowan Williams, *Christ on Trial*) Jesus is quietly pragmatic; his accusers will not believe him, listen to him, nor let him go. He says that he will sit on the right hand of God, but then uses the odd phrase, "ye say that I am" when asked directly whether he is the Son of God.

Luke's genius is to help us see Judas the betrayer and Peter the denier alongside each other without making the customary radical distinction. He says that Satan entered into Judas, and Jesus warns Peter that the devil will sift him like wheat. The two figures are still both present when dissent breaks out between the disciples. These two figures are not so far from each other as might be supposed, and they are not so far from the rest of the disciples, who are allowing the solemn Passover meal to degenerate into petty and fractious competitiveness. Jesus uses the occasion to respond generously, promising that there will be places for them all in the Kingdom (we do not know at what point Judas leaves). After the denial we are left to imagine what facial expression Peter saw, but we have no reason to doubt that it was a face of sad and generous forgiveness.

Luke's approach is a warning against separating society into good and bad, separating the law-abiding and the criminal. In demonising criminals we are not only setting them apart as a different class of people, we are also setting ourselves apart, which has two serious consequences. The first is that we are tempted to deny our own sinfulness, and the second is that we are tempted to deny our solidarity with all God's creatures, loving the sinner but hating the sin. We do not know what trials others have to face, nor the means they have for facing them. However, we do know how far we have gone ourselves, as individuals and members of society, to ensure that those who are poor and weak receive resources and strength which might reduce the temptations they face. We only have to analyse the prison population, with its high illiteracy levels, widespread mental health problems, and endemic addiction, to see the extent of our own failures.

Thursday before Easter

Epistle   1 Corinthians 11.17–34
Gospel   Luke 23.1–49

Whatever the precise form of the Institution of the Eucharist at the Last Supper (cf. Paul Bradshaw: *Eucharistic Origins*), Jesus' wish that it should be performed in his memory had gained wide acceptance by the late AD 50s when Paul was writing his First Letter to the Corinthians, but it seems to have moved its domestic base to some kind of meeting hall where the general rules of hospitality were difficult to apply. Not only were there Christians with widely different backgrounds—Jews and Gentiles, Judaisers and Pauline radicals, slaves, free artisans, and aristocrats—but there was still an underlying controversy about the status of meat offered to idols. There was not only a good deal of disorder, including drunkenness, but also a basic lack of charity (cf. James 2.1–9). What counts is not the precise form of the observance—Paul's account comprises bread and wine, though on the ship off Malta (cf. Acts 27.35) he simply broke bread—but rather its purpose and meaning. The celebration of the Eucharist is the defining, uniting, event of our Church. An occasion of such significance and power is always, as Paul sees, open to exploitation by the significant and the powerful. Paul establishes a contrast between the Church and heresy, a point that might well have been in the compilers' mind, still deeply preoccupied with what they regarded as the Eucharistic extremes of Catholic *transubstantiation* on the one hand, and radical Protestant *memorialism* on the other, to which the BCP was a middle of the road response. Although the 1552 version of the prayer book was decidedly Protestant, the settled format, contained in the 1559 version, was designed to attract at least the nominal adherence of Catholics as well as Puritans. Paul might not have recognised the precise terms of the controversy but he would have recognised the polemical rhetoric.

It might seem almost disrespectful on this most bittersweet day of the Church's calendar to refer to such controversy, but there is a more important positive point to be made than the negative observations so far. For all its controversy and evolution, the Eucharist has remained the historical, universal continuation of the reality of the incarnation, the perpetuation of Jesus' physical presence with us.

Luke's account of the trial of Jesus picks up with that incarnational controversy. The Jews, who had no notion of incarnation, were genuinely puzzled by Jesus. This can be seen in their rather muddled accusation that he is refusing tributes to Caesar and claiming to be the Christ. When Pilate asks the direct question Jesus resorts to the already remarked odd phrase, "thou sayest it". In one sense Pilate was less puzzled than the accusers. If Jesus really claimed to be the King of the Jews then to the Roman titular King of the Jews he should go. So Jesus is sent (unique to Luke's account) to the rather Janus-like figure of Herod who was known to be cruel, according to the severest of his Evangelical critics (Matthew 14.6), but who was also an authority on Judaism and had, according to Mark (6.20), killed John reluctantly, because he regarded him as holy. Herod's sadism took the form of theatre, torturing Jesus and dressing him in a gorgeous robe. How this reconciled him to Pilate it is impossible to say, because Herod had not solved Pilate's problem. He went on with the quasi-judicial process until, as a matter of policy, he finally caved in. In Luke's account, Simon of Cyrene, not Jesus, carries the cross, which explains why he is able to talk to all those who knew him. His lament over Jerusalem reflects Luke's literary and theological positioning of Jerusalem at the centre of his narrative (cf. Saint Luke the Evangelist) until, in the latter part of Acts, the emphasis moves dramatically to Rome. Typically, Jesus talks to women and, equally typically, when he arrives at his final earthly destination, Luke finds good as well as bad in the dregs of society. Jesus' forgiveness of the repentant thief is the essence of Luke's core belief that the mission of Jesus was to the poor and weak, those (in the words of a physician) who needed a physician. The repentance of the thief is shown in stark contrast to the rulers of the people who mocked. With something of the technique of Mark, the final minutes of Jesus' life shift from the wide focus of the public event to the private dialogue with the thieves, and then back again. His final cry is as submissive as his commitment at the Mount of Olives, praying with the support of the angel. The narrative closes in a way that only Luke would depict, with the women, standing at a distance, watching the terrible suffering reaching its inevitable climax.

Looking back on Luke's account, the quality that stands out is his understanding of human complexity. With the exception of the utterly simple Jesus, everyone in his narrative is plagued by a variety of factors which subtly alter their balance as the narrative unfolds. None of us, says Luke, has an unchanging set of attributes to which we stick regardless of circumstances; we shift the balance between the elements within ourselves almost without knowing it. From the dominant figures of Pilate and Herod, through to the rather caricatured figures of the religious leaders, to the women who at one point talk to Jesus but at the last can only stand far off, nobody gets through these two chapters without experiencing change. How true is that for us?

Good Friday

Collects:	*Almighty God, we beseech thee graciously to behold this thy family . . . ;*
	Almighty and everlasting God, by whose spirit the whole body of the church is governed . . . ;
	O merciful God who hast made all men . . .
Epistle	Hebrews 10.1–25
Gospel	John 19.1–37

In the working out of the theology in Hebrews it is easy to forget two words: *ecce homo* ("behold, the man"). What can sound like an ingenious salvific device is a person of flesh and blood. The man whose blood substituted the image for the shadow, who superseded the blood of animals so that the sacrifice of his life might seal the New Covenant, was mocked, tortured and killed for us, but is that the extent of God's mercy? The first Collect refers to the family of the Church, and the second is gracious enough to recognise that this comprises "all estates of men" (a reference to the reading of the Litany), but the third is most definite that Jews, Turks, Infidels, and, ominously, heretics are not covered by the saving act of Jesus unless they enter the Church's fold. All this, sadly, is common enough rhetoric. The Jews were a familiar target (cf. The Sunday Next before Easter) and the Turks, after the fall of Constantinople in 1452, pursued an aggressive anti-Christian campaign which brought them to the gates of Vienna in 1680. Infidels had been the target of the

Crusades and were still possessors of the holy places, and although all but the first had been disastrous, there was a lingering attachment to the idea. Protestantism had not been slow to requisition the Roman Church's treatment of heretics, among which some of its more radical adherents were numbered. If the ideas are in any way helpful in the abstract, the list itself is surely a sorry piece of history, best overlooked on this most solemn of all days when our minds should be fixed on the suffering and death of Jesus rather than on anachronistic and meretricious factionalism. Jesus regrets the hard-heartedness of the Jews, and the Evangelists in their different ways try to come to terms with it, but nothing can obscure the boundless generosity of the death of Jesus on the Cross and its perpetuation in the Eucharist. Before that historically transforming mystery, all theological controversy (and intrigue) must fall. We have put in peril the mysteries of Eucharist and Cross, making them, against the somewhat pious wishes of the First and Second Collects, a symbol of division rather than of unity.

The hearts were hard enough in Jerusalem on that fateful morning. Pilate did not show off Jesus in his crown and robe because he was sorry for him, but because he hoped, in this piece of theatre, to show how trivial the whole thing was and, when it failed, Pilate dismissed him. The Jews, who had their own backs to watch, kept on justifying themselves against Pilate's charge of trivia. To frighten Pilate, Jesus was portrayed as an impostor, but not even that could move Pilate who, surely in jest, referred to Jesus twice as "your king". Pilate was no doubt reflecting sarcastically on the claim of Jesus that all earthly power, including that of Pilate, came from him. The religious authorities lead Jesus away, mouthing the hypocritical platitude that they had no king but Caesar, but Pilate has the last laugh. He cites Jesus on his inscription as King of the Jews, which goads his accusers into a challenge, but the plaque remains to taunt them. After the familiar reference to Jesus' clothes (with the elaboration of the seamless garment), John's Passion takes a singular turn as Jesus commends his mother and the Apostle John to each other (cf. Saint John the Evangelist's Day). This accounts for the persistent tradition that he looked after her until she died at Ephesus near the end of the first century. In Luke, the women are far away, but here they are at the foot of the Cross. This serene Jesus drinks the proffered vinegar and simply, somewhat enigmatically, says, "it is finished." John's account is also the only one to exempt Jesus from the final, summary process of leg breaking. Instead of which, in one of the most graphic scenes in all four Passions, he calls on numerous references (Exodus 12.46; Psalm

22.16, 34.20; Isaiah 53.5; Zechariah 12.10) for the image of Jesus' side being pierced with a lance, so bereft that there is only a drop of blood, and then water.

Of all four accounts, John's brings us, through the depiction of the utter serenity of Jesus, to a point of silence. For Mark the Son of God, for Matthew the King, for Luke the Saviour, but for John, this is the Lamb of God who goes to the slaughter like the animals in Hebrews, ritually bled so that no drop of blood remains in him but is poured on the ground as tribute to the Father.

There are those who will use this saddest of occasions to reflect upon how our sin brought Jesus to his death on Calvary, and what that death means for our sinfulness and redemption. Just as I find it impossible to think about the incarnation on Christmas day without seeing the Cross, stark against the sky on a distant hill, so I cannot think on Good Friday, particularly reading the Gospel of John with its reference to Mary, without thinking of the crib where she suckled him. Milk, to blood, to water, the life cycle we share with the animals who were said to have warmed him with their breath. That this child should have come to this through us and for us is almost too great a thought to articulate as we leave church in silence.

Easter Even

Collect	*Grant, O Lord, that as we are baptized into the death . . .*
Epistle	1 Peter 3.17–22
Gospel	Matthew 27.57–66

This is perhaps the most curious day in the Church's year, the one day when we are most acutely suspended between death and new life. It is also the day in the early Church which reached its climax with the baptism of catechumens. It is therefore natural that we should consider dying the old death and being born again into new life, the essence of baptism (although, curiously, this central theme is only introduced by the Collect as a surrogate for Romans 6.9–11 included in tomorrow's Anthems).

The massive difference between "Mary Magdalene, and the other

Mary, sitting over against the sepulchre" and us, as we await the Easter Proclamation, is that they did not know what was going to happen. Not even Jesus knew what was going to happen. He had been called upon by God to fulfil a vocation which he carried out in obedience and even if he knew he was divine (cf. John's gospel, as opposed to the Synoptics), the detail was elusive, as it was to his followers even after the Resurrection. Of course, Jesus had mentioned "rising again", but the Book of Daniel, which was one of the most popular texts at the time of Jesus, was only one of many instances of late Old Testament pronouncements which, at their basest, could be interpreted as the overthrow of Roman power and, at their most exalted, could refer to an afterlife of which the Pharisees were controversial adherents. For those preparing the body of Jesus for burial, the arduous, sometimes exhilarating, often bewildering, journey had ended in failure. Whatever the fleeting triumphs, the taunts of the religious authorities and the cold sneers of the Romans would have to be endured on Sunday morning. Whatever had been in Jesus' mind had simply not worked out. The Resurrection, when it came, was an unimaginably enormous shock.

Its enormity was first confronted by the same Mary Magdalene who was sitting against the tomb and, as there are more fundamental matters for tomorrow, this is an opportune moment to consider the scandal of the omission in the Easter readings (John 20.11–18) of the first encounter between a human being and the risen Lord. Is this because it was a woman? Why was the constancy of the women in the Passion narratives overlooked when the early Church was considering its leadership? The argument is often put that if Jesus had meant women to be church leaders he would have numbered them amongst his Apostles, but the same argument could be used about Gentiles. Whatever our standpoint on the role of female leadership in the Church, we should consider these questions as far from our own prejudices as we are able.

What of the sepulchre against which the two women sat? It is a scandal (that word again) that the Church of the Holy Sepulchre in Jerusalem is the setting for the longest running inter-denominational feud in Christian history, a feud that is so bitter that it frequently breaks out in violence, and so intractable that the door-keepers of the Church are Muslim. Because the different occupiers (a better word than occupants) cannot agree on how to preserve the building from collapse, its condition continues to deteriorate, and the Sepulchre itself is only prevented from complete collapse by metal girders driven into it as a temporary measure by British Royal Engineers in 1927, following a severe earth-

quake. Tonight, on its greatest night of the year, the different denominations will intone their liturgies as noisily as possible, not so that their
prayers might reach "heaven", but that the prayers of the others will be
drowned out.

It is within the context of this betrayal that we need to consider the
themes of baptism and Resurrection in the Epistle. The history of the
Chosen People was one of going away from and returning to God, and
there is no more spectacular episode in this tension than the flood and
Noah's survival. These events prefigure the nadir and the revival realised
in the crucifixion and Resurrection, but Peter also means us to see them
as a prefigurement of Baptism. The idea of death in baptism is that we
are consenting to such a radical change in who we are that we begin a
new life in which we do not claim to be less sinful, but simply ambitious
to do the will of God. As the Collect is careful to point out, no matter what mortifications of our corrupt affections we undertake, we may
only pass to our own "joyful Resurrection" through Jesus' merits.

For those who live, no matter how falteringly, in the presence of God,
this is the loneliest day of the year, and therefore provides us with the
opportunity to remind ourselves how bleak life must be if such a period
of dead calm is prolonged through doubt or despair. We should also
consider how life must be for those who have never known the Lord
Jesus.

In some Christian traditions, we are brought out of suspense by the
lighting of the Paschal Candle in the dark of the night, followed by a
complete recital of our redemption from Genesis to the empty tomb.
The ancient Easter baptismal tradition is then remembered through the
renewal of vows. In some churches there is a revival of Easter baptism.
Whatever our tradition, we have a strange but precious space in which
to shift out of our Lenten mindset and prepare for the renewal that is to
come.

Easter Day

Anthems	1 Corinthians 5.7^{b}–8; Romans 6.9–11; 1 Corinthians 15.20–22; Doxology
Collect	*Almighty God, who through thine only-begotten son Jesus Christ hast overcome death . . .*
Epistle	Colossians 3.1–7
Gospel	John 20.1–10

Perhaps because we live in a world that is imperfect by virtue of our necessary freedom to love, we are less well able to deal with the perfect act of Resurrection than with the Crucifixion, in which we all have a part. The liturgical cycle of Easter, from the Vigil to the Ascension, is as magnificent in its affirmation as the Lenten cycle is profound in its preparation. Yet, somehow, it is difficult to rise to its level of supreme triumph. We say to each other, "Christ is risen! Alleluia!" but reply with the somewhat mundane, "He is risen indeed! Alleluia!" After the baby whom we know how to love, and the suffering servant whom we have known how to pity, comes the triumphant risen Lord, and we are somehow flat-footed. Even after two thousand years of tradition, which has retained the reality of the Resurrection at its core as the identifying *sine qua non* of Christianity, we are unsure.

If we find the concept of the perfection of God's incarnation difficult to handle, imagine how the followers of Jesus must have felt. On that Easter morning they had no theology of Resurrection other than a knowledge of the enigmatic Book of Daniel, and the split between the Pharisees and Sadducees on the issue. As we noted yesterday (Easter Eve), Jesus made statements about rising again which sound much stronger in retrospect (which, of course, is when they were written down) than they must have sounded in the heady days of fear and hope as Jesus went to his self-proclaimed, prophesied, fate.

Let us never forget that it was women, including Mary Magdalene who, according to all four Evangelists, discovered the empty tomb, and in all three Synoptic Gospels they heard news of the Resurrection from angels (Matthew 28.1–6; Mark 16.1–8; Luke 24.1–9). In John, the women simply find an empty tomb and report it to the Apostles, at which point there is something of a dynamic tension between the Apostle John's youthful competitiveness with, and deference for, Peter. Ultimately they both go into the tomb, see the discarded grave clothes and go home puzzled.

At least we have our Anthems and other readings to counter balance this most low-key account of Easter morning. Even so, both the Epistle and Collect seem reluctant to enter into the festive spirit. Although Paul in Colossians explains that the Resurrection means that we will appear with Christ in His glory, he cannot resist the usual temptation to refer to those sins which will exclude people from that experience. Although the Collect crisply states that the Resurrection has opened up for us the "gate of everlasting life", it still adopts a penitent rather than an affirmative stance. Only in the Anthems from Paul do we really receive a triple blast of affirming Resurrection theology: the first links the Passover with the Resurrection, the second affirms that death and sin have been conquered, and the third describes the span from Adam to the conquest of death (cf. The Sixth Sunday after Trinity).

It is important that Paul's necessary difficulties in formulating a theology of Resurrection should not obscure the utter simplicity and magnificence of what we are being told. To understand this we need to remind ourselves of two preceding events. In the incarnation, God erupted into history and confirmed the union of the Creator and the created. In the Crucifixion, God showed us that our wrong choices in exercising our freedom to love would not count against us. In the Resurrection those two realities were transposed by, in Carl Rahner's memorable phrase, "an irreversible promise of salvation" whereby the created will be enfolded back into the life of the Creator.

What we miss in the bewilderment and struggle of all the Resurrection accounts is a true sense of history shattered and yet perfected. Rather than, "Christ is risen", and the reply, "He is risen indeed", we might try, "Christ has freed us from earth", with the reply, "He has made us sacred", or something of the sort. Cyclical observance makes it difficult to generate a real sense of wonder and surprise, but that is what we must try to do. Without this history-shattering and history-confirming event there is no point in coming to church at all. The incarnation and the Crucifixion, taken separately or together, mean nothing to us without the Resurrection. They might, in some way we cannot understand, have some theological significance, but what would be the point of confirming our oneness with the Creator and our freedom to love without any hope of returning into the Creator? What would it mean to be Christians without the Resurrection?

It seems not to have occurred to the Apostles (with whom we must count Paul) that there was any significance in the life of Jesus without the Resurrection. The early writers did not have the crystalline perspective of an Aquinas or Rahner, but their utter faith in Resurrection, and their fearlessness in explaining it, made that later clarity possible. Not only did the Resurrection defy history, it also put immense strain on the Apostles' understanding of what history is. Theologians they were not, but, guided by the Spirit, whose coming ends the Easter cycle, they never wavered. Nor, with all our theological tradition and the benefit of hindsight, should we.

Monday in Easter Week

Collect   *Almighty God, who through thine only-begotten*
                   son Jesus Christ hast overcome death . . .
For The Epistle Acts 10.34–43
Gospel   Luke 24.13–35

Luke's account of the Resurrection chronology is radically different from the other Evangelists. Matthew (28.9), Mark (16.9), and John (21.14) agree that the first appearance of Jesus was to women in general, or Mary Magdalene in particular, somewhere near the tomb. Luke, who might be expected on the basis of the rest of his Gospel to note the prominent role of women in this most dramatic of events, does not follow the discovery of the empty tomb with a detailed account of the appearance of Jesus, but dismisses Peter's encounter with Jesus in a single line (24.34). Instead the narrative shifts to two travellers, Cleopas and, it is reasonable to assume, his wife (Mark 16.12 adds nothing), who are trying to get home to Emmaus before the light fades and, therefore, whose departure from Jerusalem must have taken place before the full impact of the day's early events became clear. They are approached by a stranger who asks for the latest news. They tell him about Jesus, their hopes, the empty tomb and the angels' announcement that Jesus is alive, but they can make nothing of it, and so the stranger "opens their eyes", but only in a theological sense. Their eyes are "holden, so that they should not know him" until the breaking of the bread in their home. This is only one aspect (cf. Tuesday in Easter Week) of the problematic nature of Jesus' post-Resurrection physical state.

The discourse of the stranger, reflecting one of Luke's major concerns in the Gospel, but even more so in Acts, significantly begins with Moses in linking Jesus with the prophetic tradition. In his sermon to Cornelius and his family in our extract from Acts, Peter further underlines the prophetic link, drawing in the baptism of John, and connecting the Crucifixion and Resurrection with the last judgment and the remission of sins. Again, significantly, Peter underlines the post-Resurrection physicality of Jesus by referring to his eating and drinking. One question is whether the references to food in acts and the Gospel are pointed or incidental.

Apart from Luke's necessary preoccupation with establishing a link between the Jewish prophetic tradition and the life, death, and Resurrection of Jesus, the key element in the Gospel is the self-conscious reference to the Eucharistic rite, which only consists in the breaking of bread (cf. Monday before Easter). Cleopas and his companion are so struck by this act that it triggers their recognition of Jesus. This raises two interesting points: firstly, that followers of Jesus other than the Twelve were present at the Institution of the Eucharist at the Last Supper; secondly, that if Cleopas' companion was indeed his wife, that presence might well have included women. Whatever the case, the impact of this repeated ritual was so great that after Jesus had gone from their presence, the two householders immediately braved the onset of night to return to Jerusalem to tell the others what had happened. Their hearts aflame, they carried Jesus' scriptural exegesis, sealed with his own special sign.

For us, the particular relevance of Peter's speech in Acts is that the good news is being proclaimed to Gentiles after a long inner struggle, which finds Peter in conflict with his own traditional instincts and those of most of his followers. The story of Cornelius, unlike that of many other Gentile converts, is not opportunistic (cf. The Second Sunday in Lent), but is an elaborately constructed set piece which ties together Peter's rooftop vision of Gentile food (recounted twice for effect) and Cornelius' vision which causes him to summon Peter. The account which Peter presents is as simple and practical as that which a soldier might expect, based on eyewitness testimony and with a simple conclusion.

One of the major underlying dynamics in these readings is that of transformation and consolidation. The obvious starting point is the Resurrection itself, which transforms the landscape of Jesus' followers from one of total disaster and defeat to one of bewilderment which takes some time to clear. It is, I think, fair to argue that in none of the Gospels is there a post-Resurrection portrayal of the followers of Jesus at ease with their new situation. By the time we reach the story of Peter and Cornelius, everything is much more clear. The Pentecost experience and the continuing active intervention of the Holy Spirit in the nascent Church enables Peter to put the post-Resurrection events into focus. There is also a strong element of transformation and focus in Luke's account of the breaking of the bread. What might seem, without the benefit of 2,000 years of Christian tradition, to be rather fragmentary accounts of the Institution of the Eucharist, are given a massively consolidating affirmation in Luke's Emmaus account. Jesus really did mean that his actions at the Last Supper should be repeated.

The most striking feature of Luke's account, given the general background of post-Resurrection bewilderment, is the decisive action of Cleopas and his companion. There is no hesitation, no doubt, no fear of being ridiculed and, one surmises, no decorous little phrases to describe this momentous revelation. The Eucharist is a decisive affirmation that Jesus has risen from the dead. How, then, can we who have the testimony of the whole of the New Testament and 2,000 years of Christian tradition, generate the same wonder at our risen Lord and the same sense of affirmation in the Eucharist?

Tuesday in Easter Week

Collect	*Almighty God, who through thine only-begotten son Jesus Christ hast overcome death . . .*
For The Epistle	Acts 13.26–41
Gospel	Luke 14.36–48

One of the mysteries of the Resurrection to whose core we will never fully penetrate is the physical nature of the risen Jesus. It is a subject which clearly confused the Evangelists. In today's Gospel, Luke has Jesus eating and drinking (referred to by Peter, cf. Monday in Easter Week), Matthew says the women held Jesus' feet (28.9), and John describes Thomas putting his hand into Jesus' wounds (20.27), but confuses the issue by telling how Jesus warned Mary Magdalene not to touch him (20.17). It also confused the disciples. A person whom they had served constantly is killed and then re-appears in a way that, if he wishes, they can recognise. He appears through locked doors—unnerving enough in itself—but he is somehow a physical presence.

This issue is crucial to our understanding of the Resurrection whose physicality is not just a metaphor, it is a precise prefigurement of our own trajectory of existence. It is an aspect of Christian doctrine, included in the Creeds, which is frequently avoided or fudged, mainly because we have been contaminated by dualism which leads us to think that parting with our bodies will be a fitting reward for earthly self-denial, when in fact celebrating with our bodies is a fitting prefigurement of eternal life. When we die we will lose our physical bodies, but when time comes to an end we will get them back. In Tom Wright's crisp phrase, "there is life after life after death" (*Simply Christian*).

We tend to drift away from an integrated view of our state into dualism, separating our body from what we call our "soul", because even as he is trying to combat the dualistic tendencies of gnosticism, Paul, living in a pagan world of self-indulgence and narcissism, too easily descends into anti-materialist diatribes. The passage in Acts is the second half of Paul's first reported sermon, preached at Pisidian Antioch, which Luke barely differentiates from Peter's sermon to the family of Cornelius (cf. Monday in Easter Week). There is an egregious contrast between the state of the risen Lord, and the corruption of earthly things which are all doomed to be wiped out in death and destruction. Far from affirming the physicality of creation, Paul seems to think in this passage that the Resurrection trumps physicality. In conquering death, the Resurrection guarantees our life after death in Christ, and it does not characterise the physical as degrading. The spiritual is in a different category from the physical, and to rank them is as absurd as saying that a Bach cantata is more worthy than a carrot. Such ranking is profoundly unhelpful and misleading but, driven by competitiveness, we frequently fall into this trap.

Against the assaults of romantic, self-abasing dualism, we must always bear three points in mind. Firstly, God created the physical world so it is as perfect in its way as everything created must be. Secondly, God chose to live among us not by appearing as a wraith but in the incarnate person of Jesus. Thirdly, neither did our risen Lord appear as a wraith but, the Evangelists, Peter and Paul all attest, was a physical presence.

In Luke, Jesus not only eats, he also invites the disciples, full of fear that they are seeing a spirit, to touch him because, he says, "a spirit hath not flesh and bones". There is something overwhelmingly touching about this invitation, underwritten by the very basic request for food which, again, leads one to wonder who was present. It was uncharacteristic for men to cook fish and prepare honey-comb in a domestic environment. They might have to barbecue at the beach, as they do today, but indoors was different. Whatever the answer, Jesus, beginning with those emblematic words, "peace be unto you", transformed a situation from cosmic fear to domestic familiarity. He then explains, yet again, as he had to Cleopas and his companion (see Monday in Easter), precisely how his mission and Resurrection conformed to the scriptural framework with which they were familiar. Finally, in a typically Lucan touch, Jesus marks out the beginning of the new mission in Jerusalem, the focal point for all of Luke's writing until the emphasis radically shifts to a Roman axis in the second part of Acts.

What Luke reports Paul as saying is an understandable aberration, given the contrast between Judaic fastidiousness and pagan abandon. We know from Paul himself how careful he was to underline the concept of the body as a spiritual temple, as a vessel which must be worthy of God (Romans 12.1). This raises some questions for our body-conscious generation. These are usually framed around sexual conduct, with the obvious condemnation of power-based and/or trivialised physical relationships, but we tend to think much less, even in this age of mounting obesity, of greed and laziness. Just because the emphasis moves, as we grow older, from the genitals to the stomach, and from the human object to the inventory of possessions, this does not mean that our self-indulgence is somehow less venal. That being the case, we would be in danger of confining sinfulness to the young and the sexually active, a stance which many glibly adopt to their own complacent self-satisfaction. In an age where excess of the kind which Paul confronted easily lures us into misunderstanding God's creation, we need to make a special effort to understand how we must, commemorating the Resurrection, fittingly celebrate the physical.

The First Sunday after Easter

Collect	*Almighty father, who has given thine only son to die for our sins . . .*
Epistle	1 John 5.4–12
Gospel	John 20.19–23

One of the problems with the Bible for contemporary readers is our culture's concern for chronology. Our historical practice is concerned with accurate dating, and our near addiction to news prompts us to want to know not just what happened, but when. Many news stories of corruption are not so much concerned with who did what, but when the Prime Minister or President knew about it. Leaders may not have done anything wrong, but they might have been involved in a cover-up. John, whose Gospel is deeply concerned with the development of Trinitarian theology, is reasonably specific in Chapter 14 (cf. Whitsunday) that after Jesus ascends into heaven He will send "down" the Holy Spirit, but here Jesus is breathing the Holy Spirit into his disciples before he ascends. There is no specific reason why the Trinitarian completion should take place after the Ascension, but we simply have to adjust to a rather more fluid and unfamiliar economy.

Fluidity is also important in the way we understand 1 John. Whether or not the two works were written by the same author (cf. Saint John the Evangelist), their concerns are very similar. Yet again, however, we need to be cautious. John cites three marks of Jesus: water (cf. Chapter 5), blood, and the Spirit. Just because these are placed next to the "Persons" of the Trinity does not mean that we can draw an automatic correspondence. The Spirit corresponds in both triads,, and it is easy to correspond blood with the Son, but the link between the Creator and the Water of Life is pleasing ywr not specific. In John 5.1–30, Jesus says to the Samaritan woman that she will only attain everlasting life if she receives the "water of life", which he will give her, and we know that he is the intermediate between the Creator and the created (John 14.6), so the correspondence makes sense, even if it is not specified.

There is, too, a rather strange apparent anomaly in the Collect which describes the death of Jesus for our sins, but the Resurrection as our means of justification (as opposed to the customary formulation classically expressed in Romans 3.24 that our justification was brought about by redemption through the Cross). As the Cross and Resurrection are integral this inconsistency is hardly significant. The Collect is on surer ground when it mentions the leaven of malice and our need to lead pure lives which signal the resumption of post-Easter business as usual. The post-Resurrection accounts are necessarily concerned with the forgiveness of sins because the event itself had radically altered the terms of trade. Before His death and Resurrection, Jesus might have proclaimed his power, and that delegated to His disciples, to forgive as late as the Last Supper (cf. Matthew 26.28), but the power looked altogether more plausible three days later. The other reason for concern with this issue was that, until the destruction of the Temple in AD 70, the Jews had a recognised and detailed system of atonement, but Christianity before the destruction, and Judaism after it, had to work out a new formulation. On one point 1 John is classically Jewish in a way that we should note carefully and seek to follow. When it talks about sin, the primary sin is the denial of the Godhead of Jesus; it is the New Testament equivalent of the Old Testament sin of blasphemy. We should never forget that in the two classical statements of the law we are to follow (Exodus 20.1–17; Deuteronomy 5.1–21), offences against the Godhead take precedence over offences against our neighbour, yet in most contemporary Christian formulations of what it means to be faithful, offences against people seem to take priority over offences against God. Atheists, after all, can be profoundly ethical, but only a belief in God would make them Christian. It is a mistake to think that to be a Christian fundamentally means to be ethical; that follows from our faith.

As we have noted elsewhere, there is a tendency for the early writers to veer towards dualism (cf. Tuesday in Easter Week), but 1 John is, above all, concerned with the earth as the perpetrator of persecution. Gone are the days when Paul (Romans 13.1–7) (cf. The Fourth Sunday after the Epiphany) could urge Christian adherence to the Roman secular state. The severity of persecution which lead Revelation to characterise Rome as Babylon (cf. Revelation 17–18) forced a temporary change of what it meant to render to Caesar. This is a point we ought to bear in mind. There has been a tendency in Western Christianity to develop theories of Church and State (cf. The Fourth Sunday after the Epiphany), but our adherence might better depend on a practical assessment of what the state does which would entitle us to make our adherence conditional. There have already been instances early in the twenty-first century where the UK state has shown signs of legislating to impose modes of conduct which go against the consciences of some Christians. The right course is to commit open civil disobedience and take the consequences, but most of us would find that very hard. It is not enough to be familiar with the principle. Much of the secular state wants to sanitise religion so that it is simply a segment of the charitable sector, prepared to fulfil public policy on the cheap. We should be clear that there is a price to pay for our co-operation, and that price is freedom from persecution by legislative means. Jesus was preparing his disciples for a hostile world not very different from our own.

The Second Sunday after Easter

Collect	*Almighty God, who hast given thine only son to be unto us a sacrifice for sin, and also an example . . .*
Epistle	1 Peter 2.19–25
Gospel	John 10.11–16

On this day which many churches will celebrate as "Good Shepherd" Sunday, it would be as well to remind ourselves that shepherds in first century Palestine were the lowest of the low (cf. The Circumcision of Christ). So when Jesus characterises himself as "the Good Shepherd", he is not taking on airs and graces. He is, in fact, making a radical proposition by presenting himself as a shepherd, but not a hireling, because all shepherds at that time were hirelings of absentee landlords. They certainly were not owners of sheep. What Jesus is saying is that he will unite the two quite separate phenomena of ownership and care within his person, making us children in God's care.

Although this appears to be a pleasingly simple image, there are numerous complexities, of which there is only space here for a few. First, we do not simply "go astray" in the fashion of sheep, but commit deliberate acts of will that separate us from God. These have entailed divine intervention in our affairs in the form of the incarnation which, in turn, directs us to the second complexity of the image. Jesus is not only the Good Shepherd in one context, he is also the innocent lamb that is slaughtered in another who, in the vivid words of Peter, "His own self bore our sins in his own body on the tree". The Collect, as usual, outlines the antithesis between the sacrifice of Jesus and our want of good behaviour, our tendency not so much to wander as to trust in our own devices.

The third complexity of the image is brought out in the Epistle, where

Peter commends the virtue of suffering. Whereas sheep may undergo cold, hunger, thirst and illness without any self-determination, we are called upon deliberately to choose suffering as part of our witness to Jesus. When he says that his own sheep know him, this is more than an instinctive reaction of the dependent to the dominant; it is a much more (although of course this is itself a metaphor) reciprocal relationship. Next, our choice to suffer is nothing to the choice which Jesus made and whose consequences, in Peter's phrases, he withstood without complaint. The two figures involved in this sacrifice, other than we sheep, are the Father and the wolf, both of whom (again in a complex metaphorical way) dictate the pattern of Jesus' offering of himself.

There is something deeply satisfying about the elegantly interlocking metaphor of Jesus as shepherd and laying down his life for us as a lamb, reflecting the very similar interlocking of Jesus offering himself as priest and victim. They are metaphors simultaneously of power and vulnerability, underlining the essential mystery of the passion as simultaneously wounding and healing. By those stripes we were healed.

Peter's conclusion that we were going astray before the Crucifixion, but are now back on course, is surely, as the Collect implies, overly optimistic. The first century perspective saw a seamless continuity from the prophesy of Isaiah and Jeremiah, through the transformative life, death and Resurrection of Jesus, and the coming of the Holy spirit to the end of earthly time. This has been complicated for us, both by an inevitable dislocation from the continuity of feeling within Judaism from King David to the destruction of the Temple at one end of the chronological spectrum to a lengthening of time itself at the other. Humanity was destined by God not to be swept up into the end of time shortly after the death of Jesus but, rather, we have lived in erratic faithfulness mirroring in our own Christian affairs the vicissitudes of the relationship between God and his Chosen People.

Yet for all its complexities, and for all our need to be careful not to think ourselves into a state of ovine moral incapacity, there is a serious sense in which, noting the Collect, the metaphor of the shepherd and the sheep works. For just as there is a difference of degree, as well as a difference of role, between shepherd and sheep, so the same difference, on a much more radical scale, exists between our Saviour and the saved. Just as the sheep that go astray cannot reorient themselves but must be rescued by the shepherd, so we could not redeem ourselves, but rely upon Jesus laying down his life for us.

How much Peter saw himself as a shepherd—or bishop—it is difficult to say, but his dialogue with Jesus at the end of John's Gospel (21.15–19; cf. Saint John the Evangelist's Day) must have run deep. Of all the metaphors from the Gospels describing the Christian condition, this is the one that has made the greatest impact, not least in the way we understand the relationship between the bishop and the flock. For many today, however, who have never visited the countryside, this metaphor and its reality in the office of Bishop must present a new set of problems. No matter how much we love the language of the shepherd and the sheep we will need to find new ways of explaining this complex of interlocking Christology which is at the core both of our dependence and our obligation to live holy lives.

The Third Sunday after Easter

Collect	*Almighty God, who shewest to them that be in error . . .*
Epistle	1 Peter 2.11–17
Gospel	John 16.16–22

The predictions which all four Gospels put into the mouth of Jesus about his death and Resurrection, particularly in John, sit somewhat uneasily with the doctrine that, in being fully human and willingly surrendering his divine powers during his incarnate life, Jesus could only have known about his forthcoming death to the extent to which he was able to manipulate events. As such he could not have known anything about his Resurrection. No wonder his disciples were puzzled. They might have vaguely comprehended the idea that the death of Jesus would conform in some way to a Biblical pattern, but any Messianic figure could not be expected to want to arrange his own death, and even a Messianic figure would have experienced some difficulties arranging it. The point, as Richard Burridge puts it (*John*), is that John invariably depicts Jesus as "being in control". At this last gathering before his death, Jesus knew that he was in trouble with the authorities for attacking them and preaching what amounted to heresy, but the outcome was uncertain.

As for the Resurrection, the only doctrine they knew was the Pharisaic belief in Resurrection at the end of time. They could not have imagined the reappearance of Jesus after his death in some sort of physical guise.

John's motive in describing Jesus' apparent riddle was to provide a grounding for the promised transformation from sorrow to joy, that temporary and painful tribulation would be followed by everlasting reward. This was a message which required constant repetition by the AD 90s when Christianity was suffering its latest bout of persecution, this time under the Emperor Domitian. As has been pointed out before (cf. The First Sunday after Easter), the behaviour of the Roman state was radically different when John was writing from the late 50s when Paul urged obedience to the civil powers. Peter appears to be writing primarily to Jews as he places them in antithesis to the Gentiles. We know that the Jews had a long-running problem with Rome (or any secular power), exacerbated by the imperial assumption of deity, which explains the trap set for Jesus in Matthew 22.15–21. The emperor Claudius expelled the Jews from Rome in AD 59, apparently out of short-term political considerations, but by the early 60s, just before this letter was written, Palestine was again in a state of foment, which culminated in the destruction of Jerusalem. At the same time, Nero had begun to persecute the Christians in Rome and so, on both counts, Peter's exhortation is particularly remarkable because he explicitly and emphatically requires obedience to the civil powers during a period of persecution.

The issue of Church and State, and the scriptural authority for rebellion (cf. The Fourth Sunday after the Epiphany), was a live issue in the sixteenth century because of "extremist" theocratic sects like the Anabaptists. In England, which had recently assumed explicitly ecclesiological authority, attempting to impose an exterior measure of religious uniformity (under pain of criminal proceedings), the issue of authority, particularly in the face of Papally backed Spanish Catholic belligerence and Puritan critique, was acute, which explains the reaction in the Collect to the Readings. It does not talk about Christ, but of "Christ's religion" in which they must "follow all such things as are agreeable", in this case to the monarch in Parliament. This was an age when people were tortured and killed by the state because their religious convictions ran counter to the orthodox and so, oddly in the context of a Eucharist, the Collect carries a threat as well as encouragement. In view of Peter's perhaps naive contrast between the faithful and the Gentiles, there is a sad irony in the spectacle of Christians killing Christians in defence of Christianity.

Setting aside the extreme case of persecution which so coloured John's writing, the Gospel (borrowing the most often used, and in many ways the tritest, analogy from the Old Testament of the joy of birth after the pain of labour, which none of the authors can have experienced) is concerned to encourage fortitude. Most of us will never face the prospect of being called upon to die for our faith but, still, we are pilgrims, and we can expect suffering as a consequence of steadfastness. Whereas the early Church faced fanatically definite opposition, our challenge is the contemporary tendency to hold any position tenuously and to abandon it at the first sign of trouble. At a more concrete level, in a world where medicine involves extended periods of poor health as well as rapid cures, we often require stamina rather than the instant courage of crisis. Who is to say that one is less or more exacting than the other? This message in John is, therefore, not a highly specific encouragement to the physically brave. We can all look forward to our everlasting reward as long as, paradoxically, we do not believe that our behaviour justifies it.

To be a pilgrim is to be permanently alert and committed, qualities which are difficult to sustain in our cacophonous world of constant competition for our attention, and a sustained campaign by global corporations to persuade us to want what we do not need. The challenges to faithfulness are different in every generation, but the message of hope is the same.

The Fourth Sunday after Easter

Collect	*O almighty God, who alone canst order the unruly wills . . .*
Epistle	James 1.17–21
Gospel	John 16.5–14

One of the unquestioned truisms of our time is that we live in an era of unprecedentedly rapid change. The assumption behind this is that we are more greatly affected by change than any previous generation in recorded history. Behind this commentary, too, there lies the worry that rapid change generates uncertainty. "Goodness knows what will happen next", we say, as if we are in a novel. Yet, at the same time, although one major source of upheaval is climatic aberration, never has meteorological forecasting been better; although we are subject to massive global capital flows, economic forecasting has never been better; and although technological change has never been more rapid, our capacity to take advantage of it has never been greater. Conversely, we think of the era when the BCP was compiled as one of rural stability, from one generation to the other, with people contentedly living in the rhythm of the cycle of the seasons. Yet even describing the mid-eighteenth century, the historian J.H. Plumb said that the single biggest factor in politics was sudden death.

When the Collect talks of change, this might not only result from sudden death but also from the exercise of arbitrary power, or a catastrophic shift of fortune. Change might not have been so rapid, but uncertainty bit much more deeply into the fabric of everyday life. No wonder the Collect contrasts these uncertainties with the fixed point where true joy may be found. In doing so, however, it makes an implicit connection between human suffering and "unruly wills", which is still a controversial topic today. As we know from discussions on the effects of climate change, those whose wills are most unruly are not those who suffer the consequences; for example, the excesses of Manhattan will obliterate the Maldives. This is not to say that there are not areas where we inflict suffering on ourselves, but the connection is more complex than that which the Collect proposes.

James, who tends much more towards the concrete and practical than the abstract theological style of Paul, points out how easy it is for us to hurt others through what we do. He is particularly concerned with rash speech and with angers and proposes that our first action in any situation must be to listen to God and to ourselves.

We are to receive with meekness the "engrafted Word", a term which naturally refers us to John. The Gospel is an extract from the great valedictory discourse, one of whose central themes is the way in which the mission of Jesus will continue after his death. The pivotal event, says Jesus, will be the sending of the Holy Spirit, which will take place after he has returned to the Father. This Trinitarian theology can easily become anthropocentrically time-bound. If we are not careful, we can take John to mean that the coming of the Spirit is only possible after the Ascension, that the moment when the Spirit proceeds from the Father and the Son (to quote the Nicene Creed) takes place in time. This is a profound misunderstanding of the coterminality of the three persons of the Godhead. What Jesus might mean is that as long as he is bodily present there is no need for a Church, but once he has ascended to the Father, the nascent Church will need the Holy Spirit.

After making sense of the Crucifixion and Resurrection, perhaps the most acute issue facing the Apostles was to grasp the nature of the God-head, faced with the risen person of Jesus and the evident fulfilment of his promise to send the Holy Spirit on the Church. Looking back from his position in the late AD 90s, John could make much better sense than the disciples of the blueprint which Jesus set out from the time when he "turned" towards Jerusalem until his Ascension. This yet again raises the central issue of how far the human Jesus understood the divine plan or, to put the matter slightly differently, what kind of theologian was Jesus if he was one at all? Nowhere more than in John's great discourse is it more important to recognise that the text has a theological purpose rather than being an historical account of what Jesus said, heard, and recalled by the "Beloved Disciple".

Understanding the timeless coterminality of the Trinity forms the basis of the emphasis in the readings on the fixedness or stability of God's purpose, compared with the forces under which we operate and the waywardness with which we behave. Our best response is surely to follow James and, in meekness, to control what we can rather than com-plaining about our helplessness and the vicissitudes of life to which we are subjected. It is a sobering exercise to list those matters over which we have control, from our own speech and deportment, to the resources we command, and the power we exercise. To acknowledge that we can only be saved through the merits of Christ, as specified in the Collect, and that we are utterly dependent on the Spirit, as the Gospel implies, does not contradict the Epistle's essential requirement that we hold our-selves responsible for our own actions. In our rapidly changing world it is tempting to renounce responsibility for our own actions by plead-ing that we have lost control of our own lives, but as a social ecology of dense communication and interdependence, while much of the change may have diluted collective power at the national level, it has massively increased our personal power.

The Fifth Sunday after Easter

Collect *O Lord, from whom all good things do come, . . .*
Epistle James 1.22–27
Gospel John 16.23–33

The final portion of Jesus' final farewell discourse before its summary in Chapter 17 contains a number of enigmas. Firstly, what should the disciples ask of the Father? Jesus says that previously they have asked nothing in his name but now they must ask that their "joy may be full". The Old Testament in general depicts people as being fatalistic rather than intercessory. The patriarchs regretted their lack of children but God announced their change of fortune on his own "initiative" rather than in response to prayer. The great prayers, such as the Psalms, praise God, regret misdeeds, ask for peace of mind, and, above all, ask for revenge on (uncircumcised) enemies, but they are largely devoid of the kind of intercession to which we are accustomed. If we take the ACTS acronym (adoration, contrition, thanksgiving, and intercession), the Old Testament put least emphasis on the last.

Secondly, matters are not made easier when Jesus says that he has finished with proverbs and will now speak plainly. The disciples acknowledge this, which enables them to affirm their belief that Jesus "came from God". Thirdly, this happy, if illogical, sequence is then capped by Jesus making two apparently contradictory statements, that his followers will be scattered and abandon him, but that he has said what he has to bring them peace. No matter, he concludes, for he has "overcome the world." The discourse also implies the forthcoming "Ascension" without being specific, which is an indication of the reason for its place in the Lectionary. In order to grasp the complexities of the farewell discourse we have to see it entirely as a theological understanding of the Trinitarian economy and its relationship with the Church and the world. Trying to understand it from the point of view of the listening disciples yields nothing but bewilderment. They would not understand the activity of the Trinitarian Economy until Pentecost and its aftermath, and they would not know what to ask for until their mission began. Yet, even as late as Acts, the traditional priorities of Jewish prayer persist.

James, ever practical, provides a clue to the change of priorities when he unites religious observance with the performance of good works. Although this connection was integral to Jewish life, it was at once purer and simpler than the Christian perception because, devoid of any clear belief in the afterlife until the development of Intertestamental Pharisaic thinking, devout Jews performed good deeds for their own sake without any thought of "banking" them as credits towards eternal life. It was that very "banking" which had triggered Luther's protest against Rome, and it partly explains Luther's reaction against the "efficacy of good works" and the unpopularity of James during the Reformation.

The Collect, in identifying God as the source of all "good things", leads us to the conclusion that we can only ask for the good and that only God can determine what that means. When we intercede we are consciously laying our concern before God and saying, in effect, that he alone knows what is good for us and those for whom we pray. Intercessory prayer is, to a great extent, prayer that reminds us of our own obligations and weaknesses so that when we pray for a sick person we are reminding ourselves to visit them. In a very basic sense, we should ask for nothing to which we are not prepared to contribute ourselves. In other words, as James would put it, prayer (or faith) is not a substitute for action.

Just as the disciples have no tradition of intercessory prayer so, conversely, our prayer tradition has become over balanced in that direction, so that the word "prayer" is used to mean to make a request. This calls to mind the most famous incident of Old Testament personal intercession (prompted by God and not by Solomon) when God asks Solomon what he wants and he (wisely) opts for wisdom. That is a high standard against which to judge our own efforts.

One imagines that if the disciples had understood Jesus they would have asked for the kind of things we, rather than Solomon, ask for. It is understandable that people who are involved in the complexities of mission and compassion should be led to intercessory prayer. Our first instinct when we see a suffering child for whom the doctors can do nothing is to pray for a remarkable recovery, or a swift end to earthly life. There is nothing wrong with this as long as we are clear that we are not lobbying. To attribute a trivial success to prayer leaves us with the uncomfortable corollary of having to attribute the failure to achieve something trivial as a failure in prayer, which brings prayer as a whole into disrepute.

John uses the term "world" in its three senses of being shorthand for wickedness, as a neutral term, and as the fruit of the Creator. In his final, triumphal phrase we are to understand that the Crucifixion overcame evil. Different explanations of how that came about account for the Reformation suspicion of James. We are not caught up in the same controversy, and almost invariably take to philanthropy more easily than theology, but in order to maintain our relationship with God we need a secure and balanced theology of prayer. Unlike the disciples, we are looking back at John's complex discourse from a Resurrection standpoint from, which we ought to be in a much better position to know how, and for what, to ask the Father.

The Ascension Day

Collect	*Grant, we beseech thee, Almighty God, that like as we do believe . . . Christ to have ascended . . .*
For The Epistle	Acts 1.1–11
Gospel	Mark 16.14–20

Theology is the search for the meaning, expressed metaphorically, of sacred mysteries. This basic search for meaning frequently descends from that sublime enterprise into attempts to describe mechanics. This leads to a number of questions. Was there a virgin birth? Was the Crucifixion an act of penal substitution? What form did Jesus' physical presence take after the Resurrection? In the context of today's feast, did Jesus literally rise from the earth, through the clouds to heaven?

Without Luke's two accounts, in today's reading from Acts and 24.50–52 of his Gospel, there would be less of a concern with mechanics and more with meaning. All the Evangelists agree that Jesus took on some kind of physical form for brief periods after the Resurrection and then returned to the Father, but Luke's graphic descriptions make us face up squarely to a questioning of events which must deeply influence our theology. If, for example, Jesus simply appeared as a wraith after his Crucifixion, it would have a profound effect upon our understanding of life after death and salvation. Similarly, the return to the Father, graphically portrayed, makes us think differently about our own return. The actual event of the Ascension in Luke is consistent with its post-Resurrection predecessors.

This very physicality of Jesus during the period between his Resurrection and Ascension naturally revolves around three central themes. Firstly, Jesus has conquered death and turned the tragedy of the Crucifixion into a triumph. Secondly, the Apostles need to be aware of their responsibilities, which will be further reinforced by the coming of the Spirit. Thirdly, having put all things in order, Jesus will return to the Father. As already noted, only Luke describes this return graphically, using it as a link between his Gospel and Acts, and only he locates the farewell on the Mount of Olives, making it yet another pivotal event associated with Jerusalem. Matthew locates the appearances of Jesus in Galilee, but leaves it at that. Mark completes his narrative at the tomb (today's Gospel was a later addition, but this was not known in the sixteenth century). John is most emphatic about the necessity of Jesus returning to the Father (chapters 13–17), but does not feel the necessity of going further, even though he locates the post-Resurrection appearances of Jesus both in Jerusalem and Galilee (some scholars believe that Chapter 22 was a later addition to John).

The rapid and profound development of Trinitarian theology was one of the first fruits of the Holy Spirit. Although it was necessarily most developed in John as the last of the Evangelists, all four Gospels show evidence of the deep understanding—which runs so counter to Judaism—that the Christian approach to God (the Father) is always through the Son and in the power of the Spirit. Such Trinitarian economy could not have been established without the return of Jesus to the Father, yet he did not return as he had come. Jesus was born of the Father outside time, but he was also born of the Virgin Mary and the Holy Spirit as an incarnate being. What, then, we are being told in the Gospels, and Luke in particular, is that, having been enfleshed, Jesus remains enfleshed in anticipation of our enfleshment at the end of time. The Ascension is therefore pivotal in the relationship between the Creator and the created because it is, literally, the last word on the eternity of the incarnation. The bridge between the divine and the human is to remain intact, serviced, if you like, by the Holy Spirit. Some of the terminology in the Nicene Creed is confusing to the contemporary intellectual climate, not just because of a quite understandable general ignorance of fourth century Greek philosophy and its associated theological disputes, but also because such terms as "person", "consubstantial", and "proceed" have so completely changed their meanings in the last 1,600 years that in some ways they are not just obscure, but actually obscure what the Creed is trying to say.

The important idea in the context of the Ascension is that Christianity is, above everything else, relational (although this and its sacramentality are both absent from the Creeds): we were created voluntarily to form a loving relationship with the Creator. Jesus was created to give physical reality to that relationship, to see it, so to speak, from our side of the fence, and the Spirit exists to maintain that relationship. Without the relationship there would be no need of the Son nor the Spirit; there would just be a God making more or less comprehensible pronouncements about the duties of creatures.

There is, apart from the theological implications, a very human aspect to the Ascension which is typically Lucan, and that is the recognition of the human need for closure. For Matthew, Mark, and John there is no real problem, but as Luke is taking the story on through Acts, he has to find a narrative approach that does not leap straight from appearances to the disciples to the coming of the Holy Spirit. Luke's solution is to see the Ascension as both an end and a beginning.

In Luke's Gospel account he describes the disciples as being joyful after the Ascension. This is a somewhat counter-intuitive notion unless, for once in their lives, they clearly understood the promise Jesus had made about the sending of the Spirit. At least they did not have long to wait for all to be made clear.

Sunday after Ascension Day

Collect	*O God the king of glory . . .*
Epistle	1 Peter 4.7–11
Gospel	John 15.26–16.4[a]

Our involvement in the Church's year makes it very difficult for us to be existential, and so the Collect has us both looking back to the Ascension and forwards to Pentecost, with the unifying prayer that the Holy Spirit may help us to follow where Jesus has ascended in his triumph. Although a certain degree of anticipation is unavoidable, occasions such as this enable us to try to put ourselves into the place of the disciples who had, in spite of warnings from Jesus (probably much less precise than those in the Gospels), undergone the shocks of his death, Resurrection and Ascension. This is not a call to empathise with the disciples or undertake a spot of role playing, but we have the opportunity for a little reflection and for gathering our thoughts after the hectic pace of events.

If we find existentialism difficult because of what we know, there are three major reasons why this was even more difficult for Peter and John's early readers. Firstly, life was precarious, even for the moderately well off, and although most people knew where their next meal was coming from, few had savings to counter the immense uncertainties of famine, disease, lawlessness, and simple bad fortune. The other two factors are specific to early Christianity, and are both referred to in today's readings. Peter reminds his readers that the end of time is near at hand and John writes about the persecution of the Church. Both of these factors would have sharpened the purpose of newly converted Christians both to the perils of believing and the rewards for resisting.

It is only fair to concede that in many ways it is much easier to be charitable, as Peter urges, if the prospect of eschatological closure is imminent. It is also true that the prospect of martyrdom, with all its fears and heightened consciousness, would have sharpened the moral sense. On the other hand, some would say that our lives are much easier. We have insurance, savings, wealth, and the ability to plan. Even with recent environmental and financial shock waves, we are still accustomed to seeing the end of time as too distant to engage us. Instead of martyrdom, the worst we can expect is a little crude insult and mild intellectual baiting, submerged in a sea of indifference.

And yet I would argue that the spiritual quest is much more difficult for us without these three major injectors of moral sharpness. Although we believe that we must show charity regardless of whether it will be reciprocated, and in the knowledge that it will not affect whether or not we will be saved, the latter misapprehension is a sharp spur to altruism. Emergency generates an extreme form of altruism. Even though the theology of charity was not so precisely fixed as it might have been for Peter's audience, one imagines that there was a sense of living in a state of emergency which led people to perform all kinds of supererogatory acts that it would not have crossed their minds to perform in normal circumstances.

It is therefore appropriate for us to reflect at this point how far our moral behaviour is a form of diluted Pelagianism. How far do we at some level "go the extra mile", not for its own sake, but because we somehow feel it will enhance our chances of salvation or, even worse, because it may raise our reputation in the eyes of the recipient or the observer? To what extent is generosity a form of peer competition? Of course the dichotomy between faith and good works is exaggerated—such dichotomies always are (cf. The Fifth Sunday after Easter)—and it would be naive to believe that salvation is attainable without both. Although it is certainly true that the relationship between the two is important, it is by no means as fundamental as theological controversy might indicate. In our personal relationships with God Our Parent and with Jesus Our Brother, it would simply be a betrayal not to behave as well as we possibly can, because that is what the relationship requires, as it also requires faith. When we think about what we do, the first question should always be put in the context of our relationship with God. The mechanics are always subsidiary.

If we can to a certain extent clear our minds of some of this historical/ theological baggage we will be in a much better position to leave ourselves open to the counsel of the Holy Spirit whose empowering of the new church we will celebrate next week. Jesus describes the Spirit's role as that of giving strength, and in the context of our lives that strength will be of a different sort from that required by martyrs. Our enemy is weakness and our need is not for a high degree of physical courage, but for stamina. In spiritual terms we are hardly likely to be sent into the arena to face murderous beasts, but we need to go to the gym every day and watch what we eat. Prayer, like going to the gym, can often be unrewarding but it builds us up in ways we do not always immediately recognise and, as for the spiritual diet, we need to be careful that what we think of as orthodoxy is not contaminated by our lazily relativist, morally indifferent, theologically cynical world. We will rediscover next week that to hide from this hostile prospect is not the proper response for a Christian. In the meantime, we have time to get ready.

Whitsunday

Collect   *God, who as at this time didst teach the hearts . . .*
For The Epistle   Acts 2.1–11
Gospel   John 14.15–31[b]

Unlike the stable for incarnation, the Cross for redemption, and the empty tomb for Resurrection, the setting of the Church's birthday truly matches its significance. The followers of Jesus (it is not clear whether the Apostles alone were inspired, cf. Acts 12–15) were suddenly struck by a massive spiritual force which drove them out of the upper room into the Temple precincts on one of the three most important days of the Jewish calendar, the feast of the First Fruits, to harvest the first fruits of the Christian mission. This was the first public declaration of the significance of the Crucifixion and Resurrection.

There are three aspects that stand out. Firstly, Jesus had told his followers to await the Holy Spirit, and they were in no doubt what had happened when it came. Secondly, they were filled with amazing courage. Jesus had sent them out to preach in villages where they knew some of the people, but now they were in Jerusalem preaching to a large and cosmopolitan festival audience. Thirdly, in a remarkable reversal of the Babel story in which humanity had been "punished" for hubris (Genesis 11), the message of salvation overcame the division of language. Naturally it is this last factor which commands most attention because of the comprehensive list of tongues which underlines the point, but that is secondary to the massive injection of power which they received to "kick start" the Church. The first half of Acts in particular is a startling testimony to the power of the Spirit.

The audience was so international because the weather made this the easiest of the three major Jewish festivals to attend (during his travels Paul was anxious to attend this feast, cf. Acts 20.16). Although the majority were Diaspora Jews, Gentiles were almost certainly present. In the Gospel, the other Judas asks why Jesus has not manifested himself to the world, and Jesus replies that doing so will be the mission of his followers. He says that the Holy Ghost will teach them all things and help them to recall all of the things that he said. That promise underwrites the theological authenticity of the New Testament, such that what it says to us about the life of Jesus, and his relationship with the Father and the Spirit, is quite independent of any discussion about historicity. In a little over half a century a revolutionary theology of the Trinity, of Word and Sacrament, of incarnation, redemption and resurrection, of charity, and the meaning of the holy and prayerful life in private and public, was constructed by the most unlikely collection of authors who transformed old genres for new purposes. At the same time, the missionary audacity of Peter, Paul, Stephen, Philip, and the rest was beyond human explanation. How else but in the power of the Spirit could so much have been accomplished?

Sadly, as she (I like to think of associated female qualities with the "Third Person") is equal in the Trinity, this is the one day on which the Spirit is seriously considered instead of being an afterthought in the Doxology. Acts is the book of the Spirit and the Church is her cure. We are the earthly manifestation of the presence of the Spirit, an outward sign of the invisible life force of salvation. Both the Collect and Gospel use the word "comfort" to describe the gift of the Spirit in the sense of "aid and comfort", which is an active assistance precisely opposite to the contemporary, passive meaning of the word.

Perhaps the Spirit suffers most from the language of "person" in Trinitarian jargon, where an active presence willed by the Father and Son would be a better idea. If talking of God makes more sense as a verb than as a noun, then that applies strongly to the Spirit who is constantly active through the Church in history. The Father is outside time, the Son has returned to the Father, but the Spirit is here, with us now, inhabiting our history and our sense of ourselves.

The Collect is courting danger when it associates the Spirit with "right judgment in all things". Too often Christians, and particularly those in authority, invoke the Spirit to underwrite their pronouncements. In the sixteenth century, spiritual and temporal leaders far too often claimed God's sanction for doubtful conduct. We call upon the Spirit, and we have sacramental means of giving added significance to the way we call, and we use our best endeavours to do God's will in the power of the Spirit, but it is dangerous to associate specific decisions with the Spirit. In this sense the Spirit informs our conscience and judgment, but does not issue decrees on matters great nor small. We pray in the power of the Spirit and in union with Christ to the Father, but it is not our power.

Our problem, if it is a problem, is our quest as pilgrims to penetrate further the sacred mysteries, and a key element in that quest is depiction. We know enough to know how inadequate are our efforts when we look at images of Jesus and even more so of the Father, but the spirit is so far beyond our reach as to make our efforts almost ridiculous. When that first great proclamation of salvation was made to the world there would have been doves waiting to be sold and sacrificed and a fire burning to receive them. I like to think that there was a wild dove looking down on Peter as he spoke.

Monday in Whitsun Week

Collect   *God, who as at this time didst teach the hearts . . .*
For The Epistle   Acts 10.34–48
Gospel   John 3.16–21

Unfortunately, the passage from Acts is not a continuation from yesterday, giving us Peter's first great sermon. Instead we have the Acts passage used on the Monday in Easter, with the addition of five verses dealing with the Spirit and baptism.

Having understood his mission to the Gentiles (Paul's dichotomy in Galatians 2.7 is somewhat self-serving), Peter, accompanied by Jewish followers, preaches to the household of Cornelius. The Holy Spirit descends upon the listeners and the Jews are surprised that the audience is behaving in much the same way as the Jews at the Feast of Pentecost. The Holy Spirit, it seems, does not discriminate between the two groups. In spite of the incident of the Syro-Phoenician woman (cf. The Second Sunday in Lent), the election of Greek speaking deacons (cf. Saint Stephen's Day) and, perhaps most shockingly, Jesus' marked sympathy for Samaritans (Luke 10.29–37, John 5), not to mention numerous scriptural inklings and very specific commands from Jesus, this still comes as a considerable shock. How the survival of a strong Jewish element in the Church might have affected its development in the second half of the first century AD is an interesting question, but the crisis defused at the Council of Jerusalem (Acts 15) was effectively snuffed out by the destruction of Jerusalem in AD 70, even though there are traces of it in the way that Matthew sets about his task (cf. The Sunday Next before Easter).

Through Peter, the Holy Spirit endows the Gentiles with visible gifts which they offer to the Jews in the form of prophesying, which in itself must have been yet another curious experience for people accustomed to their prophets fulminating against Gentiles. Then the narrative takes a profoundly sacramental turn. The descent of the Holy Spirit in Acts both prefigures the detailed theology of baptism and confirmation which, along with Eucharist, are the three traditionally combined elements of Christian initiation. These have now been so separated from each other that there is both a debate about the order of Eucharist and Confirmation after Baptism, and a move to recombine the three for adult converts. There is no record of Peter breaking bread (the first records after the Ascension refer to Paul in Acts 20.7–12, 27.35) but there is little doubt that he would have done so on this occasion.

There is a tendency to think of the Spirit almost entirely in terms of confirmation and ordination, but the presence of the Spirit is integral to sacramentality. We only have to think of the Eucharist, which cannot be celebrated without the *Epiclesis*, the calling of the Spirit to bless the elements of consecration, or of the Spirit moving on the waters (Genesis 2.1) which prefigures baptism. The Spirit is indispensable for the ordination of every member of the Royal Priesthood of God (1 Peter 2.4) which takes place in baptism, cleansing the candidate with the water of life. This is the metaphor for the sacrament used by Jesus in his talk with the Samaritan woman (John 5) and in that part of his discourse with Nicodemus which precedes today's reading (cf. Trinity Sunday). The first part of Chapter 3 makes an attractive pairing with Acts because of the natural fit of the imagery, but the second, more reflective part, takes us much further. Mission, comprising Word and Sacrament, exists within the embrace of God's purpose for humanity. God sent his Son to save not condemn, and, if we believe, we will not die. These promises lift religion out of its traditional Jewish dimension. Even for Nicodemus who, as a Pharisee, believed in the resurrection of the dead, this message is startling because it is personal. We do not rely upon God in a detached, universal way, but speak to him as an individual through our relationship with Jesus. In a strange way, Cornelius probably found the message of Peter easier to absorb than Nicodemus listening to Jesus. In the Gentile world the span of the pantheon stretched from a God-the-Father-like Zeus to the extremely earthly imperial line, and so the notion of an intermediate entity between the one and the other would not have been unfamiliar. For Nicodemus, however, the split between God and humanity was radical.

Jesus says that he was sent in love to save, which renders condemnation redundant as there is no point in it. That is why we need to ask what use it is in our own lives. It might make us feel superior, but that is no justification for hurting people. Further, what do we really mean, to take the most obvious case, when we condemn the cruelty of an authoritarian regime? Is our condemnation a noble but futile attempt to change behaviour, or is it the exercise of our moral faculty for our own self-regard? In any case we are operating from a position of ignorance. Just as we do not know the circumstances under which individuals make moral decisions, the same is true of governments. What happens after the overthrow of a dictator (e.g. in the former Yugoslavia or in Iraq) can be worse than what happened before. Condemnation and the consequent exercise of moral authority are not only morally doubtful, they are also fraught with uncertainty of outcome. On a personal scale we are only now beginning to learn about the detrimental effects in adulthood of the authoritarian rearing of children. We must be careful to avoid a similar syndrome in our dealings with all humanity, for we are all children of God.

Tuesday in Whitsun Week

Collect   *God, who as at this time didst teach the hearts . . .*
For The Epistle Acts 8.14–17
Gospel   John 10.1–10

In order to appreciate the chronological development of the theology of the Spirit's role in sacrament, it would have been better if the readings from Acts for yesterday and today had been given the other way around. In today's passage we see that the spirit's invocation through the laying on of hands is already well recognised, but that her presence in baptism is not. It was this chronological ordering of water and then the Spirit which was to lead to the later development of confirmation and its radical chronological separation from baptism. The reverse order also takes us back from the conversion of Gentiles to the conversion of Samaritans closer to home. It is therefore fascinating to consider how it was that Samaritans were baptised without the knowledge of the elders in Jerusalem, unless it was the baptism of John. As is often the case, the Jews (or, more accurately, Judeans), disliked their cousins the Samaritans even more than complete outsiders. The dispute was both political and religious. The Samaritans were the rump of the Northern Kingdom of Israel which had rebelled against Solomon's son Rehoboam (1 Kings 12), setting up their own kingdom under the notorious Jeroboam, and the rift was given new impetus in the Maccabean period. Jerusalem Jews, on the other hand (cf. Whitsunday), had no problem with its own Diaspora whose religious observance was necessarily more sketchy than their own.

The Gospel is not concerned with whom can be counted orthodox, but rather whom is fit to lead. Jesus uses the image of the sheep fold which was a protected paddock where a number of small flocks would overnight under watch. Each shepherd would call his own flock and it would form behind him to be led out into the open. Jesus is referring to Jeremiah 23 and Ezekiel 34, which accuse the religious leadership of being unfaithful. In this case the image is startling because Jesus is not saying that the sheep might transfer their loyalty from the Jewish leaders to him; he is saying that he is the automatic and proper shepherd and that the authorities are like thieves, climbing the wall of the fold, to harm the sheep. Even taking into account the kind of rhetoric and polemic which frequently characterised public religious utterance at the time, this is extremely wounding, calculated to upset the religious leadership. This reminds us of how radical were the claims which Jesus made. We are accustomed to seeing events in the considerable hindsight of the Gospels continually extended in the life of the Church. As time goes by, the Jewish leaders look more wrong and hopeless, but at the time nobody knew what would happen. False Messiahs were not unusual (Acts 5.34–41) and for all anybody knew Jesus was just another leader in the Maccabean mould. There was a long tradition of prophets attacking religious leaders without wishing to overthrow their religion, but Jesus seemed to be threatening just that. The nearest contemporary equivalent is to think of somebody claiming to be the fourth person of the Godhead.

Behind both readings there is just a hint of the origins of the new order of the episcopacy. Clearly there was a division of labour between those who baptised and those who laid on hands, even in the pre-Pauline Church, which temporarily disappeared in the unified office of the city-based bishop, before appearing again as dioceses contained larger flocks, and the metaphor which most represents the office of bishop is that of shepherd. It is sad, then, that the contemporary trend has pushed them ever further into diocesan administration, obscuring the essential simplicity and sympathy of the role. Jesus did not say that he was the good scribe, the good official or the good steward.

Two further themes, membership and ministry, also run through the two readings. Both are radical shifts from Judaism. People are born into Judaism and so it has no concept of voluntary membership. Mixed marriage, which might introduce new blood, was (and by many Jews still is) forbidden, and conversion is still rare. Likewise, there was no tradition of voluntary priesthood, and the tribe of Levi had a monopoly. Yet within a decade of Jesus' death, the apparently conservative Christian leaders had developed a view of mission which was based on a voluntary turning to Christ both in baptism and in the laying on of hands.

In our own Church there has always been a missionary imperative, but for many Christians the hereditary tradition and infant baptism have tended to blunt any feeling of voluntarism. As for the monopoly of ministry, it was never entrenched, even though the higher levels of Church and monastic hierarchies were class based until the Reformation, when they were broken both by the expansion of printing and the democratisation of education on the one hand, and by the revival of congregational affirmation, as opposed to Episcopal appointment, on the other.

Of course it does not matter how good our bishops are and how clearly they call, if we are not listening. One of the foundational principles of Protestantism, which was largely discarded because of humanity's inherent tendency towards hierarchy and organisation, was the redundancy of intermediate clergy between people and their God. Today there is a similar trend based on the hegemony of the individual as consumer. That self-image makes the ovine metaphor uncomfortable, which is no bad thing if it brings us to a more realistic assessment of our selves and our relationship with God.

Trinity Sunday

Collect	*Almighty and everlasting God, who hast given unto us thy servants grace, . . .*
For The Epistle	Revelation 4.1–11
Gospel	John 3.1–15

Many preachers say that today's is the most difficult sermon of the year. Perhaps they think that other mysteries are less mysterious, although ranking mysteries is an impossibility. Part of the problem is that we discuss mystery in metaphorical language, whose meaning changes through time (cf. The Ascension Day).

Unfortunately, today's readings do not help much. Although Revelation is stirringly encouraging and metaphorically rich, it is illustrative rather than foundational. It adds nothing to the Gospels in general, and John in particular, about the nature of the Trinity. The Gospel, too, is only marginally helpful when Jesus poses some impossible riddles to Nicodemus about rebirth in water and the Spirit, and the descending from and ascending to heaven (in his own person), but this also is much less clear in its Trinitarianism than many other passages in John.

Rather than trying to make plausible links out of unhelpful material, let us face the central questions head on: what is the Trinity? Why is it necessary to Christianity? How far can we penetrate its mystery? How can we describe these ideas in contemporary language?

There are numerous occasions for discussing the "persons" of the Trinity individually, and so our concern here is their relationship or, to use the technical term, their "economy". Both of these terms have now completely changed their meaning from the time they were used by fourth- and fifth-century theologians, and so we might today think of the Godhead as a set of symbiotic attributes. Two illustrations involving light might help. Firstly, we might say that the white light of the unity of God needs to be split into component colours to facilitate better human understanding of the divine mystery. Secondly, we might describe the combination of red, blue and green to make up every image that we see.

In terms of the Creator we can ask: why is there something? How do we account for matter if physics says it cannot be created or destroyed? What happened before the big bang? One philosophical answer is that there must have been a creative force. As Christians we believe that this is a divine entity whom we call the Creator (or God the Father), with whom we have a personal relationship, and in this case we have the physical evidence of creation. The doctrine of the incarnation accounts for the Redeemer (or the Son) and, again, we have physical evidence. Nonetheless, the concept is mind-blowing. To overcome the severe stresses imposed by it, the Councils of Nicea (325) and Chalcedon (451) described Jesus as having a divine and a human nature in one person. Today we might think of the fusing of ideas of the physical and the virtual, like a letter on a screen or emerging from a paper printer, three-dimensional haptic objects created out of thin air, and "real environments" like aircraft cockpits simulated. Accounting for the Sanctifier (or the Holy Spirit) is somewhat more difficult because, in a sense, we have to take the word of Jesus for the phenomenon or, recursively, we invoke the presence of the Spirit to account for the Spirit. We might, however, turn to science for illustrations. In the late nineteenth century, scientists were able to predict the existence of certain elements in the Periodic Table before they were found. Scientists, looking at "shifted" light, can locate planets that they cannot see, and we are now familiar with the idea of anti-matter. If, then, we believe in a personal Creator and an incarnated Redeemer, we can readily infer the presence of a Sanctifier who "comprises" the love between Father and Son.

The "necessity" (words in quotation marks to emphasise metaphor) of the incarnation to reconstitute our relationship with the Creator through the Redeemer and, in turn, the "necessity" that we should do so in the light of that incarnation, "generated" the Sanctifier. Thus, Trinitarian unity is a direct "consequence" of the unique event of the incarnation, always remembering that the economy is outside time. In rejecting this "model", other religions confine themselves to an abstract relationship with God which, it can be seen from the Old Testament, places demands upon the believer far in excess of those placed upon us. We have been told by Jesus that nothing will be asked of us for which we are not given the resources, but this places a massive obligation on us to share our good news. This is not to say that it is easy to be Christian, but our theological imagination does not have to wrestle with an unmediated, abstract God.

Thinking back to the idea of colour, it is important to recognise that we all broadly agree about such ideas as blue and red, but they do not mean precisely the same thing to each of us. Doctrine is what we have in common, but it does not make us identically Christian. There is the difference between agreeing a standard, and forcing people to standardise belief or behaviour. Science has also shown us that the Newtonian model of solid objects is conveniently practical, but the world is much more fluid than that. Quantum mechanics might help us to ask if God in Trinity should be a noun or a verb.

Theology and preaching can benefit greatly from contemporary science, not least from Richard Dawkins in his more expansive and less angry work (*Weaving The Rainbow*). We should not be frightened by the Trinity as we have the tools to make exploring this mystery enlightening and enlivening.

The First Sunday after Trinity

Collect   *O God the strength of all them that*
              put their trust in thee, . . .
Epistle   1 John 4.7–21
Gospel   Luke 16.19–31

John's first Epistle is so cumulatively overwhelming and apparently re-
petitive that there is a danger of missing some of what it says. In summary: God is love and that love is made manifest in the sending of Jesus
so that we might "live" (i.e. attain everlasting life through him). Because
God loves us, we should love one another, and in doing so God lives in
us and his love is perfected in us, and therefore he dwells in us and we
dwell in him. In that, God's love is perfected in us; we may live without
fear.

The turning point of the passage, which is easily missed and which
is, significantly, repeated, is that God's love is perfected in us, which implies that without us it would be imperfect. In one sense this is to deny
the perfection of God independent of anything created by him, but in
another sense it means that only we can fulfil God's purpose for us. In
a sense which it is hard to define, our existence is an eternal necessity
of the Godhead, even though we live in time. In other words, allowing
for the problem of the metaphorical language, the eternal, changeless
God can hardly have "decided" to create humanity as a contingent act.
This interpretation almost certainly stretches John's meaning beyond his
intention, but at the very least, the notion that our union with God involves us in some form of perfection is a great comfort. This must have
bolstered John's audience, many of whom were living in fear of persecution, which explains why he was so anxious both to allay those fears and
to set out the over-arching theology of love and salvation.

In their different ways, love and salvation are at the heart of Luke's
story of Dives and Lazarus. The man clad in purple certainly lacks love,
and is therefore deprived of salvation. He therefore asks that those he
has left behind on earth should be warned of their fate if they persist in
his ways, but this plea is rejected.

For a sixteenth century congregation, this story could hardly have
been more straightforward. Its members would have known instinc-
tively that the rich man had Christian obligations of charity, and that
the poor man had basic entitlements. In the late sixteenth century, terrible scare stories of beggars were spread as part of the campaign which

resulted in the mean spirited "Poor Law" of 1601 (which survived until the twin onslaughts of Charles Dickens and the 1930s depression). Begging in the Middle Ages, however, was confined to those who were absolutely incapable of undertaking any manual work. This explains the nature of obligation and entitlement.

In a broader perspective, people in Tudor times knew instantly where they stood in the way society was ranked, and most would have placed themselves closer to Lazarus than to Dives, thus arriving at a secure standpoint from which to view the parable. We have no such luxury. Our society is much more subtly stratified than late feudalism and we frequently find ourselves in different hierarchical relationships. When we read about city tycoons we are poor, but when we sit on the committee that determines mission giving priorities we are rich. As the economic cycle turns and markets rise and fall, we can be pitched from one state into the other. One minute we are Dives, and the next Lazarus. We are also warned against giving money to beggars and against "quick fixes" for deep-seated problems of poverty.

This Janus-like ambivalence ought to enliven us to the necessity of exercising responsibilities as Dives, because we are soon to become Lazarus, but it never quite works that way. Nor should it. We do not exercise graciousness, clemency or generosity in the hope that our conduct will be reciprocated. From a practical point of view this is hardly likely, as the power exercised over us, and that which we exercise over others, is progressive and linear, rather than reciprocal. In any case, the quality of love is that it goes on and on, and is not a boomerang. We should act out of generosity regardless of the conduct of others which might impinge on us.

Luke being Luke, this parable is not as simple as it appears, because of the divine rejection of Dives' plea for a moral messenger to be sent to his brothers. The refusal is both practical and salvific. At the practical level, we all know, as the most literate society in history, how little what we learn influences what we do. Whether we are thinking of morality, history, psychology or simply the life-broadening experience of novel reading, the instances where we change are so infrequent that we can identify them. At the salvific, level the Gospel intersects with both the Epistle and Collect in declaring that salvation is not vicarious. We can, with God's help, only care for our own souls, a point which would not have been lost on post-Reformation worshippers recently deprived of the popular Roman practice of declaring indulgences. The point is further hammered home by the converse observation in Luke that Lazarus could not help Dives once he had been condemned to "hell".

Underlying the readings is the antithesis between loving and not loving, between perfection in, and separation from, God. In living out our contemporary meaning of love, we must be careful not to typecast ourselves too firmly. Our temptation will always be to cast ourselves as Lazarus, but if we examine ourselves closely we will almost certainly find that we are Dives.

The Second Sunday after Trinity

Collect	O Lord, who never failest to help and govern . . .
Epistle	1 John 3.13–24
Gospel	Luke 14.16–24

One of the dangers of set forms of words is that they are taken at "face value", as if there were an obvious, even definitive, interpretation. This then becomes an obstacle to, rather than a starting point for, deep re- flection. Taken at its face value, for example, the Collect strikes balances between help and governance on the one hand, and fear and love on the other, but these conceal a deeper historical reality. Whereas sixteenth- century sensibilities would have been far more sharply attuned to gov- ernance and fear, ours tend much more towards help and love. It is not that the Tudor age did not recognise the primacy of love proclaimed by Jesus nor that contemporary Christians always act in that spirit rather than in fear of divine reprisal, but simply that the theological orienta- tion has shifted from the negative to the positive. Yet the formula in the Collect stays the same.

The parable of the banquet is a good starting point for analysing our motives, questioning the extent to which we act out of love or fear. At one level, the story is about flouted hospitality, but at a deeper level it is about the lure of earthly concerns keeping us from enjoying eternal life. Let us say that we are not as venal as the three who refuse to go to the banquet, recognising that it is more important than our earthly concerns, but is our attendance the result of a genuine yearning for the banquet or are we frightened of what will happen if we do not give up our familiar pleasures? To what extent are we driven by the rather dubi- ous notions of "hell fire" and how far are we being purely altruistic? Such is the complexity of life, and such are the multiple layers of self-analysis, self-delusion and self-reference which make up our perception of self that it is impossible to say. We are perfectly capable of characterising ourselves as pragmatic for fear of appearing too pious and, conversely, capable of persuading ourselves that we are being pious when we are being pragmatic.

As the Epistle points out, our conflict over priorities is not purely internal; we can be influenced by what goes on around us. We will, says John, be hated for what we are and what we do. At the time of writing this was literally true, but we live in a much less confrontational environment. Although Christianity is now intellectually marginal, the most we can expect is a withering comment about the futility of religion or, perhaps worse still, benign indifference to the life we have chosen, which is now generally dismissed as a "lifestyle choice" rather than a faithful commitment. Nonetheless, peer pressure is apt to chip away at our firm resolve. A good example of this is the increasing tendency of Sunday activities to keep us—and, much worse, our children—from church attendance. We argue, quite rightly, that we must be with children in many of their activities out of a sense of duty, regardless of our personal preference. This might include standing on the touch line on a wet winter afternoon, but why do we not see that part of that duty is to take children to church and, if necessary, to rank this above other activities? If we rank rugby practice above church on behalf of our children, what can we expect from them? If an activity on Sunday morning is so central to a child's life that it cannot be given up, then we should be campaigning for a more flexible worship pattern.

There is also a widespread shallowing and coarsening of social sensibility, threatening the very fabric of Christian life, which is difficult to avoid and even more difficult to combat, and it is not a very radical shift from passivity to acceptance. We complain to each other, but rarely to perpetrators, and because of our passivity the few who do complain are branded as unrepresentative or even cranks.

But John asks us to go much further than intellectual combat. We are to love not just in our words but in our deeds. Again, we need to examine our motives. To what extent is our giving guilt-driven, a token that we know we could and should do better? To what extent do we use professionals, paid for by taxation or by our voluntary contributions, to do the work which we should be doing, such as caring for the elderly, visiting the sick, or helping people to climb out of poverty and degradation? Are we simply buying off our obligations in a modern form of indulgences?

Because parables are necessarily outlines of possibilities, it is easy to turn their messages into caricatures, but in this case, as opposed to that of the story of Dives and Lazarus (cf. The First Sunday after Trinity), most of us can identify with those who refused the banquet rather than those who accepted the surprise invitation. It is, therefore, salutary to remember that it is precisely those people who attended the banquet who are the recipients of our vicarious concern. How would we have fared if we had turned up at the banquet and been sat next to one of these?

However different we are in sensibility from Tudor times, we share this in common: that we find it difficult to love the poor, downgrading our response to duty or worse. From our contemporary standpoint it is easy to scorn governance and fear but equally easy to see why they exert such power over our behaviour.

The Third Sunday after Trinity

Collect	*O Lord, we beseech Thee mercifully to hear us; . . .*
Epistle	1 Peter 5.5–11
Gospel	Luke 15.1–10

Although they are almost invariably joined together, as they are in to-day's Gospel, the stories of the shepherd and the housewife are very different. Money was a rare article in the peasant lives of first century Palestine, barter being the norm except for Temple offerings and major transactions such as land transfers. The most widespread and frequent use of money was for the payment of dowries, and because peasant homes lacked secure storage, the safest place for money was to sew it into the bride's garments. We can therefore readily understand how a woman would have worried and searched if she lost part of her dowry, and how she might have celebrated when she found what was lost. The story of the lost sheep, on the other hand, is totally irrational. A shepherd with 100 sheep, all of which led precarious lives, would have been courting catastrophe if he had abandoned 99 for one that was lost. Here is the shepherd, sentimentally returning with the lost sheep over his shoulders, to find the remainder of the flock ravaged and scattered! The absentee landlord will sack him; his life is ruined! The only thing lower than a shepherd is an unemployed shepherd.

The very irrationality of the shepherd reinforces the message in the Collect and Epistle of our need, respectively of God's "mighty" aid or "mighty" hand. The Epistle then goes on to describe the devil's threat in the form of a prowling lion, thus completing the vivid antithesis in the readings between the predatory lion and the helpless sheep. The Collect and Peter both emphasise that our best defence lies in steadiness. Perhaps the Collect is somewhat optimistic when it says that we have been given "an hearty desire to pray", but we can at least recognise the need to be "sober and vigilant".

Again we are confronted with the problem of the connection between behaviour and salvation, something of a sixteenth-century obsession, which explains its prominence in the BCP. The Collect does not specifically link our desire to pray with our benefiting from the "mighty aid" which will defend us from all dangers and adversities. Peter complicates the issue somewhat by saying that God gives grace to the humble, which would seem to indicate some kind of link between behaviour and heavenly favour. We might at this point also notice the preamble to the Gospel stories in which Luke sets the scene so that the two lost and found stories are specifically aimed at "publicans and sinners." It is all too easy to become sentimental about the crowd and the lost sheep, but Luke means to set the opposite tone. It is precisely because those listening to Jesus are not virtuous—and might best be represented by an almost worthless, scrawny, errant sheep—that they need the irrational love of God, irrational because it does not depend on a transparent, predictable formula.

The starting point for grasping the importance of all three readings is for us to count ourselves with the publicans and sinners and to see the scrawny sheep as our personal icon. Only then can we put our own worth, represented by our faith and works, into perspective. In the face of our own inadequacies in both, it seems somewhat futile to debate which of the two is more likely to secure salvation, as the answer, surely, is neither.

The reaction of the Pharisees and scribes, denouncing Jesus for mixing with and eating with sinners, is both predictable and depressing. Steeped in the Law, their religion was one which values fixed rules which, when broken, required fixed atonements. It was this mechanistic approach which Jesus and, later, Paul much more vehemently, rejected. It would be a mistake to put contemporary words into Paul's mouth but when he says, echoed by Peter, that we are totally dependent upon Jesus for our salvation he is surely invoking the image of humanity as broken. Not necessarily in the extreme language of "original sin", but in the sense that imperfection is a necessary human attribute which enables us to exercise the function for which we were created, to love God freely.

The connection between imperfection, or brokenness, and freedom is the most fundamental dynamic in our lives, which is why its interpretation spans the whole range of philosophical and emotional possibility from Pelagian positivism to fatalism. The tendency in the sixteenth century, immediately after Luther, was to emphasise the imperfection rather than the exercise of freedom. There are large numbers of Christians today who yoke freedom and imperfection in a negative way, seeing perfection as conformity with "plain" morality. Conversely, yoking the two positively shifts the balance from fear to love. Further, if we do not allow ourselves to see past our condition to its consequences then we are falling short. We were not made to languish in our imperfection but to take risks for love, for a necessary consequence of imperfection is that there is no love without risk.

In a way which is impossible to understand, in abandoning the flock for the one sheep, Jesus was taking a risk for us so that we might take a risk for him. We should therefore neither take comfort in the routine of the Pharisees and scribes on the one hand, nor in the abjectness of being publicans and sinners on the other. We should learn from Mary that to be humble is not to be passive; to exercise the freedom to love in our imperfect state is as good as it gets.

The Fourth Sunday after Trinity

Collect   *O God, the protector of all who trust in Thee . . .*
Epistle   Romans 8.18–23
Gospel   Luke 6.36–42

Luke is so full of optimism that it seems a shame to dampen it but, as the Psalmist would testify, our good is not usually returned with equal good, and rarely does the giver of more than fair measure receive even fair measure in return. Even if Luke is right, what can Jesus mean by this optimism? He is referring to the relationship between the Creator and the created, between God and us, where none of the "normal" rules apply, and where we can fully rely on being given infinitely more than we have given. It is important to be clear about this; Jesus is talking about the "terms of trade" between the divine and the human. He is not talking about the human hope that "what goes around comes around". We might hope that it does, but we should not act in that expectation, neither should it be our motive.

The Gospel is Luke's highly concentrated account in Chapter 6 of the "Sermon on the Plain" which covers roughly the same ground as Matthew 5–7 given from "The Mount" (cf. All Saints' Day). This impactedness accounts for the somewhat sudden lurch with which Jesus then cites the short parable of the blind leading the blind and, again, we need to be clear what we are being told. This is not an invitation for us to work out whether we are blind or whether we are leading the blind. The central message is that we are all blind and quite incapable of leading each other, but must instead rely upon the grace of God. Then, in a characteristic modification of metaphor, Luke moves from blindness to what impedes sight, the beam in the eye. If we are so blind that we cannot lead, then we certainly cannot judge, but, being Luke, the metaphor is not that simple. We can, in fact, attempt to remove the beam from the eye of another, but only once we have removed our own. If we accept the grace of God in humility and simplicity we will be of much service to our neighbours.

Paul has been wrestling with very similar ideas in the first half of Romans, and in this extract he is coming towards the half-way climax in a style almost as concentrated in its impact as Luke. Aware of the futility of what we can do for ourselves, we "groan within" in anticipation of our bodily resurrection when we will enjoy the "glorious liberty of the children of God", which, says Paul, is not to be compared with our present sufferings. Of course, what Paul saw in the context of eschatological immediacy looks very different to us, who expect to be judged over the whole span of our lives rather than over a short period of intense preparation.

Typically, Luke is concerned with individual responsibility, which is why his version of the beatitudes is couched in terms of a direct address from Jesus to his audience, "blessed are you", whereas Matthew, much more concerned with the corporate entity of the Christian community, employs indirect address with "blessed are they". There is always a temptation to think of ethics in terms of abstract propositions, and so it helps to have Luke's very direct style to prompt us into more urgent reflection.

Rather than thinking about motes and beams as a form of moral currency, it might be more helpful to think about our individual relationship
with the people with whom we deal. To what extent am I downplaying
my own failings in order to give me the self-appointed "moral authority"
to judge somebody else?

Not far below the surface of many readings is the tension between
divine judgment, human moralising, and civil justice. Pragmatists will
rightly point out that reserving judgment for God is a position that can
only be sustained in an ideal world. Moreover, constructing frameworks
within which moral judgments can be made is necessary in a complex
and uncertain world, and the very imperfections from which we suffer
require a degree of civil justice. The problem arises when we confuse
these approximate distinctions, taking on the divine role or citing human laws as if they were of divine origin. Both Paul and Luke emphasise
the dangers of this confusion, but it is apparently a weakness we find
hard to counter, because the somewhat harsh characterisation of helpless "groaning" in Paul, and the metaphor of total blindness in Luke,
leave us little to do when we have been created as social, busy creatures.
Luke's concluding get-out clause is therefore comforting. As long as we
admit our limitations, there is scope for us to be morally active.

Both of these passages are characterised by a high degree of intensity
which arises not only from the seriousness of the content, but also because of the emphasis on the personal. Abstractions may be necessary to
human survival, giving us patterns within which we can locate certain
kinds of behaviour, but, in the end, it is the relationship between God
and the individual, and vice versa, that really counts. While it is true,
seen from the divine perspective, that we can do nothing but lead each
other into the ditch, from the human perspective we operate in a world
of limited vision, both in clarity and scope. It is when we remember this
that we operate within our proper limits, but when we forget, the trouble
really starts. Imagine a soap opera without the complexities caused by
the exercise of moral superiority!

The Fifth Sunday after Trinity

Collect   *Grant, O Lord, we beseech Thee that*
              the course of this world . . .
Epistle   1 Peter 3.8–15[a]
Gospel   Luke 5.1–11

Because the Gospels are written as a series of vignettes, things seem to happen suddenly, with very sharp edges. In Luke 1, for example, the scene shifts rapidly between the house of Mary and the house of Elizabeth. In Luke 2 the scene shifts between Bethlehem, the Temple, and then the Temple some twelve years later. In Chapter 3 John the Baptist bursts onto the scene. There is the synagogue reading, the death threat, and miracles in Chapter 4. And yet here we are in Chapter 5, with Jesus performing the miracle of the fish prior to recruiting Peter. It almost certainly did not happen so episodically in real life. It is a pleasant walk from Nazareth to the Lake, though the return journey is a bit of a climb, and there would have been plenty of contact between Nazareth and the lake towns, particularly with Tiberias. It is also hardly likely that Jesus appeared one morning and announced the start of his mission. Luke 4 implies that Jesus was in the habit of reading and preaching in the Synagogue and there is a strong suggestion among some authors, particularly Vermes, that Jesus was a disciple of John before his arrest. Whether or not this is true, the two were cousins and would have been well known to each other and their extended families and clans. A few days living in a rural community without broadcasting very soon brings home the point that people have very little to talk about, notice everything, no matter how slight, and weave endless minor variations on the same few themes.

It cannot, then, have been a surprise to Peter when Jesus came recruiting, but the manner of the encounter is, as such things are, no less remarkable for being awaited. Peter has had a very bad night, catching nothing, so Jesus makes amends, but also ensures that Peter's fishing career ends temporarily on a high note. Peter, recognising the miracle that Jesus has performed, dismisses himself as unworthy, and Jesus transforms the fishing from fish to men. This could not have been accomplished overnight. Family businesses were hereditary and members of cartels which ensured that there were not too many boats for the market (a kind of self-regulated Galilee Common Fisheries policy). It was not the custom for small family businesses to hire casual labour. It is therefore misleading to think of the recruitment of the disciples as a dramatic series of boat-mooring and tool-downing. It is almost certain, too, that the Apostles were not full-time followers of Jesus, but put in a spot of fishing, or whatever, when occasion offered. It is not irreverent, for example, for Peter to go fishing so soon after the Resurrection (John 21.3). What we are looking at here is slow, steadily increasing commitment, an extra burden on top of everything else. To be a disciple was not to escape from drudgery, it was to take on extra work. In that respect, we can model our Christian lives on the disciples, not by becoming full time ministers, but by living out our Christianity in ordinary life and in Church ministry.

It is only possible to connect the Peter of that lakeside calling with the writer of the Epistles if we take seriously the active intervention of the Holy Spirit. How else could we account for the transformation? The Epistle is full of sharp contrast and economical writing, the tone is as certain as Gospel depictions of him are indecisive, and there is a sense of concentrated professionalism. At another level, there is the customary contrast between knowing what we must do, and the failure to do it. It is a danger of which all teachers must be aware. It is often said today, incorrectly, that to preach one thing and to do another is hypocritical, but that would only be true if we claimed to be more than we are and better than those we teach. The real fault is to claim not to be sinners.

Perhaps Peter is most eloquent on the subject of suffering. "If ye suffer for righteousness' sake, happy are ye", he says, with an inevitable backward glance which travels from the early days of his calling (and the healing of his mother-in-law), past the tribulations of trying to come to terms with the message of Jesus, past the horrible trauma of his denial and the Crucifixion, past the incomprehensible events of the Resurrection, Ascension and the coming of the Holy Spirit, to his present responsibilities and his hard-headed assessment of likely violent death. Of all the Apostles, his life was the one which experienced the most ups and downs, which adds weight to what he says, just as Paul is at his most powerful when he combines his teaching with accounts of suffering.

The outrageous haul of fish was a wonder and a promise, a wonder that would sustain him through all his trials and a promise that, as a fisher of men, he would bring many to Christ. No matter how many adventures a fisherman has, there is always one tale to which he warmly returns. No matter how difficult things became, there was always this inspirational illustration of God's power and promise to which he could return, reminding him of the inextricable link between suffering and righteousness. He could no more have thought of the haul of fish as an accident than he could have thought of Pentecost as a freak event.

The Sixth Sunday after Trinity

Collect   *O God, who hast prepared for them that*
                     love Thee such good things . . .
Epistle   Romans 6.3–11
Gospel   Matthew 5.20–26

One of the aspects of criminal justice that most puzzles people is the balance it strikes between motive and outcome. While the layman might want three motorists who have killed a pedestrian to be given identical sentences (usually the severest available, regardless of the evidence), the justice system recognises that the first was driving dangerously while over the legal limit for alcohol, the second was in a hurry, a little distracted, and drove carelessly, while the third struck a man who emerged from behind a stationary vehicle and walked straight into the path of a car. While the distinction between the first two and the third is readily recognised, that between the first two often is not. This is the kind of distinction which Jesus is trying to draw between his kind of righteousness and that of the Pharisees; he says that motive matters. To continue with our motoring illustrations, Jesus says that if we are determined to run somebody over but she gets out of the way, that is morally as bad as succeeding, because it is the intention that counts. Further, whenever we transgress but do not reconcile ourselves immediately to our victim, we will suffer the great punishment of being "denied heaven".

These kind of encouragements in the Gospel, which imperfect humanity needs, are set against the most condensed and emphatic account of Paul's theology of baptism and Resurrection. The ideas are so familiar that they are easy to gloss over without due attention. Because we were baptised into Jesus' death we will rise again because he rose. This is an interlocking two-part statement of immense weight, which makes nonsense of debates in the sixteenth century and today about the relative merits of the Crucifixion and Resurrection as focal points for belief. Without the Crucifixion there would be no Resurrection, and without the Resurrection the Crucifixion would say nothing to us. The first point is relatively clear, but the second seems more difficult to hammer home as there are some Christians who genuinely believe that the act of Atonement in the Crucifixion is not a necessary, but a sufficient, precondition for the Christian life. If that were the case then why did Jesus not immediately ascend to the Father after his death? The "answer" is that the bridge between the divine and the human, which the incarnation initiated, could only be completed by a promise so concretely expressed by the divine being of Jesus that it could be grasped by humanity. Carl Rahner (*Foundations of Christian Faith*) talks about the Resurrection as the "irreversible offer" of salvation, a kind of underwriting of what was promised in the Incarnation and secured in the Crucifixion (my own interpretation).

Yet as we contemplate the prospect of rising in glory, we have to admit that Paul's "old man", so needful of the advice in Matthew, is ever present. Theology is one thing, life quite another, and that is the ambivalence in which Christians live, as testimony of the nexus between the human and divine, which is what gives Christianity its peculiar tension, its triumph and remorse. Given what is "on offer" in Paul, it would seem churlish not to take absolutely seriously the advice in Matthew. We are being offered so much in exchange for so little, and all that we have to do is use the resources which we have been given to make proper choices in our relationships with God and our neighbour. So why is this so difficult?

The usual, glib answer is that we are sinners and therefore doomed to fail. This, to venture briefly into philosophy, is a profoundly Platonic idea which compares human phenomena unfavourably with "spiritual" or otherworldly archetypes which are perfect, thus dooming all earthly things to imperfection. This idea has had much more influence on European thought than its Aristotelian counterpart, which turns Plato on its head, by saying that human achievement lies in creating phenomena where the whole is more than the sum of the parts. This latter position does not deny human imperfection, but it helps us to see ourselves more constructively. Theologically, we might say that imperfection, rather than being something to be regretted, to be compared unfavourably with perfection, is the defining quality of humanity, because it is only in a state of imperfection that we are free to choose, to exercise our free will to love rather than not to love. Set in the context of post-Reformation neo-Platonic Lutheran Protestantism, this is a rather counterintuitive concept to grasp. The alternative, first clearly advanced by St Augustine, another neo-Platonist, encapsulated in the concept of original sin,

is that although we do have free will, we are born with a moral handi-
cap and, even in the bosom of the Church, live in a permanent state of
"chasing the game". Some would argue that this difference of approach
is profoundly theological, but it might be a matter of psychology and
temperament. Luther was a pessimist with low self-esteem who, to a
certain extent, found that Paul's view of righteousness chimed in with
his own private needs and it is easy to entangle the two. Instead of trying to bully or coax each other into accepting one outlook or the other
we would be much better off according respect to those whose outlook
differs from our own.

The Seventh Sunday after Trinity

Collect   *Lord of all power and might, . . .*
Epistle   Romans 6.19–23
Gospel   Mark: 8.1–9

Jesus could never have written Romans. This is not an intellectual observation—as Peter and James are ample testimony of how people of
humble origin, moved by the events they have seen and prompted by
the Holy Spirit, can write formative theology—but a psychological one.
Where Jesus is gentle, Paul can be brutal. In this extract he is telling
his readers—whom, remember, he has never met—that they have been
slaves to wickedness, and that they are still so corrupt that he has to con-
descend to them. Somewhat confusingly he then says that, because they
are reformed, they can expect everlasting life and not the death which
is the wage of sin. Regardless of the not unusual muddle Paul gets into
when he tries to use metaphors, the message is clear enough: that faith
in Jesus is the source of everlasting life.

The Collect reflects Paul's message, but its judicious choice of words
is significant. It calls for an increase in us of "true religion" and for nour-
ishment with "all goodness", but it pointedly does not mention the sacrament of the Holy Eucharist which is often said to be the motif behind
the Gospel. This is the slightest of the six accounts in the Gospels of
Jesus' miracles of feeding: 5,000 in Matthew 14.15–20, Mark 6.34–44,
Luke 9.10–17, and John 6.5–15 (cf. The Fourth Sunday in Lent; The
Twenty-Fifth Sunday after Trinity); 4,000 in Matthew 15.32–38; and

today's account in Mark. There are two curiosities in the Lectionary. Firstly, as there are so many accounts, why is John used twice? Secondly, the ranking in this case of Mark over Matthew, who was foremost in the sixteenth century, and regarded as the origin of Mark rather than vice versa.

Rather than think of the feeding miracles simply as Eucharistic harbingers—a hotly contested thesis—the logical starting point might be the feeding of the Jews in the wilderness with manna from above. The Chosen People had been liberated but were hardly grateful, goading Moses at every turn because of their perceived grievances, to one of which manna was the response, so it was not food for the righteous, but for everyone, regardless of their conduct. Likewise, Jesus did not organise a vetting system before feeding people. The divine food, therefore, whether it came from Yahweh or the hands of Jesus, was not distributed in relation to moral merit, nor could it be if we accept that we do nothing meritorious of ourselves. In that sense, Christianity has been equivocal, the Eucharist being so important in its life and to its people that withholding it has been used as a weapon. The medieval Church habitually used denial of the sacraments as a spiritual/political weapon and today there are those who wish to use the same weapon to deny the Eucharist to gay people on the grounds that they are unrepentant sinners. The contemporary variant is for people to withhold themselves from the Fellowship of the Eucharist on the ground that they are pure, and the remaining participants are sinners. These thoughts may seem far away from the central point, but they are not. Fitness for Eucharist is a matter of conscience, and it is not for anyone to question that fitness. What is remarkable about all six accounts of mass feeding is that they took place because the compassion of Jesus was aroused.

Returning, then, to the initial question, these six accounts can only be taken as a prefiguration of the Eucharist if we accept it as a gift freely given to those who humbly believe that they are worthy of it. Christ, from the Jewish perspective, was reliving the wandering in the wilderness. Christ, from the Christian perspective, was anticipating the gift of Himself in sacrifice for sin. In either case, the primary motive is generosity not judgment. The true significance of the feeding of the 4,000 is that it took place in Gentile territory, and that is why it is not a repetition of the feeding of the 5,000.

The idea of literal prefiguration is much more difficult to sustain. Did Jesus know, when he was distributing the bread and fish, that he would later offer Himself at the Last Supper? We will never know, but the fact that six similar accounts occur in the Gospels means that the Evangelists counted them as singularly important stories, which in turn underlines the importance they place on the Institution of the Eucharist. This importance was denied by some sixteenth-century Zwingli-inspired English reformers. Perhaps they mistook the late medieval ritualism for the essence; a mistake which other reformers, who followed Luther and Calvin, did not make. Instead, they clung to the centrality of Eucharist, but radically simplified the ritual and made the text accessible in the BCP. Yet it would take 400 years for the Eucharist to regain its centrality in the Church of England, although that reality is still not beyond controversy.

Having courted controversy, we might best return to the beginning. Jesus could never have written Romans, but that is to affirm, rather than to deny, the importance of theological diversity, and the importance of respecting it. Current theological controversies, like all their major predecessors, are attempts to de-construct mystery and, therefore, to put less stress on the idea of faith, a proceeding which Paul would have found dangerous and which we might regard as a fatal crossing of the boundary from theology into the philosophy of religion. The paradox of the sixteenth century was that it restored the Pauline concept of faith while down-playing the centrality of mystery.

The Eighth Sunday after Trinity

Collect   *O God, whose never-failing providence*
                     ordereth all things . . .
Epistle   Romans 8.12–17
Gospel   Matthew 7.15–21

At first sight the Gospel appears to be optimistic, declaring, "by their fruits ye will know them". After all, there is no such thing as a discovered con-man because if he is discovered then he is no longer conning. So of one thing we can be certain, if we are to detect dishonesty we must either be very lucky or highly skilled.

This was an acute problem in the middle of the sixteenth century, when the established religion of England lurched from Henrican mercurial Catholicism, to Edwardian Puritanism, and back to Marian Catholicism, before settling uneasily into the Elizabethan pragmatism which is our heritage. In seeking to discern the divine will, it was often difficult to know whether the discernment was genuinely religious or merely political. To quote just one telling phrase from J. W. Allen, "Church lands made stout Protestants" (*Political Thought in The 16th Century*). Today we suffer from a rather different problem; instead of having to judge the sincerity of a spiritual guide in a political context, we have to judge in a dizzyingly pluralist context. People make and remake themselves so that they become collections of experiences and aspirations, a kind of psychological bricolage. Consequently, they have the capacity to re-engineer themselves as circumstances change, playing on our unwillingness to challenge and our short memories. At the time of Jesus, the uncertainty of pantheism, resembling our contemporary condition, was prevalent, although it was not of much concern to the Jews. The steady bifurcation of Christianity from classical Judaism caused tensions which are an important background element to Matthew's Gospel. We know from 1 Corinthians 1.11–12 that there were at least four competing factions (Paul, Apollos, Peter and Christ) and Matthew probably knew of these and some additional variants.

Our customary response to the warning against ravening wolves is to cite obvious threats such as consumerism, spiritualism, and secularism, but their very obviousness ought to reduce their threat. Much more pernicious from a Christian perspective are fanaticism, narcissism, and individualism, which reduce the mysterious span of the Christian experience to such statements as, "the Lord has told me to reform our accountancy system", declared by a missionary in West Africa. This may sound absurd but, particularly in "born again" circles, it is common to attribute to "the Lord" a decision which is, and should be, pragmatically secular. False prophesy uses sacred authority for an opinion or a course of action as a way of spiritually blackmailing opponents, or people with a different outlook, into submission or uniformity. Although the Holy Spirit moves in mysterious ways, nobody in the sixteenth century supposed that religious decisions had anything to do with principle, let alone God. In our own day, it is quite customary for "Church politics" to determine where we officially stand, but the authorities find it hard to resist invoking the Holy Spirit in their aid.

If, then, there is a weakness in the extract from Romans, it is that Paul sees the issues as far too clear-cut. We are either flesh or spirit, adopted children of Christ or not, and he makes these distinctions in the power of the Spirit. At least the evidence tells us that Paul was not as certain of this as these statements suggest—elsewhere in Romans he depicts God's purposes, realised through Jesus, as cosmic rather than particular. However, the irreversible damage has been done, such that some authoritarian Christians, faced with contradictions between the Gospel reports of what Jesus said and the letters of Paul, frequently choose the latter.

Together, the readings present us with a warning. Authoritarian Christianity might just be tolerable if it were not for the inevitable existence of false prophets; power in the hands of the unscrupulous is immensely dangerous. Given the inevitability of falsehood, we would be wise to be deeply suspicious of authoritarianism which runs counter to the teaching and behaviour of Jesus, and we would need to find a very particular reason to tolerate it. Until recently, this warning might have seemed redundant in a Church of England, which observed the mutual tolerance of necessity from its founding 400 years ago, but fundamentalist theological domination is back in vogue, naturally supported in every detail by the aforesaid Holy Spirit. Paul's overriding message of the centrality of love in which we must all be united is obscured by a myriad of more proscriptive statements, which is why confining one's biblical access to Sunday reading, or quoting fragments of text selectively, is fatally misleading.

Having pointed out the dangers, it is only fair to note, however, that the intention of the combined effect of the readings is to tell us that it is easy to distinguish good from bad, truth from falsehood and, by implication, those who will be saved from those who will not. How far we can agree with this is both a matter of theological inclination and temperament on the one hand, and a matter of our general outlook and experience of life on the other, but, in view of the way in which people of strong opinions generally behave, it might be as well to be sceptical. There have been too many occasions when we have known them by their fruits but too late, when we would be better off knowing them by their seeds.

The Ninth Sunday after Trinity

Collect   *Grant to us, Lord, we beseech Thee, the spirit to*
                     think and do always such things as be rightful . . .
Epistle   1 Corinthians 10.1–13
Gospel   Luke 16.1–9

We are in a world of moral equivocation. A steward is accused of wasting his master's goods, and is condemned without being asked to explain himself. He gathers allies through discounting his master's debts, and is commended for it. The passage concludes with a piece of irony about Mammon, righteousness, and eternity that is so deep that it is impenetrable to us today.

Paul's account of the Jews in the wilderness is scarcely clearer. Paul's actual and our spiritual ancestors were "baptized unto Moses", ate the same "spiritual meat", drank the same "spiritual drink" from the rock, "and that rock was Christ". This possibly relates to Paul's idea in Galatians 4.22–31 that the Christian tradition really begins with Abraham, passes to Moses, but then somehow bypasses a huge slab of Jewish history until it settles on John the Baptist. If so, this theological inter-working of Abraham, Moses and Jesus must be approached with caution. It is one thing to say that Moses prefigures Christ, but quite another to say that Christ was an operative force in the conduct of Moses. We ought, too, to note here that the reference to producing drinking water from a rock is itself deeply equivocal. The accounts of the events in Exodus 15.23 and 17.1–8 are relatively undramatic, but in Numbers 20.1–13 the faithlessness of the Jews is used as a pretext for excluding Moses from entering into the Promised Land. The accounts, therefore, are subject to the theological aims of their authors, and one suspects a good deal of this in Paul. This is not a bad thing in itself, but a phenomenon which should make us wary of naive or "plain" interpretation. Paul then travels to firmer, familiar ground, citing the evils that befell the Jews in the wilderness for their various sins, and reminding us that these are warnings of what will happen to us. Paul's conclusion makes something of a nonsense of the aforementioned when he says that God is faithful and will not allow us to be tempted past our ability.

There is a place for moral clarity, but it is sometimes helpful to acknowledge the real presence of moral complexity. Let us start with the Jews in the wilderness. Far from being the simple narrative which emerges from a highly selective reading, the accounts of what happened between the flight from Egypt and the death of Moses are immensely complex and contradictory. The acid test which I frequently apply, as a former director of plays, is how would I set the scene. Here we have people who are almost starving and parched to death, who are given water from rocks and manna and quails from heaven, but who herd cattle and possess great wealth. For reasons which appear to be entirely arbitrary—the punishment is not by any means for the worst of their collective offences—they are condemned to 40 years in the wilderness. They are wretched and rich, powerless and harassed. How are they expected to react logically to a set of messy and often inexplicable events? There is no shape to the narrative, and it is therefore not surprising that there is no coherent moral response.

Turning to the steward, what are we to make of a master who threatens summary dismissal without the opportunity for self-defence and then applauds a blatant misuse of his own resources? How might such behaviour shape the conduct of a steward? Is he supposed to behave honestly or dishonestly to further the ends of his master? The ideal answer to this question is that we should always behave morally no matter what immoral demands are placed on us by our superiors, but it is not always clear whether such demands are moral. It is a brave person who would risk the wrath of a superior over a marginal matter which might lead to dismissal, a stance which might look admirable to the moralist, but which would be less welcome to the hard-pressed wife, the hungry child, and the strictly impartial bank manager.

None of this excuses acts which separate us from God, but it is impossible to be effectively pastoral if we simply apply a set of rules abstracted even from a million instances, for to be pastoral is to be a person of the instance. There are burdens to be shared, doubts to be explored, areas of individual and joint responsibility to be settled. Consciences must be informed, wills strengthened, minds uncluttered, principles clarified, in an iterative process which shuttles between the instance and the principles, between the concrete and the abstract.

What we have to recognise is that Paul's account of Israelite behaviour in the desert is a tradition, not a workshop in moral response. We can learn very little from it other than the link he makes between good conduct and divine approbation, but it is a case where the detail obscures rather than illuminates. For different reasons the same effect is created in this passage of Luke. It is impossible to arrive at a clear principle from what we are told about the master and his steward. On the basis of the text, we are not sure whether to imitate the behaviour or avoid it.

From the corpus of Jesus' teaching we know we must certainly not imitate the steward, but a corpus cannot afford many apparent anomalies such as this.

The Tenth Sunday after Trinity

Collect	*Let Thy merciful ears, O Lord, be open . . .*
Epistle	1 Corinthians 12.1–11
Gospel	Luke 19.41–47[a]

If we are not careful, time plays tricks, and we rewrite history by accident. The chronological sequence in today's readings begins with Jesus approaching Jerusalem from the South, climbing steadily towards it until he sees its skyline, dominated by the impressive and beautiful Herodian Temple at the South-East corner. His followers encourage him to stop and look. In Luke this works on two levels. Firstly, there is the centrality of the Temple in Judaism, which is one of the motifs which runs through Luke and Acts. Secondly, there is the sclerotic, law-bound Temple establishment, which represents opposition to Jesus' revolutionary message of love and personal commitment. The last of the Prophets is looking upon a way of worship which stood in opposition to them even before a permanent site was found for the Ark of the Covenant. Part of that opposition was created by the Temple's never-ending need for cash for building projects and repairs, which in turn led to financial transactions between the people and the priesthood in addition to the traditional priestly portion of animal sacrifice. Symbolically, Jesus, acting as a prophet, attacks the Temple trade as an act of protest against the whole paraphernalia of ritual and graft, which would have appealed particularly to sixteenth-century Reformers who drew parallels between the Pharisees and the Papacy, and believed that their simple ways were the ways of Jesus Himself.

Reformers of the mid-sixteenth century would also have been in sympathy with Paul's dilemma in a nascent Church which was forced to embrace both the priestly and prophetic traditions. They looked back with reverence to a time when each person established a relationship with God without the intermediary encumbrance of the (Roman) Church and, while they were not naive enough to believe that the primitive church could be replicated in Tudor England, they thought that access to the Bible and more austere church practice would go some way to realising early simplicity. Yet the price that the Reformation had to pay for biblical autonomy was a degree of religious radicalism that not even the most robust political settlement could embrace. Today we would probably regard as paradoxical a Church which was rigidly ecclesiologically conformist and scripturally libertarian. However, it was not an issue which seriously worried either the secular or spiritual authorities who reserved the right to limit freedom whenever it threatened stability, a position which Paul appears to adopt in the latter part of 1 Corinthians. He values all gifts and all points of view, but his overriding concern from the opening attack on schism (1 Corinthians 1.11–18) is that the Church should live in unity, defined not by statute but by mutual love.

Between Jesus' sighting of the Temple and his cleansing act there is a "fast forward" to the destruction of the Temple and its form of worship. To an extent for which he is given no credit, because the victim in his sights was Jesus, Caiaphas (John 11.49–50) was right when he considered the death of one man as a fair price to pay for religious stability. It was this very failure of the Temple establishment to detach itself successfully from religious and political insurrection which led to its eradication.

The questions for us from these readings are both profound and immediate. Firstly, although we manage reasonably well to contain the priestly and the prophetic within the Church, we are less successful at achieving a balance between uniformity and liberty. Why should the governance of the Church be ever more weighty as its numbers decline, and why should the transformation from a conforming to an affirming Church induce more rather than less governance? Might it be that there are many in positions of church leadership who would prefer conforming to affirming? Secondly, what price are we paying for placing external conformity above the integrity of personal commitment? Are we really insisting that nobody is capable of a personal commitment to Jesus unless their public, ascertainable behaviour conforms to an imposed standard of uniformity? Thirdly, what are the chances of survival of any institution which exalts style over substance? This is not a distinction which the Pharisees would have understood, because for them the style, how they did things, was the substance of what they did. We do not know better, but we necessarily know differently. Having broken away from a (partly caricatured) Roman tyranny, it seems odd that we should be in danger of establishing our own home-grown variety in the shape of an Anglican Covenant.

Luke's final sentence is significant. One of the shortcomings of Temple religion was the priority of ritual over understanding which the Rabbinical Diaspora was to correct. Paul looks at the problem from the other extreme when he wishes to give priority to teaching and prophesy over the self-realisation of speaking in tongues. The Reformation, based on scholarship, was to promote education and preaching as its core values. Today, in spite of the rhetoric, in spite of what we say we want in schools for our children, we live our lives in a paradoxical welter of irrational assertion and prejudice, and ever more minute regulation which makes a nonsense of a society containing more university graduates than at any time in our history. If most church congregations only knew as much about the contents of their Bibles as they do about their professions, society would be much less in danger of physical and social collapse.

The Eleventh Sunday after Trinity

Collect   *O God, who declarest Thy mighty power . . .*
Epistle   1 Corinthians 15.1–11
Gospel   Luke 18.9–14

The danger of parables which, in typically Lucan fashion, set up dichotomies, is that instead of asking us to see both sides of an issue, they invite us to identify with one of the protagonists. In this case, most of us are well enough conditioned to know which we should choose. We have been schooled to opt for the homely humility of the publican and to suspect the prickly pride of the Pharisee, naturally opting for the easier solution, playing the role of the person of whom not much is expected. God, however, "sees through" moral double bluffs.

Modern psychology has taught us that this approach to self-understanding is simplistic. Far from being transparent to ourselves and others, we think and act at a variety of levels, so that in this case we are neither exclusively Pharisees nor publicans. Some of us experience the two states chronologically by a radical change in our condition, but most of us experience something of each simultaneously. That is precisely the case of Paul, who recognises that without the grace of God he is nothing and that the Law, as he would express it (Romans) is of "non effect", but it does not stop him, deep down, from being a Pharisee as well as an Apostle.

Whereas Paul is alive to his inner contradiction, we are always in danger of not being so acute. We think that pleading guilty like the publican will let us off the hook, but it will not. Do we really think, particularly those of us who hold some position of influence, responsibility, or power—who have something of the Pharisee about us—that we will get away with hiding at the bottom table, pretending that what we say and do is of no account? Jesus is warning us against false pride, but we might equally be cautious of false modesty which is just as bad. Our model should be Paul, who is always torn between the two.

At a superficial level, we have the contradiction, already noted, between the Law and Grace but there is also the very obvious matter of Paul's status. In Corinth, as we know from Chapter 1 of this letter, Paul was trying to damp down factionalism, and one of the factions was almost certainly made up of people who had seen, or who said they had seen, Jesus. Others claimed that whatever Paul's pretensions, Peter was superior to him. In his efforts to unify the factions, Paul appeals strongly to his ecclesiological inheritance, starting with the Resurrection and going through a succession of the appearances of Jesus before attaching himself to the end of the line. Typically, he somewhat weakens the advantage he has so carefully built up by calling himself "the least of the Apostles".

In the light of these thoughts and our personal experience, let us look again at Luke's parable. As usual, we have stereotypical, caricatured figures without anomalous features. They have been created to make a point not about Pharisees—they are incidental—but about us and the way we view ourselves. The second point follows from this. Jesus is not saying that there ought not to be Pharisees, nor that publicans who have sinned are a particularly good thing. He never denies the importance of the role of the Pharisees, and publicly consents to the Roman imposition of taxation. The caricatures simply illustrate the extremes to which we occasionally push ourselves. Thirdly—and this relates both to Paul and to the Collect—it does not matter who we are, we all depend on grace. The Pharisee's problem is his belief in moral and salvific self-sufficiency, which links with the fourth important point. The metaphor of the banquet pecking order is pragmatic at one level—the potential shame of being publicly demoted is powerful—but also refers to God as our sole means of salvation. Humility lies not in self-deprecation, but in understanding the relationship—or, rather, the lack of it—between what we are and which place at the table we are asked to occupy.

Pharisaic credibility rested on a tradition which stretched back to the end of the Jewish exile in Babylon, when most of the oral and fragmented scriptural tradition was consolidated. Paul's strategy for combating this formidable tradition is to sketch a Resurrection chronology which underpins his other teaching, as some great figures in the early Church, and some 500 others, saw Jesus after he had risen. His position is strengthened by the Pharisees' own belief in Resurrection, although they did not have in mind Jesus' kind of Resurrection on earth.

So torn is Paul that his almost simultaneous hectoring and self-deprecation is a common stylistic feature of most of his writing. This often makes for uncomfortable reading, and it reflects what should be our chronic discomfort. Like him, but at a much greater chronological remove, we are children of the Resurrection and witnesses of Christ, called upon to live in the world and make the best of its challenges. We are Pharisees and we are publicans and as we know from history and contemporary public life, the more we are Pharisees the more in danger we are of becoming publicans—power corrupts—but that cannot excuse us from taking the risk. Sanctity, as we can see from Paul, is turbulent, but the way in which we describe it frequently bares more resemblance to "good breeding"—many people colloquially described as such are simply well-mannered—which begs the question of whether an established Church has any room for saints.

The Twelfth Sunday after Trinity

Collect	*Almighty and everlasting God, who art always more ready to hear than we to pray, . . .*
Epistle	2 Corinthians 3.4–9
Gospel	Mark 7.31–37

The Collect is a fine example of knowing when to put practice above theory. In this case we know the relationship which we should have with God, but we are incapable of fully living. The Collect notes that God is more ready to hear than we are to pray, and is accustomed to give more than we deserve or can imagine. It then customarily asks for mercy but, in a strikingly unusual phrase, asks for forgiveness in those matters "whereof our conscience is afraid".

Nobody knew more about consciences that were afraid than Moses, who is a prefigurement of Jesus as the divine intermediary, in token of which he shone when he had been in the presence of the Lord. The context in which he led his people was one of upheaval and bewilderment, spiritual uplift and sharp retribution, representing followers who consequently oscillated violently between complete awe and crude self-indulgence. This was wearing enough for Moses, but the other aspect of his representation was the pressure of literally being in the presence of God. The worse the behaviour, the more intense the prostration. The glory with which he was rewarded, says Paul, was great in itself, symbolised by his physical appearance, but that was nothing to the glory which we will encounter through the intercession of Jesus. In a slightly tangential metaphor, Paul compares the glory of Moses with the tablets of stone and then, by extension, compares the tablets of stone with the Christian ambition of observing the spirit rather than simply the letter of the Law. So, one stage further back, we reach the logical foundation that "our sufficiency is of God".

Throughout his mission, Jesus demonstrates the sufficiency of faith in God through performing acts of power, not to show his own powers but to confirm the power of the Father on whose behalf he is acting. The Jews never quite understood the intercessory role of Jesus. They saw what he did and they attributed it to Him, finding the link which he made with the Father deeply troubling. As long as he could perform mighty works while not making any claims of kinship with the Father, he could be accepted as a prophet, but once he made those claims he was in a heretical danger zone. Many Christians (particularly some "fundamentalist" sects in North America) share this problem of intercessory connectivity, having very little interest in Jesus, but many more Christians experience the reverse problem with the Father/Son relationship, concentrating on the life and teaching of Jesus to the exclusion of the Father.

All of the Abrahamic religions require a complex balance between reliance on God and personal responsibility, but the unique factor in Christianity is the way in which Jesus makes both of these aspects of our creatureliness more concrete. Whereas Moses solved this problem through a strict code, which was the recognised approach of his times, Paul repeatedly emphasises how this will no longer be adequate. Both the relationship with God, and the commitment to neighbour, have to be much more personal.

The very concreteness of Jesus also allows us to see our relationship with God much more clearly. The Collect's observation that we ask much less of God than we might is instructive because it tells us of the narrowness of our spiritual ambition. We tend to get stuck in our spiritual ways for a wide variety of reasons, but let us think of just three. Firstly, intercessory prayer tends to close down the spiritual horizon and ambition, making our relationship with God mundane and habitual, extracting the wonder from it. Secondly, our very familiarity with scripture in general and the Gospels in particular can rob the texts of their wonder. This is a particular danger when our primary concern is trying to extract a contemporary "meaning" from a complex text. Thirdly, many of us abandon theological development when we leave school in a way we would never abandon our vocational or professional development. One of the reasons why we choose a vocation or hobby is the way in which the beauty of it fills us with wonder. We have traditionally thought of God in terms of wonder without understanding its cause, which is the beauty of the relationship.

Addressing all three factors involves frightening our consciences. Taking risks with prayer, with our understanding of scripture and with our theological reflection, should test us to the limit whereas staying within our spiritual comfort zone gives us a sense of security. Yet, Jesus did not deal in security, his mission was to widen and deepen our personal relationship with God. What makes this area of consciousness particularly difficult is that deep relationships are profoundly paradoxical. The more secure they are, the more they encourage exploration into areas of insecurity, a theological replica of the heightened experience of being in love. A further paradox is that one of the things we talk about most is love, when we know it is barely susceptible to language; the same is true of our relationship with God, which is hardly surprising as it is the ultimate manifestation of love. Another way, then, of understanding conscience might be to say that the more critical our commitment, the more sensitive our conscience, which might best explain our fear. Yet with God we need not fear going too far, asking too much, or taking too much. Therein lies the paradox of responsibility and dependence.

The Thirteenth Sunday after Trinity

Collect   *Almighty and merciful God, of*
                 whose only gift it cometh . . .
Epistle   Galatians 3.16–22
Gospel   Luke 10.13ᵇ–37

The parable of the Good Samaritan falls into that dangerous category of easily adopted caricature (cf. The Eleventh Sunday after Trinity) which tempts us to identify wholly with one of the characters, and who would not choose to be the Samaritan? There we are, walking down the road behind the priest and the Levite, who cross over to the other side while we keep fearlessly on, not crossing, bent on helping the stranger who is yet our own brother. To imagine the enormity of this generosity we might want to imagine stopping our car to help a tattoo-covered victim, a drug addict, a beggar or an immigrant, who might yet possess a knife. Yet as a culture we tend to shy away from what we call "getting involved". We prefer to drive past criminal incidents and even serious accidents in case we are called upon to give evidence, we allow appalling public behaviour in case the perpetrators turn nasty on us, and we are reluctant to help disabled people, we tell ourselves, in case this embarrasses them. We are the culture that sees nothing, hears nothing, and tells nothing. If matters had turned out slightly differently in Western Europe we would have turned a blind eye to Jewish persecution. In that light, it is best to be realistic about our individual and corporate behaviour. During the twenty-first century, the United Kingdom has been almost hysterically xenophobic, lumping together criminals, impoverished immigrants, asylum seekers, war victims, and workers from European Union countries, into a vast melting pot of the despised and hated. Collectively, as a culture, the only reason for which we might cross the street to the Samaritan would be to kick him, and most of us would stand by at the other side of the street, watching the kicking and saying nothing. An acid test of our Good Samaritanism might be to ask how often we have had the courage at a dinner or party to stop a racist in their tracks by saying that their language is unacceptable. Let us be clear, the parable of the Good Samaritan does not say that we are to tolerate Samaritans or speak well of them, nor that they are to be accorded publicly acknowledged civil rights by the authorities, or even that we are to follow a "politically correct" course of action to avoid the public utterance of unacceptable intolerance. It says that we have to go out of our way to help the most despised and rejected people in our communities. Having considered all these factors carefully, it might now be time to choose our role in the parable. Sadly, I fear, most of us will find that we are priests or Levites.

Yet we need not be so frightened in our ambitions to do good. The Gospel begins with Jesus welcoming back his unlikely band of preachers from their first missionary journey, thanking God for what they have done. If they could do it in an atmosphere of uncertainty, how much easier is it for us as children of the Resurrection to bear public witness to God. Jesus then goes on to explain in the clearest possible terms that loving God and our neighbour are inseparable. It follows that if we do not love our neighbour, we do not love God, and we do not therefore have the option of loving God, but choosing who is our neighbour.

Under the dispensation Jesus was describing, however, the choice was not so clear cut. Faithfulness to God was defined by adherence to the Law, which included detailed injunctions on what was clean and unclean, acceptable and unacceptable. What was revolutionary about Jesus was that he elevated love above the Law. In Galatians, Paul makes rather an intellectual mess of this (though of course we do not know the precise nature of his tangles with his conservative opponents), but the main point he is trying to make is that the Law, for all its virtues, is imperfect and that it has been superseded by the New Covenant established by Jesus. His "logic" is that the first covenant with Abraham preceded his circumcision, which signalled the birth of the Law.

The distinction between love and the Law brings us full circle. In the early twenty-first century, we have used the civil law to try to regulate the influx of people from other countries, and there may well be perfectly good and prudent reasons for doing this, but if we are to act in good faith, we must not do the right thing for the wrong reason. Advancing a law on limits to immigration to protect stability and assist the assimilation process is quite a different matter from proposing the same law because we think that immigration threatens our level of income and wealth. To an extent we hardly notice because it is so ingrained, the radical call of Christianity has been seriously toned down by civil laws enacted by a nominally Christian society. The parable is more than a personal challenge, it also has an important civic dimension, because what inhibited the priest and the Levite was not a personal disinclination to help the injured man, but a legal and social climate which made it impossible for them to imagine providing assistance. We are in danger of a similar deadening of our moral sense.

The Fourteenth Sunday after Trinity

Collect   *Almighty and everlasting God, give*
                     unto us the increase of faith, . . .
Epistle   Galatians 5.16–24
Gospel   Luke 17.11–19

Imagine being one of the nine cured lepers who decides not to thank Jesus for curing them. It seems incomprehensible. Quite apart from any religious obligation to worship or moral obligation to contribute, there is, at the very least, the matter of politeness. As Jesus cured people to bear witness to the power of the Father and not to be thanked, good manners are not the central point of the incident, but this is the aspect of it which forms a link with the Epistle.

The logic behind "zero tolerance" policies is that they make a connection between poor behaviour in small things and the development of criminality. In this context, what such policies say is that if lepers do not thank the people who cure them they will increasingly take everything for granted and, in turn, will take everything without asking for it, before finally taking anything they like regardless of ownership or consequences. Whether or not this is borne out by evidence, it certainly plays to our instinct that, for whatever complex of causes, people develop bad behaviour.

In the Epistle, the contrast between the list of vices and virtues is stark, as is the dichotomy between "flesh" and "spirit" to which they are respectively assigned. It is all too easy to use this division as a starting point for a slide into dualism, but the concluding thought of the passage runs decisively counter to this by saying that, ". . . they that are Christ's have crucified the flesh". This metaphor of Crucifixion takes us immediately to Christ Himself, whose sacrifice was not some kind of spiritual gesture, but was profoundly and cruelly physical. It follows that although our physical bodies may manifest wickedness, they are not of themselves wicked, and it is this latter view which is dangerously dualist. It is therefore extremely important to handle this kind of rhetorical passage of Paul with care, because he frequently appears to be dualist when what he is actually saying is that the difference between "flesh" and "spirit" is the difference between those who are and are not committed to Christ; or, to put it in Pauline terms, committed to the Law or to Christ's transforming power.

To Paul and to us, that transformation is seen through the retrospective lens of Resurrection and Crucifixion, but to the lepers it must have seemed much more simple. Here was a miracle worker who might cure them. They were not only sick with an incurable and frightening disease, it was one that turned them into such outcasts that it even broke down the division between Jew and Samaritan. They had to show themselves to the priests after their cure to be readmitted into society, and it was no doubt renewed inclusion that tempted the nine Jews to seek their families. Perhaps the Samaritan realised in the moments after his cure that he had lost his nine fellow sufferers and would never see them again, as the bond of captivity was broken.

Whichever way we look at it, the story is oddly sad. After all, although Jesus says to the Samaritan that his faith has caused the cure, those who had no faith and did not worship Jesus in gratitude were also cured. That is why it is always dangerous to make a link between what we see in the conduct of others and what God "sees". We have no idea why Jesus cured the other nine and, as we have noted elsewhere, our danger is always to cast ourselves as the attractive character—in this case the Samaritan—instead of seeing ourselves as less clear-cut.

The other reason why the story is sad is because it tells us how quickly we move from one ambition to another. In our own day, this most vividly takes the form of refugees who are close to death from starvation, whose only wish is to receive food to live, but who, having received it, protest that their other wishes are not being adequately fulfilled. Our behaviour is often the same, though in a less extreme sense. One moment we are desperate for something which we regard as vitally important and then, having attained it, we are immediately desperate to attain something else. This is the best of us and the worst of us, but in this story it is the latter.

What Jesus might have seen in the Samaritan was the capacity to worship unconditionally, regardless of what actually happened to him. The tradition of such commitment is catalogued in the Book of Job. The acid test is the reversal of the Samaritan's actual outcome. Would he have worshipped Jesus, as Job continued to worship God, if he had not been cured? This is a question we need to ask ourselves frequently, to guard us from reducing worship to intercession and result-related thanksgiving. The ease with which we fall into this trap is frequently seized upon by atheist critics, who rightly say that if we attribute finding a car parking space to a successful prayer then we must equally attribute the failure to find one either to our prayer or God's response. This is an apparently harmless game we play with ourselves which can easily become dangerous, leading us, at either extreme, into fatalism or obsession. Worship, after all, is about God's due, not our needs.

The Fifteenth Sunday after Trinity

Collect   *Keep, we beseech Thee, O Lord, Thy church . . .*
Epistle   Galatians 6.11–18
Gospel   Matthew 6.24–34

What is a church? It is the question at the heart of both Galatians and Matthew's Gospel and, although the two authors tackle the question in different ways, they agree that it exists because people have made choices. It is not an external phenomenon that has been "dropped from heaven", but is a collection of assenting worshippers.

The choice on which Paul concentrates uses the rather ugly short-hand language of circumcision and its opposite. Those who have chosen the option of the Church have chosen a moral or spiritual circumcision as opposed to the strictly physical circumcision which Jews undergo when they assent to their law-based Covenant. But this is somewhat crude. If we buy into the dichotomy too comprehensively, we will find ourselves thinking that all Jews must have been legalists and all Christians moralists. Even if this was the external distinction (and even that is doubtful), there are too many moralists in the Jewish tradition and too many legalists in the Christian tradition to make this a wholly credible way of looking at things.

Matthew's vision of Church is much more challenging. Jesus says that we must be a community which simply lives from day to day without worrying about what we will eat or wear. I suspect this is as troubling to contemporary Christians as the injunction against divorce and remarriage, so it is important to understand the context. Firstly, Matthew was writing at a time when Christians thought that the last judgment was very close at hand, something that would happen in their lifetime. This produced the kind of earthly denial which we see in Acts 2.44. Secondly, however, this way of looking at earthly existence is not uniform by any means as we can see in Paul's great anxiety to show the money-loving Corinthians that he had worked hard at his tent-making and would accept nothing from them. Thirdly, there is a simple paradox in the idea that the Lord will provide for those who do not plan. Others, acting on behalf of the Lord, must do the planning, which is the whole point of holding goods in common. Theoretically, nobody worries because planning takes care of want.

To argue that we cannot live like the lilies of the field, however, is not to say that we should be selfish. In a world of extreme wealth and poverty it is important that we develop a coherent attitude to our use of worldly goods. This is an area where the personal and the political come into sharp contact and so it is important to be honest with ourselves and careful with those with whom we disagree.

Here are three proposals as a starting point for a discussion, always granting that there are many other starting points. Firstly, that we should only tolerate a difference in income and wealth if that difference is to the advantage of the least well off. Examples would include accumulating capital to invest and hire labour, using wealth to preserve art, and acquiring books so that we can instruct others. Secondly, that we should only acquire possessions if they in some way conform to the first rule or if they enhance the spiritual life of ourselves and those we serve. Examples would include using resources to make us more morally sensitive, collecting goods to enhance the community, and using goods to broaden the outlook of the community. Thirdly, the conditions in the first two rules may need to be modified in a serious crisis. Examples would include disposing of valued possessions to raise money for famine relief, giving something we value to somebody who needs it more, and selling Church treasures in a crisis.

It is important to note that the two areas where we have most difficulty—love and money—are precisely those where the ideal seems most difficult to approach. That is why we are urged to seek mutual support by choosing to be part of a church where we will be less lonely when we are trying to make honest choices about love and money. To aspire to the ideals of Jesus as hermits is given to very few of us. This is why the Christian way of life is corporate and why, incidentally, the claim that one can be a Christian but not attend church is highly questionable.

Perhaps the most important idea to bear in mind is that of the corrosiveness of anxiety. There is a paradox in the development of civilisation that the better the capacity for storage, the more anxious we become. As long as we can store nothing we are forced to behave like the lilies of the field but, as Jesus frequently remarked, barns are powerful symbols of greed and planning. It is these two factors, particularly when they are yoked together, which cause anxiety. We might, on that basis, formulate a fourth rule about the ownership of income and wealth. We should not own anything that makes us anxious. This is both morally positive and personally beneficial, a combination which does not readily present itself when we are trying to do what is right. So often, we assume that anxiety is inevitable, but it almost always arises not from external factors over which we have no control, but from the choices we make. Choice is at the heart of what we are, as individuals and as members of a church.

The Sixteenth Sunday after Trinity

Collect	*O Lord, we beseech Thee, let thy continual pity . . .*
Epistle	Ephesians 3.13–21
Gospel	Luke 7.11–17

Perhaps it is the sparseness of the narrative that accounts for the relative obscurity of the boy of Nain compared, say, with the account of Lazarus in John 11, and it is one of those many occasions when we would really appreciate more detail. Did Jesus know the dead boy and his mother? Did she ask him to intervene, or was it a spontaneous act? The account talks of many people, but Jesus did not preach, he simply told the mother not to weep and, although he acted out of compassion, the effect seems to have been stunning. There is the same sense of awe in Paul's account of God's love which "passeth knowledge", and the Collect prays that the Church may be cleansed by "continual pity". In all three cases there is a complete lack of calculation, of trying to assess the quantity or quality of God's love, making nonsense of the all too human question, "how much do you love me?"

One way of looking at the history of Christianity is to see it as a struggle between the ideas of God's unconditional love on the one hand, and the notions of "divine retribution" and the moral dimension of witness on the other. The concept of unconditionality is difficult but simple, whereas the idea of retribution is easy but complex. The conflict reached its height in the Lutheran Reformation which was, ostensibly, a revolt against prudential ethics, and a return to a recognition of the unconditional. On that point at least, Protestantism, as unable as Catholicism to keep out of the private lives of believers, soon reverted to a much more prudential stance. The problem of this approach for Christianity is that it receives no support from the teaching and conduct of Jesus. Just as he did not ask any of the thousands he fed whether they were worthy of his miracle (cf. The Seventh Sunday after Trinity), he did not ask the widow how well she had behaved, or whether her son deserved a spectacular second chance. The problem with God's unconditionality is that it is as unfathomable as God. We are so used to measuring, counting, calculating, trading, fining, and giving that we cannot help ourselves. We have to think about space and time, clothes and clocks, buildings and bridges, structures and stresses, nutrition and navigation. Our functional lives are full of numbers, but so are our stories. From the time we are children we are subjected to and deeply affected by numerical truth and exaggeration. In a sense that it is difficult to articulate, our idea of infinity is not really about a different category of reality, but is, rather, an idea of something beyond number, like more music to play, chocolates to eat, or cars to drive than we will ever have time for in life. That is why we quite often articulate life after death as similar to life on earth, but with unlimited access to earthly pleasures.

To this extent, prudential morality is an understandable anthropological, but an inadequate theological, response to the infinite. One way of approaching the issue is to imagine that we are in a permanent condition of dependency and joy, replicating the experience of the widow of Nain on a daily basis for as long as we live. In spite of what goes wrong with our earthly lives, with our jobs, finances, achievements, and relationships, we are still in that state. The way we normally describe this to ourselves is "gratitude", but that is a conditional word. In the sense that God does not want anything, words which imply reciprocity are redundant.

The core of our problem is that there is a paradox in unconditionality which requires reciprocal unconditionality. Just as God loves us unconditionally, we are required to love God unconditionally, and while the first proposition requires a struggle to comprehend, the second, more critically, requires a struggle to act. There is, however, a truth at the heart of our condition which Luther comprehended; there is nothing we can do to reciprocate God's love just as there was nothing that the widow could offer Jesus equal to the value of what he did for her.

We are blessed with an irremediably asymmetrical arrangement with God. No other kind would be possible in a relationship between the Creator and the created. We naturally try to express this in terms of ourselves, because we find any discussion of the idea of God too difficult to encompass. The paradox of theology is that it must try to use words to "capture" the idea of God, but it must equally be open to being encompassed by God. Most words, and all numbers, however, are the enemies of wonder and mystery, intent on reducing reality to terms which we can grasp and control. There lies the key to adopting a proper stance as a creature, and it is the Creator who controls, not the creature.

The Collect strikes a jarring note with its idea that we are subjects of God's pity, presumably because we are sinners, fallen or flawed. The natural response is to ask why a God who created in love would create something to be pitied. The answer is that pity is not a form of condescension. Even though it is generally perceived only to operate in an ecology of inequality, its driving forces are mutuality, respect, and recognition of God in the other, which might lead us to ask whether equality in itself is not simply a numerical concept.

The Seventeenth Sunday after Trinity

Collect	*Lord, we pray thee that Thy grace may always prevent . . .*
Epistle	Ephesians 4.1–6
Gospel	Luke 14.1–11

During a visit to Israel, my hotel lift automatically stopped at every floor on the Sabbath. My first reaction was irritation at what seemed like a rather nit-picking approach to rule keeping. Why would it matter if I pressed the odd button? On reflection, however, I saw a profound seriousness in the prohibition. For the rich and active the Sabbath was a restraint against endless grafting, for the poor it was a protection against exploitation, and for all it was a chance to curb the instinctive, the compulsive and the aggressive, to be deliberative and reflective. As we have found to our cost in secular Europe, the only way that the Sabbath retains its power is if it is universally observed. Even if we refrain from work and shopping to attend church twice or three times on Sundays, our physical and mental space is still contaminated. The Pharisees were right to insist on strict observance, but what they failed to see was the underlying reason for it. Self-restraint and reflection are of little worth if we are as hard-hearted on Monday as we were on Saturday. The enforced day of calm is not to be spent in grim resentment of time wasted and opportunities lost, but is supposed to give us the chance to orient ourselves positively towards God, our neighbour, and creation. On that basis, argued Jesus, it was perfectly proper to do good on the Sabbath, and it wasn't the action of brain or hand which counted, but to what end they were turned. In other words, Jesus was pointing out the difference between appearance and meaning. Luke then links this with an apparently unrelated parable about precedence at a banquet. Jesus, customarily combining principle with pragmatism, says that we should not over-estimate our own social significance by going to the top table but should, rather, start well below the salt, from which position there is only one way to go. Today at a mass catering function such self-denial might, at worst, result in receiving food that is a little scrappy and less than hot, but in Jesus' day the sacrifice was much greater. Society was much more stratified, so that everybody would notice where everyone else sat and this was reflected in the quality of what was served. So when Jesus urged his listeners to deny themselves, he was talking about reality and not, as we might suppose today, about symbolism. The two parts of the Gospel, therefore, alert us to the importance of distinguishing between reality and appearance, and urge us to reflect not only on what we are doing, but why we are doing it.

Paul, a Pharisee himself, was well aware of the dangers of confusing appearance with reality, and he urges the Ephesians to follow their vocation to Christ with "all lowliness and meekness, with long-suffering, forbearing one another in love; endeavouring to keep the unity of the Spirit in the bond of peace." As I write, the Anglican Communion is considering the adoption of a Covenant in the name of unity which contains sanctions to enforce uniformity, making Paul's plea all the more urgent. As long as we have been able to tactfully retain an appearance of unity by "turning a blind eye", the individual and corporate cost has been low, but the price of real unity, of forbearance, of ranking love above judgment, is, we are discovering, very high indeed. Appearing not to know and doing nothing comes naturally, being known to know and doing nothing calls for immense restraint.

For all its impediments to social justice, personal development, intellectual enquiry, cultural diversity, and openness to the unexpected opportunity, socially stratified society does have the advantage of enabling dialogue to take place under mutually accepted rules. The problem of a society based on individualism, as we have learned in politics, and are now learning in the Anglican Communion, is that we have lost the means of respectful dialogue. We believe that self-assertion is not only a right, but a positive social benefit and, to compound this, we exercise power almost without noticing. Of course, that is what the Pharisees did, but what others do is not our moral problem.

This continual exercise of self-will and power imposes enormous stress on us and pours ever more adrenalin and contention into society. In the face of this evident crisis, some will continue to try to turn the clock back by restoring the nineteenth-century Sabbath, but we will more likely have to learn how to build our own Sabbaths. We who do not labour from dawn until dusk and then collapse in exhaustion can surely restrain the brain and hand, and leave ourselves open to the Word of God in Scripture and in silence, as a regular feature of our daily lives.

Reflecting both Jesus and St Paul, the call to reflection is pragmatic, as well as principled. If we consider the amount of repetition, assertion, impromptu decisions and opinions, tedium, and trivia in our lives and the degree to which we try to mitigate these by consumption and escapism, it is obvious that there is a better way. That way, which we should seek for ourselves and our Christian communities, is also the necessary precondition for resolving the problems of the Church community at large. The argument about the Anglican Covenant, which is a proxy for the argument about gay clergy, has little to do with God. It is a dispute about authority and morals in the context of deep-rooted social attitudes to sexuality. Those who urge sexual restraint should practice verbal self-restraint.

The Eighteenth Sunday after Trinity

Collect	*Lord, we beseech thee, grant thy people grace to withstand the temptations of the world, the flesh, and the devil . . .*
Epistle	1 Corinthians 1.4–8
Gospel	Matthew 22.34–46

Living in a city which was a byword for every kind of vice, there was nothing that anybody could teach the Corinthians about the world and the flesh (cf. The Sunday called Sexagesima) but, conversely, they were pretty indifferent when it came to the devil. The phrase of the Collect rings out in a unmistakably Pauline way, and no doubt he had something of the kind in mind when he began his momentous First Letter to them concerned, as always, with eschatological closure (cf. The Sixth Sunday after the Epiphany).

There was something deeply troubled and "millennial" in the sixteenth century, which drew it to desperate moralising in general and to Paul in particular. Whether the Reformation was a cause or a symptom of this turbulence might merely be a matter of intellectual fascination were it not for the resulting "Pharisaical" fanaticism. This had a profound effect on individual and social conduct, combating the world, the flesh, and the devil, with exegesis, moral force, and state power.

In a way which should not be exaggerated, the contrast between pre-Reformation Christianity and the Reformation is not dissimilar to the contrast between Jesus and the Pharisees, including Paul. The question Jesus is asked arises from a characteristically moralist standpoint as to ask what is the greatest commandment is to require a ranking process which allows for censure to be measured out with precision. A contemporary example would be the question: is it more sinful to be gay or to be homophobic? There is no answer, not least because sin is about motive rather than outcome, but with the "last judgment" in the offing, such hair-splitting can seem important.

Although Jesus constantly preached the coming of the Kingdom, he seems not to have understood this in a quasi-judicial way. When asked about the Commandments he gives an irreproachably simple answer which eschews any notion of ranking the sins of the flesh. To understand why he took a much more open view of the question, we have to refer to the second part of the Gospel which contains some complex theological by-play. However, its central point is so inescapable that it ultimately, as Matthew says, stops the discussion between Jesus and his questioners until his trial. No matter what his virtues were as a man, as a teacher, and icon of holy living, Jesus was the son of God and could not be expected to look at moral questions from an anthropocentric perspective. It is this freedom from baggage and cant which is one of his most telling advantages, and accounts for his continuing attractiveness. In a way which is difficult to characterise precisely, Jesus the God made man, as opposed to Jesus the atoning victim, lost some of that attractiveness in the sixteenth century with its quasi-theocratic obsessiveness. We have to remember that, uniquely in Western Christian history, Christians slaughtered each other in the name of "right" religion for almost two centuries after the Reformation (cf. The Fourth Sunday after the Epiphany). To be relaxed in the context of the fifteenth century imitation of Jesus did not mean that how people behaved did not matter, it simply meant that goodness should be lived for itself and not because of threats from the civil or religious powers nor from the fear of Armageddon.

The tension between the consistently constructive teaching of Jesus, and Paul's tendency in his worst moments to sink into Pharisaical judgment, should not be dismissed nor exaggerated. Jesus was preaching from a utopian standpoint; Paul, on the other hand, was struggling to found his Church on earth, which involved tangling in a practical way with the world and the flesh as well as the devil, and Paul's worst moments are far fewer than his best.

Living the holy life for its own sake, outside the confines of eschatological closure, presents us with a much greater problem than that faced by Paul's Corinthians, and it puts us firmly in the crowd listening to Jesus. We are to live by the two great commandments regardless of external pressures one way or the other. This will frequently mean resisting all kinds of specific and implied peer and social pressures, the most pressing of which is the seemingly inexorable social pressure to judge the moral conduct of others as a precondition of a bewildering variety of ostracisms. Paradoxically, the argument for self-restraint (cf. The Seventeenth Sunday after Trinity) is in need of forceful advocacy. Just as crises always bring authoritarianism, so our own state of comfort and ease has, in spite of what we say and think, summed up in that ridiculously upper class cliché "the nanny state", brought about a condition of unsurpassed individual personal freedom, which has taxed our powers of self-governance. In a corporate context, this freedom has radically transformed Christianity from a conforming to an affirming community, which in turn calls for a degree of self-commitment for its own sake whose value is much greater than any thought or act, no matter how good in its effect, generated by fear. During the next decades when the ecological crisis alters the balance away from individual freedom and towards the exercise of governing authority, one of our challenges will be to change our lifestyle not just out of niggardly obedience or even self-preservation, but as a way of following Jesus by doing the right thing for the right reason.

The Nineteenth Sunday after Trinity

Collect   *O God, forasmuch as without thee we*
              are not able to please thee; . . .
Epistle   Ephesians 4.17–32
Gospel   Matthew 9.1–8

If only the distinction between the behaviour of believers and non-be-lievers was as clear cut as Paul implies. He draws a stark contrast be-tween the ways of the Gentiles and believers, using the metaphor of the "old man" and the "new man" to show how radical is the break between the bad behaviour of the unbeliever and the virtue of the convert. Much as we, from a Christian standpoint, like this to be true, we should ask ourselves whether Christians behave markedly differently from every-body else. What actually distinguishes us is our ambition to please God and our acceptance, neatly summed up in the Collect, that without God we cannot please Him.

This is a strange kind of love which appears to base our ability to love God on our dependency upon Him, but that way of looking at things springs from our proper desire to love each other reciprocally as equals. In our divine relationship, the reciprocity is asymmetrical and there is no question of equality and, therefore, no danger of dependency in the ordinary sense, in which unequal relationships damage self-esteem, and lead to the destruction of love through the exercise of power. Our rela-tionship with God is not one of dependency in the human sense because we are categorically different, being creatures of the Creator. Yet in one way our relationship with God is strikingly similar to our closest human relationships, in that both result from deliberate and often painful and hesitant choice. We do not and cannot love easily or simply because love is not like that, and so we can learn about heavenly love from the way we understand human love and vice versa. What we learn from our love of God is our inability to survive autonomously, and what we learn from human love is the ability to make choices which generate intensity.

One of love's chief enemies is abstraction, reducing it to sets of rules which are generally held to hold true, and this is as dangerous to divine as to earthly love, as it tends to result in a conservative view of reality, ruling out serendipity and radically altered states of perceiving and be-ing. This innate conservatism explains why the religious leaders found it so difficult to come to terms with Jesus. Their grievance operated at two separate but related levels. Firstly, and fundamentally, Jesus was claiming a right to forgive sins which they could not accept. Secondly, and more importantly from their perspective, though less radical, Jesus was changing the way that sins were forgiven by eliminating the whole of the Deuteronomical tradition. He claimed to have found a way of forgiving sins that cut out animal sacrifice and the Levitical monopoly. Sad to say, after the founding of the Church and Paul's mission, it was not long before there was a new priestly monopoly, with its tendency to accumulate all kinds of heterogeneous baggage that, over time, became fused into a pretence of human logic and divine fiat.

The man who was sick had faith, not a theory—as long as he was cured he did not mind how—which raises questions about the nature of theology. One of its purposes, which arises from the fundamental human capacity, is the search for patterns, for coherent meaning in apparent chaos. As scientists admit, the problem arises that we think we are being objective, when we are actually imposing patterns on the evidence. This is the shortcoming from which the reading from Ephesians suffers. Paul's argument about believers and Gentiles is not only a crude generalisation, it is also based on a rag-bag of assertions which oscillate between reality and aspiration. One minute he is saying how we are, the next how we should be. As we have noted, the evidence is by no means clear-cut, and we should always be wary of being led by an ecclesiastical "closed shop" into seeing apartness where it does not exist. Distinction usually leads to the tribal tendency to build inwardly focused support mechanisms, to define otherness in a hostile way and, in consequence, to make identity defensive and defined by negatives. We apparently know what it is not to be British, but find it hard to say what it is. There were good historical reasons why the Jews were internally focused, but Jesus, and Paul for that matter, were supposed to have changed all that. Underlying much of what Matthew writes is the question of what it means to be a Christian community, a Church, and we need to ask that question with the man of faith in mind: if our human purpose is to acknowledge our creation in love, that we might love God and our neighbour, what role does the Church play? If part of the answer is that we create a corporate identity, how far does that need to be definitive, in our specific case, Credal? And how far dare we extend our inclusiveness before our identity, our differentiation, our sense of ourselves as a community, is lost? Exploring this last question practically involves a high level of personal and corporate risk, to which Judaism at the time of Jesus was strongly averse. We need to ask ourselves whether we are radically different, whether we want a relationship with God which has the same potential, at a different level, for surprise and discovery that we prize in our most intimate human relationships.

The Twentieth Sunday after Trinity

Collect	*O almighty and most merciful God, of thy bountiful goodness keep us . . .*
Epistle	Ephesians 5.15–21
Gospel	Matthew 22.1–14

The way in which Archbishop Stephen Langton divided the New Testament into chapters c. 1227 is not always logical, and can be misleading because our notion of a chapter comprises ideas such as coherence, unity and structure. Although today's Gospel parable of the wedding banquet is placed at the beginning of Chapter 22, it is actually the last and least significant of three parables, the preceding being the Two Sons (21.28–32) and the Vineyard Tenants (21.33–46), which almost certainly drove the religious authorities to seek to prosecute Jesus. The issue in question which introduces these three parables is that of authority. Given that the Pharisees believe in an after-life, who are its earthly gate keepers? Jesus, at the very least, challenges the Pharisee monopoly. Firstly, in a manoeuvre which reminds one of Thomas More in *A Man for All Seasons*, Jesus refuses to cite the source of his authority because they will not come clean about John the Baptist (Matthew 21.23–27). Secondly, he says that the people who actually do the work are more important than those who pretend to do it and, crucially, he then accuses them of being impostors and murderers, rejecting the genuine Kingdom, "the stone which the builder rejected".

After this dense and dramatic set of arguments in Chapter 21, which might be characterised symphonically as a short but telling first movement, a short *minuet* for the second movement, and a long and serious slow third movement, this parable of the wedding banquet might be characterised as a rather showy *rondo finale*, certainly not to be taken so seriously as the other three. Jesus again says that the Pharisees are to be replaced in the Kingdom by "the good and the bad" who are apparently trawled at random from society. They are installed in the Kingdom and the King of the Banquet destroys the absentees, but there is one man wearing the wrong clothes, and he is discredited. These ideas sit uncomfortably together: if the Kingdom is for the good and the bad alike, surely that has to include Pharisees, whichever way you characterise them? If the servant has let all the guests in, whose fault is it that one person is not wearing the right clothes and, in any case, is there any such thing as the right clothes? Or might Matthew have transposed the story so that Jesus was portraying Himself as the person not wearing the right clothes?

Of course, none of these questions would have been asked by the compilers of the Lectionary. Firstly, they would have been attracted by the apparent randomness of salvation which, some thought at the time, divorced it from personal behaviour. Secondly, they were committed to taking every word of the Bible at the same weight, denying a latitude of understanding which, paradoxically, late medieval Christianity enjoyed prior to the explosion of Renaissance-generated Biblical criticism. Thirdly, the idea of "form criticism"—recognising different literary attributes to the text—had not as yet been crystallised. It is therefore important to recognise that this is one of those instances where many of us stand in a very different relationship to the text from those who chose it.

The passage from Ephesians casts a uniquely liturgical light on our relationship to God and the Kingdom. Paul, who was most frequently concerned with the relationship—or lack of it—between personal conduct and salvation, emphasises that we will only attain the Kingdom through proper worship; a predictable stance, given his own Pharisaic origins. So, in a sense which makes neatness impossible, the Epistle is emphasising those very elements upon which Jesus appeared to cast some doubt.

The idea of the Kingdom is at the core of all three parables, and this raises the critical question of what we think Jesus meant by this mystery, and what we mean by it. For Jesus the critical point is that his role is intermediary and that the realisation of the Kingdom involves the restoration of the true relationship between the Creator ("the Father") and the created. It would be disturbing if it meant something radically different for us, but we have been not so much led astray as blown off course by the mighty rhetorical gales of Revelation. This has imprinted on our tradition deep resonances of place and posture, of drama and experience so that the theological simplicity of the idea of being enfolded back into perfect unity with the Creator has been complicated by a massive dose of fantasy. Where Jesus quite comfortably talks in terms of kingdoms and thrones as a way of illustrating his point, our respect for the Bible has led us to take the images of that kingdom far too literally. What we are promised, from the calling of Abraham until the last words of John's Gospel, is a restoration whose beauty and completeness are impossible to conceive, bearing no relationship to the literary gargoyles of Revelation. The transcendence is underlined in the last three chapters, but our problem is that we cannot appreciate the full texture of the book's conclusion without reading what goes before. As always, our ambition to enter more fully into the mystery of Godhead inevitably involves adding colour to what is so transparent that we cannot see it, and the danger is that we disfigure what we seek with human desire. Even so, it is better to leave a finger print than not touch.

The Twenty-First Sunday after Trinity

Collect   *Grant, we beseech Thee, merciful Lord, to*
              Thy faithful people pardon and peace . . .
Epistle   Ephesians 6.10–20
Gospel   John 4.46^b–54

One of the strangest flaws in the exegesis of the letters of Paul is the failure to take him literally when he is discussing contemporary politics. Consider the following: "we wrestle not against flesh and blood, but against principalities, against powers, against the rulers of the darkness of this world, against spiritual wickedness in high places." Interpreting this simply to mean that Paul opposed immorality or was simply warning against "the devil" is surely a threadbare explanation. It is difficult to see how this cannot be taken as a direct assault on the Roman administration in general, and its emperors in particular. As successive emperors declared themselves to be gods, such attacks were not only seditious, but blasphemous, and would have brought Paul into serious danger if the Empire had had a greater capacity for spying. Ancient empires which extended over large territories spread their administration very thin, concerned only with taxation, food supply, and security against invasion and insurrection. Nonetheless, local governors had draconian powers (Acts 16.22–24), and Paul was therefore vulnerable not only to Jewish conservatives (cf. Galatians), opportunists (Acts 16.16–20), and the self-interested (Acts 19:24–27), but also from the governing classes who owed their position to Roman patronage. Republican probity, harsh but consistent and ubiquitous, was now literally legendary, replaced by tyranny which was capricious and inconsistent. At the same time, like all waves of the *nouveau riche*, imperial favourites compensated in ostentation and excess for what they lacked in subtlety and good taste. In such circumstances it is natural that Paul should have turned to the military metaphor of armour, shield and helmet when considering the moral confrontation with egregious wickedness. At the time of Jesus there was no less contempt by the Jews for the Romans, not least because of the divine pretensions of their rulers, but it was much less tangible than it was by the time of Claudius. It is therefore surprising that today's Gospel only gives the impression of rather general condemnation.

Whether the nobleman was a foreigner or simply a Jewish vassal who had "sold out", there seems to have been no hostility towards him. In any case, Jesus would not have been one to choose to heal or not on the basis of political allegiance. His reference to Naaman (Luke 4.27), for example, scandalised his hearers. As usual, Jesus' criterion was not conduct or background but faith. In an age of comparative medical ignorance there was a clear two-part dynamic in operation. Firstly, people were much more frightened by illness because it was much more prevalent, more often fatal and hardly understood, a combination which led to a much greater emphasis on faith than science. Secondly, in the Jewish tradition, the idea of healing was not frequently associated with faith. In the Greek-speaking part of the Empire the medical model, in the idea of catharsis, had sacred overtones (cf. the Temple of Esklepios and the Forum at Epidaurus), but in this there was no trace of a relationship between worship and cure. So whether the nobleman was a Jew or a Greek, the circumstances of his request were unusual.

For Paul, the dichotomy between private Christian virtue and public pagan vice could not be more clear-cut. How far should we condemn the conduct of civil powers who claim to base their decisions on ethical and social values of Christian origin? Paul had a large target, but took aim at considerable risk. Our target may be smaller but so, proportionately, is the risk. We might also observe the maxim that people in a democracy get the government they deserve, so we might consider ourselves partly responsible for what we regard as government shortcomings. We should also face up to the somewhat taboo question of whether the values of Christianity more neatly align with a particular party or outlook.

Paul's response was couched in terms of a military metaphor, but we are indebted to Susan Sontag for pointing out the dangers of this form of language. How helpful is it to an understanding of Christianity to say that we must "fight the good fight" or depict ourselves as "Christian soldiers"? The rejoinder might be that these are only metaphors, but what use are they when they mean the opposite of what we intend, or mean nothing?

One remarkable aspect of the miracle in John is that it was achieved— like that of the Centurion's servant (Luke 7.2; the accounts may have a single origin), and unlike the healing of the ancient world and, largely, our own—remotely. The nobleman had to believe it had happened even if he did not see it, and if he did not believe it had happened it would not have happened. He did not ask for a sign. Even if we pray in faith and not because we expect to inspect the divine credentials, it is human to wish to discern patterns, to make connections, but we do not know how prayer works. Jesus asked us to pray to the Father through him for our wants—however God determines them—but he never promised direct causality between the prayer and the response. The world, which Paul condemned for its immorality, has more faith in the causality and patterns of science than in God's mysterious healing power, but seems no sounder for that. It is understandable in a military empire that Paul should have used his metaphor, but we might better think about healing than fighting.

The Twenty-Second Sunday after Trinity

Collect   *Lord, we beseech Thee to keep Thy*
                     household the church . . .
Epistle   Philippians 1.3–11
Gospel   Matthew 18.21–35

Of all the master and servant parables in the Gospels, this account of the open-hearted master and the mean-spirited servant is apparently the easiest to understand, reflecting directly the Lord's Prayer. The master's good work is not imitated by his servant, as the result of which he is punished. In human terms, the retributive action of the master is perfectly understandable, but how closely should the conduct of these two be linked? Is Jesus saying that just as we are forgiven we should forgive, or is he rather saying that we will not be forgiven unless we forgive? More likely the latter, otherwise the master's conduct would be unreasonable, and yet we should not confuse what we might call the "transmission" of forgiveness with the "transmission" of virtue. The simplest example of transmission is that although our parents are gratified if we return their love, they are much more so if we love our children the way they loved us. In other words, transmission is not a boomerang, we do things because we do them, regardless of what may or may not come back. On this basis, the master might want to punish the servant or take back his initial generous offer, but he did not make that offer conditionally on the good behaviour of the servant. Conditional giving is an extremely doubtful proceeding and its grip on contemporary ethics is fatal to the kind of love which Jesus preached. The master's proper reaction should have been summed up in the phrase, "more in sorrow than anger", as he had every right to be sorrowful but no right to be angry. It turns out, then, that this is far from a simple parable which provides a clear illustration of the principles of the Lord's Prayer. Our obligation to forgive our neighbour as God forgives us is a totally separate proposition from that which says that our forgiveness must be conditional upon the behaviour of the forgiven, towards us or anyone else. We must forgive because we forgive because we forgive.

Unconditionality is the hallmark of a good work and, although Paul involves his own personal trials in his account of generosity, he is saved from egotistical excess by his ready acknowledgment that he does no good work except through God's grace. Thus, he tells the Philippians from his prison cell that Jesus, quite literally, performs good works through them, a sentiment strongly echoed in the Collect.

The dynamics of good works and forgiveness are fused in the idea of unconditionality. That reading is confirmed by the Gospel discussion between Jesus and Peter which precedes the parable of the master and servant. Peter asks how often he must forgive, and Jesus gives the inevitable answer that forgiveness must be unlimited, beyond calculation. If he had been asked the same question about the performance of good works, he would have said the same thing. As "fallen" people, regardless of how we understand the term (my personal understanding is most closely reflected by Shakespeare and Rayment-Pickard), we are forced to fall back on an element of predictable reciprocity, rather than unlimited transmission which accounts for our legal and fiscal systems. Twenty-first century social arrangements could not survive without laws and taxes; nonetheless, the imperfections of both are nothing to the imperfections which have rendered both necessary. Our culture is both unforgiving and unremitting, and our reaction to complexity in the public sector is to blame officials and politicians when we have lazily, or even selfishly, handed them the problems we are not prepared to solve for ourselves. This further leads to the ethically disastrous position where we think that what they do is somehow divorced from what we would do. If we are really so virtuous, why do we not take back responsibility for difficult decisions? The simple answer is that we have made a contract with politicians whereby we will let them take all the difficult decisions and reserve the right to abuse them for what they do on our behalf. We do not see them as symbols of our brokenness but, hypocritically, as enemies of our virtue.

One of the deepest sadnesses of our age, as with every other, is that there is massive evidence that forgiveness and generosity are much more effective for the benefactor, the recipient, and society in general, than vengeance and meanness. The reasonable objection to this characterisation is that civil justice is not vengeance and fiscal prudence is not meanness, but to exact retribution and to make generosity conditional are both contractual arrangements which Jesus clearly opposes.

Matthew's account of Jesus' teaching, therefore, needs to be considered very carefully. It begins with Jesus laying down an unconditional principle of forgiveness, which he yokes with unconditional generosity. We need to ask how far we can live that unconditional life and how far civil arrangements reflect our "fallen" selves. One approximate formulation might be that the less self-disciplined and generous we are, the more civil power society requires to attain a degree of stability. History teaches us, however, that civil instruments can only achieve stability. They cannot generate altruism, and their failure to do so both in revolutionary France and the Soviet Union led to the most disastrous consequences. The freeloader's reliance upon the moral integrity of others is an illusion, as is the notion that virtue can be imposed. Like truth, goodness cannot result from duress. In any case, the only starting point for social improvement is ourselves.

The Twenty-Third Sunday after Trinity

Collect   *O God, our refuge and strength . . .*
Epistle   Philippians 3.17–21
Gospel   Matthew 22.15–22

In spite of a relentless struggle throughout the history of Christianity carried on by such theological giants as St Augustine, St Thomas Aquinas and Calvin, Gnosticism is alive and well (cf. Shakespeare and Rayment-Pickard). The struggle was commenced by St Paul, but it is sometimes difficult to see this because of his lapses into what looks like Gnosticism's defining propositions: that the spiritual and physical are separate and that the former is superior to the latter. It is difficult to read a phrase like "vile bodies" without drawing the wrong conclusion. The root of Paul's problem is what we would now call a "category error". He compares our bodies with Christ's risen and ascended body to our disadvantage, but we would say that the two phenomena cannot be compared at all, and that the comparison is therefore meaningless. Nonetheless, the Gnostic tradition continues to divide and to rank the spiritual and physical on the basis of this error, ignoring the confirmatory conclusion of each major act of creation in Genesis, which describes it as "good", culminating in the creation of humanity which is characterised as "very good". Of course there is a difference between the creator and the created, but it is not a relationship of inferiority and superiority. We would not, for example, describe the *Mona Lisa* as inferior to Leonardo da Vinci. To understand the point more fully, we should remember that Gnosticism was a neo-Platonist phenomenon, in which everything physical was regarded as an imperfect representation of a perfect archetype. The Christian response in witness and mission is to acknowledge that we are imperfect, but to affirm our freedom to love by being what we are: human, and therefore an indissoluble union of the physical and the divine, whose perfect pattern was Our Saviour Jesus Christ.

We might say that the struggle actually began with Jesus who was called upon by the Pharisees to denigrate earthly powers. For reasons both of prudence and principle, Jesus was not prepared to satisfy his critics. He confirmed the propriety of different things—as we would say, "horses for courses".

How can we account for Gnosticism's persistent attraction? One explanation is that a traditional tendency to dissect creation so that groups give themselves the power to include and exclude—a chronic clerical tendency—has been reinforced by a breakdown in every kind of apparent stability. Economics, politics, entertainment, social mores and Christian witness are no longer continually evolving phenomena with the occasional discontinuous eruption. They all present themselves in a state of headlong fragmentation, so that contemporary commentators frequently say that what matters is not a product (what a phenomenon creates or articulates), but a process (how a phenomenon behaves). This "post-modernist" way of looking (or, rather, innumerable ways of looking) is intensely threatening to people who need to know where they are, where they belong, and who does not belong. The position of gay people in society, therefore, is properly characterised merely as the "presenting issue". If it were not this, it would be some other phenomenon which would manifest the aggressive response of the insecure. Although this issue may be significant in itself, it is minor compared with the emerging tendency to wish to divide creation along racial or religious lines. To call for the Church to be inclusive is not, on this basis, a liberal, "politically correct" fetish, but a fundamental Christian principle decreed by the Creator, manifested in the Redeemer, and confirmed by the Sanctifier.

Jesus' attitude to the civil power was generous in the context of Roman occupation, much more generous than most of us manage (cf. The Twenty-Second Sunday after Trinity). Here we exercise a different kind of dualism, in which we rank ourselves above politics instead of seeing politics as a direct representation of our aspirations, or lack of them. Our mantra is that politicians are dishonest, but our question should be how honest are we about politics. Our instinctive dualism is summed up in the nostrum that religion and politics do not mix, which is simply an embellishment of the Pharisaic trap. Our worry is that political disagreement may spill over into religious disagreement, but so it should. Perhaps for most of us, the political outlook comes first, but as Christians the different ways we understand our witness should be the starting points for creative discussion, which should then feed into our politics.

Looking more broadly, the distinction which Jesus makes may no longer be so clear cut. In his time, politics was about such basic issues as taxation and security, where a safe distinction could be made, but in an age where the civil power needs to legislate in profoundly ethical areas such as the definition of life, the nature of properly constituted relationships, the balance between parents and teachers in the rearing of children, and the balance between justice within a generation and between generations, Christians, individually and collectively, need to ask difficult questions about the relationship between themselves and the civil powers. To dismiss them simply as unprincipled, heartless, or un-christian is inadequate. Frequently the "presenting issue" in this discussion is disestablishment, but the more important issue is how we can live as Christians in a democracy without betraying Our Lord through compromise or dogmatism, by saying respectively that there are no lines, or that the lines are immutable. In the final analysis, however, we should never forget that rendering to Caesar is, in effect, rendering to ourselves, for we are Caesar now.

The Twenty-Fourth Sunday after Trinity

Collect	*O Lord, we beseech Thee, absolve Thy people from their offences . . .*
Epistle	Colossians 1.3–12
Gospel	Matthew 9.18–26

From the beginning of November (cf. All Saints' Day) until the end of Advent, one of our major concerns is the nature of our faults, and the necessity of turning again to God.

In the second half of the twentieth century, the Church underwent a crisis over the notion of sin. This was partly because of the growing realisation that judging people on the basis of their external behaviour was unjustified, but also because of a deeper, related suspicion of blanket concepts. There might, too, have been more than a hint of reluctance to accept the idea of personalised sin. Consequently, there is now a generation of Christians growing up without any deep understanding of what sin might be, who would prefer to think that evil is disembodied.

The Collect speaks for its generation in taking the idea of sin, individual and corporate, extremely seriously. Although we may feel that the late medieval practice of purchasing indulgences to mitigate the harmful effects of sin was primitive and verging on the idolatrous, the practice at least shows how closely people then connected the idea of sin with their salvific prospects. They actually believed that sin could bar them from heaven. In an age of scant medical knowledge, they thought of sin as a spiritual sickness that could easily lead to spiritual death or, worse, to perpetual torture. This is why stories of sickness and healing are so important in the Gospels. They provide physical parables about spiritual states. If you have faith in God, as did both the servant and the woman with the haemorrhage, you will be cured.

There are at least three reasons for supposing that we do not take the ideas of an earlier age seriously. Firstly, the Sacrament of Reconciliation (formerly known as Confession) has almost completely died out of Anglican usage. We no longer examine ourselves as individuals and force ourselves to articulate our shortcomings to a priest. Most of us are satisfied with a collective act of penitence at the beginning of the Eucharist or an Office which does not involve a serious examination of conscience. What we are doing, in effect, is depersonalising our sinfulness. Secondly, we have developed an understanding of how behaviour is conditioned by our biological inheritance, and physical and social environments, although we disagree about the balance between what we call nature and nurture. Yet, we often take the further step of using these very proper tools to eliminate any notion of personal responsibility. Society is to blame for all our individual and collective ills, and, in turn, this transforms people who might be deliberately behaving badly into victims. Thirdly, in complex societies like ours, we find it convenient not to take sole responsibility for anything. We are knowing in matters of causality and complexity.

Which naturally leads to the core question: what is sin? The notion against which the Church must be constantly on its guard is that sin is some kind of score card of infractions, mainly concerning sexual misconduct. A starting point for answering the question might be to think of the evil that will befall us if we deliberately choose not to love God or our neighbour. In other words, sin is not so much a question of outcome but of motive. By making choices not to love we put distance between ourselves and God. Christians believe that such distance is neither inevitable nor permanent. We believe in a God of love who forgives us if we ask, on the basis that to ask is to recognise the error of the choices we have made.

The two sufferers in the Gospel played very different roles. The woman with the haemorrhage of many years shows absolute faith in Jesus and is cured. The young girl has to rely upon the intercession of her father. Yet both are cured. It is impossible, says both of these stories, to work out a mechanics of forgiveness which relies upon some quasi-contractual relationship between the Creator and the created. Rather, we should recognise who we are and how God is. We were created to choose and that freedom of choice leads inevitably to wrong choices. As God created us to choose, there is an absolute guarantee that we will always be given the means of rectifying our wrong choices and of narrowing the distance between ourselves and the Creator. Sin is not so much a matter of wiping slates, as of retaining our determination to lean towards God in our minds, and in our spiritual pilgrimage. Sometimes we will turn away and lose ground but, then, with determination we may turn back, encouraged by seeing Jesus upon the road ahead of us, always leading, always there.

God, on the other hand, created out of love and would not create creatures free to love so that they might be trapped forever in imperfection and unhappiness. The difference between the Creator and the created is that, for God, love is a state of existence, whereas for us it is consequent upon freedom of choice, the domain of risk. The deeper the love the greater the risk. This is a warning to the comfortable who in the message of Revelation to the Church of Laodicea (3.15–16), are neither hot nor cold. We must beware of being tepid, of being cautious. We are the Church of love, not social prudence.

The Twenty-Fifth Sunday after Trinity

Collect　　　　　*Stir up, we beseech Thee, O Lord, . . .*
For The Epistle　Jeremiah 23.5–8
Gospel　　　　　John 6.5–14

On this, the last Sunday of the Church's year, we are presented with one of the most memorable Collects, which may stand as a summary for all its fellows, combining personal responsibility with a proper humility that we can do nothing of ourselves. There is a passage from Jeremiah which both promises the Kingdom and looks forward to Advent, and a Gospel reading which elaborates the much simpler account of a feeding miracle (cf. The Seventh Sunday after Trinity).

Jeremiah, quite incorrectly caricatured as a pessimist (on the basis of Lamentations, which he almost certainly did not write) is foretelling the end of the Jewish exile which has scarcely begun. Having spent so much of his spiritual and political capital foretelling the fall of Israel when the Kings and leaders wanted to hear no such thing, once the invasion was upon Jerusalem and the exile process under way, he adopted a quite proper prophetic heterodoxy by seeing the bright side in the shape of a reconstitution of the line of King David. The specific reference to the line of David was taken by all the Evangelists to portend the birth of Jesus but, at a broader level, the story of the Chosen People foreshadowed the establishment of the Kingdom. In this context, John's account of the feeding of the 5,000 might be taken to foreshadow the Kingdom of Heaven where Jesus will reign.

Not surprisingly, Jeremiah and John disagree about essentials. From the outset of his prophetic career Jeremiah said that only a few of the inhabitants of Jerusalem, those who volunteered to go into exile and abandon their homes, would survive to form the nucleus of the return. The rest, those who refused to volunteer for exile, would be destroyed. John, on the other hand, in his account of the feeding miracle, does not stipulate any conditions for being fed, for entering the Kingdom.

On this day of summing up, of thinking of our journey from awaiting the Christ child to contemplating the Kingdom, we might want to bear three things in mind. Firstly, the story of Jesus which we have read in all four Gospels is born out of the soil of prophesy. To be a Christian is not simply to worship Jesus as Lord, it is to recognise the primacy of the Creator God who chose a people to be a special instrument of salvation, to be a kind of theological sounding board. Secondly, in spite of all the rhetoric of sin and judgment, of degrees of spiritual and social hierarchy, of ritual and righteousness, we should never forget that Jesus asked no questions of those who took his bread and fish. He had already been clear enough that the tax collectors and prostitutes were at the head of the heavenly queue. We are members of a Church of Jesus, and not a Church which simply looks to the Old Testament. Thirdly, the Church in which we live is not a static entity which can freeze its understanding of what God wants of us, seeking truth afresh in each generation. The Holy Spirit has not ceased to operate just because people are no longer writing documents to be included in scripture. Just as the reformers of the sixteenth century were not satisfied with the formulations of the medieval papacy, so we should not be satisfied with simply uncritically accepting and repeating the formulae of the reformers. Theology is not a rule-based methodology for determining right doctrine, it is a dynamic discipline which seeks to enrich the encounter between the created and the Creator.

Above all, as we consider Jeremiah and John, we may more clearly understand that, whatever else it might be at both an individual and corporate level, the holy life is concerned with a direct, personal relationship with God, in dialogue and silence. Jeremiah suffered for his

encounters with God, but he persisted because there was no alternative; faithfulness involved dialogue and communication. John, too, is
concerned above all else with Jesus the communicator, with Jesus the
intercessor, with Jesus who preached the coming of the Kingdom, and
who suffered for preaching a Gospel of encounter with the Father.

Jeremiah's prophesy of return from exile foreshadows our ultimate
return from the exile of earth to the peace of the Kingdom. This is not to
say that the earth does not possess pleasantness (few of us are anxious to
leave it when called) and, indeed, Jeremiah was at pains to point out that
exile would have its pleasures. Yet perhaps the greatest danger we face is
to separate the two experiences in too radical a fashion. The author who
has taken up more space than any other in this collection is St Paul, who
struggled against a Gnostic-derived dualism, but often fell into the trap
he was urging others to avoid.

Finally, we need to consider, in the light of everything we have
thought and said, what we mean by the Kingdom. As a starting point,
we might say that to be in the Kingdom is to be enfolded back into the
perfect love of the Creator who deemed that we should live an earthly
life that we might freely choose to love God. To be free to make that
choice is the most amazing attribute of creatureliness and, living with
that choice, we should consider our life on earth not as the occupation
of a blighted waiting room outside the heavenly gates but as the enjoy-
ment of a miraculous privilege.

Saint Andrew's Day
(November 30)

Collect	Almighty God, who didst give such grace
	unto Thy holy Apostle Saint Andrew, . . .
Epistle	Romans 10.9–21
Gospel	Matthew 4.18–22

Although Matthew's Gospel portrays Andrew and his elder brother Pe-
ter being called by Jesus simultaneously, John 1.35–42 (the choice of
Matthew rather than John on this occasion is inexplicable) describes
Andrew, the disciple of John the Baptist, being called before Peter, as the

first of all of Jesus' disciples. Accordingly, the Greek Orthodox Church designates him the "Protocletos" which, together with the traditionally accepted accounts of his journeys and death, explains his huge popularity as a patron of countries including Scotland, Greece, Russia and Romania, and of such occupations as rope making and singing. For although Peter played a much more prominent role than his younger brother, there is still an attractive, if speculative, symmetry in their careers. Peter founded the Patriarchate (ultimately the Papacy) of Rome and Andrew founded the Patriarchate of Constantinople. Peter became the anchor of the Western Church and Andrew, in addition to his role in Constantinople, is supposed to have reached the mouth of the Volga and paved the way for Russian Christianity. Peter is supposed to have begged to be crucified head down, whereas Andrew is said to have begged to be crucified at 45 degrees to the ground, iconised in the Saltire Cross.

Whereas Peter receives full but equivocal coverage in the New Testament, we know very little about Andrew. As the Collect says, he came swiftly and willingly to Jesus (John 1.40–42). He proposed to Jesus, with that mixture of bravado and caution which is often seen in younger brothers, that the five loaves and two fishes might be of some use (John 6.8), and he was part of the intermediate chain when some Greeks wanted to talk to Jesus (John 12.22). He is mentioned only once in Acts 1.3. Yet even that handful of references is more than some of his fellow Apostles can boast.

The passage from Romans contains a quantity of appropriate markers: public confession of the Resurrection without shame, no difference between Jew and Greek, the importance of the preacher, the ends of the earth, and the centrality of Moses and Isaiah. It particularly emphasises personal witness, and this must have been of crucial importance to the emerging Church. We only have written testimony of very few pioneers, but whether or not Christian expansion can be specifically tied to known people and places, e.g. Andrew at Astrakhan, we can chart the rapid expansion brought about by people other than Paul, who not infrequently arrived at places where Christianity had arrived before him. In the specific case of the Black Sea coast, whether or not it was actually Andrew who sowed the seed, the Church of Smyrna was thriving by the early AD 90s (cf. Revelation 2.8–11; the Epistles of Bishops Polycarp and Ignatius of Antioch). It is impossible, even with Acts and the Epistles, fully to imagine the condition of Apostleship: the vivid memories of Jesus, the inner dynamic of the Holy Spirit, the courage to move outside familiar territory and culture, the danger of travel, the hostility of Jews and Greeks, and the thrill of conversion.

The central theme of the Gospel and Andrew's life is that of being first. Whatever reticence we may possess (in the case of English people the collective attribute is surely exaggerated) is now fortified by a contemporary suspicion of leadership. The motive of self-aggrandisement has been hopelessly entangled with the necessity of clarity, such that when people are direct in their speech or action they are accused of being arrogant. Yet more than a century of being equivocal for Christ has served no good purpose. Those who resent the Christian mission are not likely to be less hostile just because we are less direct. Andrew was speaking first to Jews, before whom he appeared as a traitor, and then to Greeks who would automatically have considered him, as he actually was, an intellectual inferior. Yet Christianity is neither for the unthinkingly conservative nor the clever. Its demands are radical, simple and necessarily manifest themselves in different ways at different times. To be first is to risk hostility aimed directly and pointedly at the person and the message. Those who stand back can modify what they wish to say in the light of reaction to earlier participants, and persuade themselves that they have preserved their integrity, but the best guarantee of preserving integrity is to be first and fearless.

A highly specific way of being first which refers back to Andrew and his fellow workers is the need to forge theology which engineers the Good News into new places and situations without subverting the message. The term "engineering" is used deliberately here; the radical change in transport from the horse to the car provides swifter travel. It might be opposed by those who prefer slow or more picturesque transport, but as the purpose of travel is to get from one place to another, for all their drawbacks, cars are more effective than horses. The same kind of change can affect the way we formulate our human responses to the mystery of the divine. The conservative spirit (cf. Armstrong) naturally seeks reform through restoring a better past, but the problem for us is that the 39 Articles, written in that spirit, were heavily dependent upon their theological and political contexts. Some will be able to assent to every word, but others may feel that, for example, the text is hostile to— or at least does not adequately deal with—ecumenism. Even in the age of spiritual conservatism theology never ossified, and we must see that it does not do so in our world of change.

Saint Thomas the Apostle
(December 21)

Collect	*Almighty and everlasting God, who . . . didst suffer thy holy Apostle Thomas to be doubtful . . .*
Epistle	Ephesians 2.19–22
Gospel	John 20–24–31

Politicians, artists and celebrities with long and distinguished careers are often remembered for one error of judgment, and this is the fate of Thomas. No matter that he urged his fellow disciples (John 11.16) to prepare to die with Jesus, nor that he almost certainly did die for Christ, doubting has become associated with his name as firmly as cake burning with King Alfred, or philandering with President Clinton. It is therefore particularly sad that we do not know more of Thomas's career. There are a number of apocryphal writings ascribed to him, including a "gospel", or written about him, and there is a tradition that he preached the Gospel in India, and was martyred and buried in Edessa.

The Collect prays that we should be so steadfast in our belief in Jesus that we never doubt, and as long as our faith is analogous to a sturdy structure founded on rock, as described in Ephesians, this is possible if still difficult, but that is to confuse faith with empirical validation. It was all very well for Paul, who had seen Jesus in a vision (cf. The Conversion of Saint Paul), and his contemporaries, decades after the event to think of the Resurrection as an obvious, empirical fact, and to characterise faith in it accordingly, but when Thomas was confronted with the narrative of the Resurrection, he was unsure as the disciples had been when they received news. Today's Gospel is very different in tone from the preceding verses, and all three Synoptics describe post-Resurrection disbelief, confusion and fear. As with Judas and betrayal, Thomas has been left, partially in caricature, carrying the can for his brethren. Conversely, we who have two millennia of hindsight are beset by doubts, regardless of the theological significance we assign to it, about the actuality of the event. Thomas was told a story about Jesus which the narrators hardly believed themselves. Their hesitation was understandable. There was no tradition of bodily resurrection in Judaism. They were being asked to believe something outside their frame of reference. In a different way that is also our state. Our culture is so completely bound up with evidence based phenomena and rational argument—the *Logos*—that it has almost completely lost any notion of the mysterious—the

Mythos—which is a necessary attribute of the divine. In a way that he would not have recognised, Thomas might be a contemporary patron saint of culture.

The doubts which we should suffer, however, are quite independent of intellectual fashion. To put it another way, we are involved in a life-long quest to become closer to God, and that quest is not possible if our theology—our attempts to better understand mystery—is static (cf. Saint Andrew's Day). Although history attests to the power of "simple faith", we must be careful of complacency which arises out of a lack of introspection and exploration. When the Godhead becomes a formula and not the "senior" partner in a relationship, then our faith is in danger. What atheists fail to see is that Christianity is fundamentally relational, not doctrinal, and that God is much more like a verb than a noun.

It is therefore vital that we separate atheist criticism from Christian self-criticism. Many devout Christians suffer guilt from doubt because we quite properly recognise that we do not believe in God in the way in which we believe in cheese or China. Nor should we. To classify God alongside physical objects is clearly, outside the remarkable case of the incarnation, a misunderstanding of the issue and is, in the contemporary jargon, a "category error". Put almost naively, if we could prove the existence of God then it wouldn't be God. Philosophy seeks proof of an object; Christians seek truth in a relationship.

Part of the "Thomas problem" is the growing tendency to see the Bible as a rationalist textbook, similar to a work of history or physics, where physical objects are central. That has two catastrophic consequences. Firstly, there are so many real, concrete contradictions in the scriptural library that to claim otherwise is to discredit the essence of the text. Secondly, because nobody finds it possible to accept every word literally, the picking and choosing reduces the whole exercise to a farce which brings great discredit upon our sacred texts. Simply to claim that the Bible is inspired by God because it says it is, is a circular—and anyway, the wrong— argument. The Bible is the Word of God because we have faith that it is, but in having faith we are inevitably subject to doubt. This phenomenon of varying adhesion is similar to the vicissitude of prayer, where we sometimes feel that absolutely nothing is happening.

If we have no doubt we have nothing at all. Whatever Thomas thought would happen after the Crucifixion, it is hardly likely that he or anybody else was expecting a Resurrection event which had physical attributes. Progress and penetration are the results of doubt, and its crowning glory is surprise (cf. Rowan Williams, *Christ on Trial* p15). Jesus, after all, was not harsh to Thomas, but he did bless those who believe without empirical evidence. To ask such questions as whether the risen Jesus had a body like ours is the wrong kind of question, because the mechanics are insignificant compared with the mysterious reality.

The Conversion of Saint Paul
(January 25)

Collect	*O God, who through the preaching of the blessed Apostle Saint Paul, . . .*
For The Epistle	Acts 9.1–22
Gospel	Matthew 19.27–30

No other single event after Pentecost is so important in the life of the early Church as the Conversion of Paul which is recounted three times in Acts (22.6–16; 26.12–18). The narrative, as opposed to the retrospective, account of the events wrenches Acts from its miraculous but somewhat leisurely course into a new level of activity and, it must be admitted, controversy. Apart from the "presenting case" of the need for Gentile circumcision, which was apparently settled by the Council of Jerusalem (Acts 15), there were deeper underlying tensions. Paul was a Rabbi initially on the side of the persecutors, whereas Peter was a fisherman carrying the guilt of denial. Paul was a lawyer and theologian, Peter was impetuous and unsystematic. Paul claimed to be the Apostle of the Gentiles (Galatians 2.7–8), whereas Peter also made that claim (Acts 15.7). When they ultimately clashed, the convert shamed the stalwart (Galatians 2.11–16). How far that tension was creative, and how far destructive to Peter's preaching of a simple message, we will never know, but the question is begged by the Collect, which urges us to follow Paul's doctrine. For all his legality and system, Paul was forging theology "on the hoof", formulating it in response to a random set of questions, which was not an ideal basis for developing theology systematically. What the Collect almost certainly has in mind is Paul's supposedly central doctrine of justification by faith alone, which was Luther's highly personal *Deus ex machina*, but which was rapidly assumed as the major doctrinal breakthrough, separating Protestant reformers from Catholic conservatives. That breach has largely been healed, but the dispute still rages within the Anglican Communion in the slightly different language of "penal substitution". Another strand of doctrine which the sixteenth century embraced as part of a general return to neo-Platonism, was Paul's tendency to fall into flesh/spirit or body/soul dualism. This cast of mind was enormously boosted by the particular coincidence of the Reformation with the arrival in Europe of sexually transmitted diseases from North America, which wrought havoc outside their endemic ecology (although not so great as that which was wrought by European influenza and measles exported to the Americas). There was also a "political" need to downgrade Peter, which implicitly meant upgrading Paul. This might explain why there were—and still are—Christians who, consciously or otherwise, rank Paul's doctrine above Jesus' teaching, a situation which, as we know from 1 Corinthians 1, would have shocked Paul. He always was, and constantly referred to himself as, a servant of the Gospel, and he approaches doctrine with a mixture of directness and self-deprecation which is often the style of shy people forced into positions of authority. Certainly his humility is underestimated and under-emulated by his admirers.

In considering his global, primarily doctrinal, impact we should not forget the immediate effects of Paul's conversion. The Church lost a powerful enemy and gained a powerful friend (although his welcome varied between petrified and cautious). The link between the Old Testament and the mission of Jesus was put firmly in place long before the Evangelists began to write, and the focus of mission was diversified so that the ultimate catastrophe of Palestinian Judaism only had a marginal effect. The whole enterprise received an intellectual boost necessary for serious discussion with Greek speakers accustomed to an open dialogue on religion and philosophy, which was alien to Jews brought up in a profoundly conservative theology and culture. Indeed, one of Paul's great gifts is his ability to imagine himself outside Jewish tradition, even though the results were frequently rough, psychologically, theologically, and textually.

Describing the events on the road to Damascus as a "conversion", as opposed, say, to a radical transformation, is somewhat misleading, as Paul never thought of himself as anything other than a fully devout Jew and meticulous Pharisee who, in accepting the general doctrine of the resurrection of the body, had simply accepted Jesus as a very special case. There is admittedly something of the tactical in his use of this argument in his own defence (Acts 23.6), but the sense of scriptural and doctrinal continuity in his writing is at least as strong as the setting of a new course, to such an extent that some of the complex discussions into which he was drawn by conservative Jews (notably in Galatians) must have puzzled Gentiles in the extreme. Paul's mission would have been much easier had he been able to make a cleaner break with his past although this would have given developing Christianity a different theological tone.

Yet however jagged his profile, his achievements are massive. The unbreakable bond between the Old and New Testaments, the consolidation of Trinity, a cosmic interpretation of the sacramentality of baptism, the first account of the Institution of the Holy Eucharist, the metamorphosis of the Jewish tradition of animal sacrifice into the unique sacrifice of Jesus, a theology of the Cross and Resurrection, the development of the concept of the holy life springing from volunteer behaviour not observance of the law, the entrenchment of the three great motifs of faith, hope, and charity, and the summation of all of these in a soteriology, which survived beyond the period when eschatological closure was believed to be imminent. Paul is such a massive figure that we are always in danger of exceeding his wish that we should take him at his word. For, as the thirteenth, he counted himself as the least among the Apostles (1 Corinthians 15.9).

The Presentation of Christ in The Temple
Commonly Called The Purification of Saint Mary the Virgin (February 2)

Collect	*Almighty and everlasting God, we humbly beseech thy majesty, . . .*
For The Epistle	Malachi 3.1–5
Gospel	Luke 2.22–40

Mary was the most serious casualty of the English Reformation. This liturgical microcosm provides three pieces of evidence. Firstly, the use of "Saint Mary" is a deliberate downgrading of the mother of God. Secondly, the Collect fails to mention Mary. Thirdly, the choice of Malachi over Isaiah 7.14 is odd (cf. The Annunciation of the Blessed Virgin Mary).

The statement that the Feast was "commonly known" as the Purification when it was actually commonly known as Candlemas is another snub, but as the use of candles was controversial in the Elizabethan Church, this is hardly surprising.

The doctrine of the virgin birth was never in question because it was Credal, but late medieval excess in substituting homely Marian devotion for what had become highly complex and almost clerically exclusive devotion to Christ, met with a reformist reaction which was particularly radical in England, arguably the place where Mary had been most venerated. An analysis of BCP readings shows that she is almost eliminated from the Nativity story, and accorded the minimum possible notice in the two feast days devoted to her.

The theme of purification dominates the Collect and Malachi but occupies only half a verse in Luke, who is much more interested in the presentation of the first-born to the service of God. This theme is then reinforced by the stories of Simeon and Anna, whose service to God is meticulously catalogued by Luke. Malachi's view of the Messiah is somewhat astringent. He will come as a refining fire, but only the priestly classes and the wicked have anything to fear. The poor and the lonely will receive comfort. That comfort is extended by Simeon to Gentiles but it comes at a price, namely that Mary will suffer for her motherhood.

The point of the Temple Presentation is that it was a lifelong commitment. Unlike John, who was declared a Nazarite (Luke 1.15), Jesus was not marked out in any special way (although his residence in Nazareth, as opposed to Bethlehem, might be a mistranslation of "Nazarite" as "Nazarene") and yet he is immediately identified by Simeon and Anna. Typically, Luke prepares us for the scene by recounting the promise of the Holy Ghost that Simeon would live to see the birth of the Messiah, who would be the "consolation of Israel", but he is moved in the *Nunc Dimittis* to extend the promise of the child to the whole world. Luke is fond of presenting key characters in pairs, so Simeon and Anna are matched not with Mary and Joseph but with Mary and Jesus, who are yoked in lifelong service.

Lifelong service requires a high degree of faithfulness, and this characteristic unites the four main characters. Simeon and Anna had seen the triumph of Rome over a divided and declining Israel, and Mary's faithfulness, says Simeon, is to be severely tested. The three protagonists could not have imagined the quality or the depth of faithfulness that would be required of Jesus, but from their different standpoints, they knew that it would be unique. Simeon's prayer reflects a generosity of outlook which accords with Luke's perspective. It is not that the Messiah's message to the Gentiles will be incidental to Jewish concern but, rather, that the mission to the Gentiles, whatever form it takes, will bring glory upon Israel. Looked at from a post-Crucifixion perspective, that is a remarkably generous way of looking at things. Whatever the vicissitudes of Christ's life, promised in an address to Mary, the ultimate result would be the extension of the Kingdom to Gentiles, which would redound to the benefit of the Jews. It was a perspective which was, unfortunately, rapidly lost in the narrow and ultimately homicidal interpretations of the Passion narratives, particularly Matthew (cf. The Sunday Next before Easter) and, to a lesser extent John.

Lifelong service, faithfulness and generosity of outlook are all Marian characteristics to which we should aspire, but the gradations of equivalence are sometimes difficult to comprehend. We are imperfect human beings, sinners in need of repentance, and she, whom we must imitate, was born without sin. Jesus, whom we and she must imitate, was God incarnate who, though he laid aside his glory, was still God. Late medieval Christians found the imitation of Mary an easier concept to handle than the imitation of Christ. The Reformation apparently raised the bar in singling out Jesus and consigning saints, including Mary, to a marginal position, but the higher standard was not actually real, because sacrifice and intercession were replaced by justification and the doctrine of "the elect" who had no need of intercession. The theological outlook became less human, more cerebral. The holy life was no easier, but it was easier to think that it was. Yet for all these possible explanations for the Reformation dynamic which so brutally sidelined Mary, there must be more than a suspicion that it was caused by one of the all too frequent outbreaks of misogyny which survived clerical marriage. Perhaps the safe devotion for celibates was redundant, but the comfort it brought to the poorly educated was very great, and its deprivation deeply felt. The Church of England, supposedly "reformed" but not Protestant, still has problems with Marianism, tending to brand it as Roman Catholic. In this age of broken families sustained by lone parents, there is a new and vital role for Mary, particularly among the suffering, in the slums beyond the regular call of Anglicanism.

Saint Matthias's Day
(February 24)

Collect	*Almighty God, who . . . didst choose*
	Thy faithful servant Matthias . . .
For The Epistle	Acts 1.15–26
Gospel	Matthew 11.25–30

Just about everything we know of Matthias is contained in the reading from Acts. There are some traditions about his death and burial and the transportation of his bones, but none of this amounts to much theologically or historically. He will be forever remembered for his passive part in this remarkable story at the beginning of Acts. Peter clearly thought that it was an absolute necessity, within a few days of the Ascension, to restore the Apostolic quota to twelve, to correspond with the tribes of Israel. Justus and Matthias were short-listed as having been with Jesus since his baptism by John, and Matthias was elected by the ancient Jewish tradition of drawing lots.

The lurid picture which Peter paints of the treason and death of Judas stands in stark contrast with the concluding lines of the Gospel: "my yoke is easy, and my burden is light". We are told by Jesus that we will not be asked to do anything for which we will not be given the resources, but Judas, who had the privilege of personal contact with Jesus, turned his back on such resources and chose the fatal way. We will never know why; the portraits we have of Judas are pseudo-history written with the gift of hindsight, and with more than an element of scapegoating in them. We know that Judas committed the actual act of betrayal and that Peter openly spoke his denial of Jesus, but all the Apostles initially fled at the arrest of Jesus, although Peter and John stayed on the fringes through the trial, and John came to the Cross. We must also presume that Justus and Matthias also fled when Jesus was arrested.

This passage in Acts raises three key issues. Firstly, the practice of scapegoating was, in many ways, benign in the Jewish tradition. It acted as a communal moral purgative and allowed people to start their lives again after a period of unfaithfulness, but the sacrifice involved an animal not a human being. Today whenever something goes wrong there is a strong temptation to find one person who has to take the blame for all the rest of us. We have even evolved a slightly ironic tone when we say "society is to blame" because that would implicate us. We do not want to consider that individual acts of vicious youth crime result from a callous and coarse culture, ranking money over parenting, sensation over self-control, gratification over self-denial, and self-interest over society. We remember the initial maxim of former Prime Minister Blair only in part: we applaud his "tough on crime", but tend to forget "tough on the causes of crime". In a way which we do not like to accept, our selfishness and self-satisfaction are the causes of crime. As such we are collectively the causes of crime. Criminals emerge from amongst us.

Secondly, the act of scapegoating allows us to divide society into the just and the unjust, the righteous and the unrighteous, the saint and the sinner. Part of that segregation arises from economic stratification, effected by the rich who want to separate themselves radically from the poor. Not since slavery have the economic classes been more segregated and stratified. Most middle class people can now go through life without any knowledge of real poverty and degradation, except when they visit poor countries on holiday and accidentally take a wrong turning into a slum. Having divided ourselves from our poorer brothers and sisters, and having arranged everything to our social and economic advantage, we then compound the evil by looking down on those we have abandoned.

The third message is most sharply set out at the beginning of Tom Wolf's *The Bonfire of The Vanities* in which Sherman McCoy, simply by taking the wrong turn off a freeway, has his whole life completely wrecked. There is a whole literature of "what if?", and its popularity relies upon our recognition of its basic truth: some of us are not found out, are plausible liars, cannot use violence effectively, are warned in time. One minute we are acting as a criminal and then something happens which nudges us out of the fatal path. What we ascribe to virtue might simply be a matter of luck. How can we square these ideas with a providential God? The not very spectacular answer lies in the nature of relationship rather than doctrine. Only God knows what hand we were dealt and how we have played it. To elevate this private realm to generalisations about ethics or the conduct of others is to misunderstand our purpose as creatures.

The story of Matthias reminds us that we do not know what is to happen to us. One minute he is saying his prayers with the whole company of disciples, the next he is one of two candidates for an awesome position and then he is elected. Difficult though this situation may be, it is not so bad as suffering a sudden reversal such as the one which, for whatever reason, Judas suffered. We should not need to be reminded that life is uncertain, and that self-satisfaction is a rather shallow emotion. There are some games in which players are dealt a fixed number of cards which they then play, but in most games one plays cards and receives new ones. We never know what card God will deal next and to whom.

The Annunciation of The Blessed Virgin Mary
(March 25)

Collect	*We beseech thee, O Lord, pour thy grace into our hearts . . .*
For The Epistle	Isaiah 7.10–15
Gospel	Luke 1.26–38

The change of title between today and the Purification may be an accident, but the omission of any mention of Mary from the Collect (cf. The Presentation of Christ in the Temple) is not. It is yet another calculated affront to the Mother of God, which cuts more deeply because sixteenth-century Christians would have accepted the doctrine of the virgin birth, based on our reading from Isaiah, without question. The very doctrine accounts for the retention of the feast in the reformed Lectionary. Subsequent translations of the Isaiah passage (notably the NRSV, now in common use) render "virgin" in Isaiah 7.14 as young woman. In the Jewish tradition, young and unmarried women were all supposed to be virgins, so the terms were more or less interchangeable. The Credal doctrine of the virgin birth can easily obscure the fundamental truth of the nature of the incarnation: that Jesus need be no less the son of God because he was the physical son of Joseph, acting as an agent of the Holy Spirit, in precisely the same way that Mary acted. The problem with the traditional understanding of the doctrine is that it is very close to neo-Platonic dualism, elevating the spiritual above the physical, requiring a "virtual" as opposed to an actual conception. The way that the Isaiah verse was later taken up by the Evangelists also casts a rather odd light on the Christian view of marriage.

For many Christians, Mary is not a person; she is a bundle of doctrines, such the virgin birth (not to be confused with the Immaculate Conception) and the Assumption. In recent years this has been overtaken by the notion summed up in the hymn words, "Blessed Mary, teenage mother", but that has the shortcoming of relegating her into a kind of nudge and wink situation. Single mother? Virgin birth? Holy Spirit? You must be joking! None of this should detract from the mysterious and ominous commitment undertaken by Mary. At some stage, she and Joseph were asked to take responsibility for an unborn child who would be unique in the history of Israel, and the world. At the very least they risked ridicule and social stigma, but the much greater risk was that they would be accused of blasphemy, the very offence which ultimately led to the death of Jesus.

What draws us to Mary is not the bundle of doctrines associated with her, but the personal, unconditional, uncomplicated commitment and the personal story, the ready acceptance of God's commission, the lowly birth scene, the life of a refugee in Egypt, the often troubled mother of a strange child, and the sad scene at the foot of the Cross foretold by Simeon. Yet we must remember that what is said of Mary is not all idyllic. According to Mark she suffered rejection by her son (3.31–35), whose behaviour was so unconventional that the family thought he was mad and should be hidden away (3.21). Her commitment was uncomplicated, but her life was not. This should alert us to the human qualities of Mary. Just as we proclaim the incarnation as the willingness of God to share our humanity, we should claim Mary's acceptance as undertaken on behalf of us all. The gross misunderstanding of the role of Mary in Christian iconography arises from the way in which she is set apart. She is first among the saints, but that means that she is first among humanity who acted on our behalf to facilitate the incarnation. In a mysterious way, then, humanity is implicated in the incarnation effected by God.

Neither should we allow the doctrinal superstructure and its facile repetition to obscure the magnitude of Mary's commitment as it must have appeared to her. The angel (or whatever the mode of the divine communication) was frighteningly specific. Her son would be the successor of David and, stretching back, the successor of Abraham, and this kingdom of her son was to last forever. In the atmosphere of apocalyptic Israel, this was both incalculable and frightening. Yet Mary's response was not to quibble about the broad picture, but simply to ask about the private mechanics. Here the genius of Luke and his customary use of pairing emerges in the reassurance of Elizabeth's pregnancy. We can take no better comfort from this encounter than from the verse succeeding the reading, which has Mary setting out to help Elizabeth. Her response was spontaneous and practical and, later still, when they meet, Mary's response, echoing 1 Samuel 2.1–10 (cf. Saint Luke the Evangelist), is again not doctrinal but practical.

As this is only one of two occasions when Mary is specifically honoured in the calendar, it is appropriate to consider her place in the twenty-first century Church. Firstly, she should be in our hearts and beyond controversy. Doctrine is only an incomplete and provisional way of expressing aspects of the divine mystery, and that should not obscure her commitment. Secondly, we should try to move away from that coldness which has considered all addresses to Mary as idolatrous. If people derive a special comfort from contemplating her life and virtue, why should it be denied? Thirdly, the strange absence of the *Magnificat* in the Lectionary (in spite of its daily Evensong appearance) should not obscure Mary's commitment to justice. Finally, we must recognise her, set apart in some ways, as our most ideal human embodiment. She bore the child who saved us on our behalf.

Saint Mark's Day
(April 25)

Collect	*O Almighty God, who hast instructed Thy Holy Church with the heavenly doctrine of Thy Evangelist Saint Mark . . .*
Epistle	Ephesians 4.7–16
Gospel	John 15.1–11

At the time when this Lectionary was compiled, it was believed that Mark was an off-shoot of Matthew, whereas contemporary scholarship indicates that Matthew is a development of Mark, who invented the Gospel format for a Syrian audience in the late AD 60s or early 70s. This explains his few appearances in the Lectionary—his Gospel is not even chosen for today. By tradition, Mark fled naked after Jesus' arrest (Mark 14.51–52), lived with his mother in a Christian community (Acts 12.25), preached with Paul and (possibly) his cousin or uncle Barnabas in Cyprus (Acts 13.5), fell out with Paul (Acts 13.13), and returned to Cyprus with Barnabas (15.37–39). He was then reconciled with Paul (Colossians 4.10; 2 Timothy 4.11; Philemon 24) and was closely associated with Peter, who called him "son" (1 Peter 5.13). These references, however, may refer to different people and they are all contested. He is said to have founded the Diocese of Alexandria, and been martyred there in AD 68. He is patron saint of Venice.

I have always thought of Mark as the ancient equivalent of a journalist (cf. Monday before Easter), because he always cuts to the heart of an issue, never resting for a moment, even when the narrative becomes more detailed in the chapters on the Passion and death of Jesus. Rowan Williams, in *Christ on Trial*, likens Mark's Gospel to a film script and this says much the same thing about his style. Nonetheless, the Collect is absolutely correct, in spite of that stylistic sharpness, in saying that Mark is concerned with doctrine. He begins his Gospel with the clearest possible introductory line, "The beginning of the Gospel of Jesus Christ, the Son of God." Thereafter, the fact that he never wastes a word does not mean that he is in any way superficial. His Gospel contains three alternative endings, the first of which leaves the disciples in a state of fear.

Perhaps his most distinctive narrative feature is his emphasis on the precariousness and secrecy of Jesus' mission, which presents us with considerable problems of interpretation. Precisely why did Jesus want to keep his mighty works secret? There have been a variety of theories, none very convincing, relating to the danger from the authorities, the danger of being misunderstood, and the need to prepare the disciples before launching a full blown mission. Of the three, the last is the most convincing, particularly if we accept that Mark, along with the other Synoptics, seems to indicate that the mission of Jesus only lasted something like a year, as opposed to the Johannine mission that implies two, or even three, years.

It is not easy to see why the two readings were chosen (other than a specific reference in the Gospel to Evangelists) for today and how they relate to each other. The Gospel is perhaps the most elegant passage, echoing Psalm 81, of Jesus' Maundy Thursday discourse on love, which here takes on both a mystical and a practical dimension. As branches of the sacred vine, our productivity, the quality of our fruit, depends upon the personal relationship we have in God. To be fruit on a vine is a quintessentially passive metaphor, which is why it points so directly to faith. We are totally dependent on the heavenly gardener. Although the Epistle is linked with the gospel through its introductory reference to grace, the passage then goes on to elaborate on the subject of sound doctrine, echoing the Collect, and to the familiar Pauline image of the Church as a human body. This is also the passage which refers to the idea that Jesus descended into the underworld between his death and

Resurrection. It is an odd notion, except that it is an early attempt to work out how the Crucifixion and Resurrection are supposed to free those who died before these events took place, an issue that had largely been worked out by the time that John was writing his more elevated, even cosmic, account of Jesus. Paul then goes on to sketch the practical purpose of the post-Resurrection phase of Jesus' mission, which was the establishment of followers to ensure sound doctrine.

Sound doctrine was the overriding concern of the sixteenth-century reformers, as witnessed in the emphasis of the Collect and the choice of the Epistle, but perhaps one additional reason why Mark was not particularly popular in the sixteenth century was, in spite of the Collect's perception, the notion that Mark had very little to say on doctrine, in comparison with the authors of our readings. His simple, straightforward message, that Jesus was the Son of God, was not in dispute in the sixteenth century. Rather, it was taken for granted, and it would have been unthinkable to question it, but most theological controversies are not questions of "what?" but "how?" This is perhaps why the complexity of Paul was far more often invoked in the sixteenth century than the simplicity of Mark. Yet today we might want to adopt precisely the opposite strategy. In an age which is not the least bit interested in the doctrinal facility required to deconstruct Paul, our key task is to project a clear, consistent message that cuts through postmodern ambiguities of response.

Mark is the Gospel of mission. If we want to tell people about the meaning of the life of Jesus in a way that they can most readily grasp, it is to Mark that we should most advisedly turn. Styles change through time, and Mark's time is now.

Saint Philip and Saint James's Day
(May 1)

Collect	O Almighty God, whom truly to know is everlasting life . . .
Epistle	James 1.1–12
Gospel	John 14.1–14

The identity of James, son of Alpheus (or James "the less") is difficult to establish, because no words are attributed to him in the New Testament, and he is irretrievably conflated with "James the Brother of the Lord" (Galatians 1.19), the author of an Epistle, the first Bishop of Jerusalem (Acts 15), and a "pillar" of the Church (Galatians 2.9). He is said to have been martyred by the Jews in Spring AD 62. Philip, on the other hand, is much better represented, but only in John. His calling with Peter and Andrew (1.44), his part in the feeding of the 5,000 (6.5–7), his mediation with foreigners wishing to see Jesus (12.21–23), and his request to be shown the Father (14.8–9) are all mentioned. He is supposed to have preached in Greece, Syria, and Phrygia and to have been martyred by Crucifixion at Hierapolis. He is not to be confused with Philip the deacon and Evangelist (Acts 6.5, 8.4–40, 21.8–9). There is nothing obvious connecting the two Apostles.

James opens his Epistle with a bewilderingly hurried synopsis of major topics including temptation, faith, wisdom, constancy, liberality, and salvation. Not surprisingly, given what follows, James is particularly concerned with practical benevolence and its connection with eternal life, a point of view so inimical to doctrinally radical Protestants seeking an artificial degree of polarity with Rome, that they said that he was unbiblical.

The theme of constancy in James links with the Gospel opening where Jesus tells his disciples not to be troubled but, on this most ominous of nights, they clearly are. Thomas asks how they can know the way to which Jesus replies that he is, "the way, the truth and the life". Philip asks how they may know the Father, to which Jesus replies that anyone who knows him knows the Father. The passage concludes with Jesus again reassuring his listeners by saying that whatever is asked in his name will be granted.

Although the theology of the two readings is largely identical, James can look back on the events leading up to the death of Jesus with a degree of tranquillity unavailable to John the narrator. Of all the letter writers

James is the calmest, the most straightforward, the most comforting, the least doctrinal, in tune with the dilemmas of daily life. He even makes falling from wealth sound comfortable! John, on the other hand, can only realise his cosmic vision through an intense and often troubled theological enquiry unparalleled even in Paul.

The questions from Thomas and Philip deal with two of the recurring themes in the Gospel, the subjects which are the core of systematic theology, the nature of God and how we know. The answer to the first, the invocation of Jesus as the intermediary to the Father, is complicated in this context by his imminent death. What kind of intermediary can he be when he is no longer listening to his disciples and praying on their behalf to the Father? With our post-Resurrection perspective, the idea that Jesus is our heavenly intercessor is as familiar as was the experience of the Apostles that he was their earthly intercessor. Likewise, our response to the second question, in what way is Jesus "the way, the truth and the life", has been given a radical post-Resurrection meaning which the disciples clearly could not grasp. To them Jesus was literally what he said he was. His leadership and mission was a matter of experience, not doctrine.

Initially, doctrine emerged from experience, but as the memory of Jesus became more distant, obscured rather than clarified by secondary sources, the danger increased of the two becoming separated. A Jewish tendency towards uniformity of observance, a Platonic tendency towards abstract perfection separated from, rather than built on, experience, and the tendency of an emerging hierarchy to have its own way in matters great and small, coalesced to rank the brokennness of experience below the wholeness of doctrine. This was then seen as a coherent set of answers rather than garbled questions. The sixteenth-century controversy over the connection between "justification by faith" and "good works" is only one example of a tendency to elevate doctrine above experience, a neo-Platonic tendency which diverts us from our true purpose as creatures. We were created to love God and, as creatures, this means relating our experience to our personal relationship with the Creator. Our dealings with God's children are dealings with God. We cannot have a doctrine of God which is radically different from our ethic of life. Thus, when we say that Jesus is, "the way, the truth and the life" we must ask how that relates to the way we travel, the truth we tell and the life we live. Here, too, there has been a tendency to try and impose a doctrine of uniformity of response upon the infinite diversity of humanity. Jesus' reassurance that his Father's house has many mansions can, however, be taken too far in the other direction to justify denominational wilfulness and individual self-indulgence.

In the light of our tendency to substitute the uniform abstractions of doctrine for the diverse pressure of being human, Philip's question about the nature of the Father, and Jesus' reply that he is the unique earthly manifestation of the Father, establishes a vital link between what we say as individuals, and how it is heard. The incarnation is not simply a Chalcedonian device to square a Greek philosophical circle, it is the vital highway which allows us to walk towards God as he walks towards us.

Saint Barnabas the Apostle
(June 11)

Collect	*O Lord God almighty, who didst endue*
	thy holy Apostle Barnabas . . .
For The Epistle	Acts 11.22–30
Gospel	John 15.12–16

Barnabas, originally Joseph, is ranked, like Paul, as an Apostle although he was not converted from Judaism until shortly after Pentecost. A Levite of Cyprus, he was frequently in Jerusalem, was related to John Mark (Acts 12.12; Colossians 3.10) and owned land in Cyprus (Levites were not allowed to own land in Israel), which he sold for the cause (Acts 4.36–37). He was an outstanding preacher, the converted Paul's sponsor (Acts 9.27), who brought him to Antioch where, as the reading shows, they worked together until the mission to Cyprus (13.1–3). This came about, ironically, because of the Christian Diaspora induced by Paul's persecution. They worked under great hardship in Asia Minor (Acts 13.14–26), where Paul was almost killed (Acts 14.19). On returning to Antioch, threatened by Jewish conservatives, they spoke at the Council of Jerusalem (Acts 15.1–35). When further missionary activity was contemplated, Paul and Barnabas disagreed over the role of John Mark (cf. Saint Mark's Day) and separated (Acts 15.36–40). Subsequently, Paul refers to Barnabas (1 Corinthians 9.5–6) which shows that their friendship was unimpaired, and later John Mark was attached to Paul in Rome

(Colossians 4.10), which might indicate that Barnabas had died. Traditions about his death are unreliable, but it seems that he was highly unusual in dying a tranquil death in his homeland. What we remember Barnabas for most is his generous reception of the Gentiles, his recognition of Paul, and his warmth for John Mark, which later yielded abundant fruit.

There is something very touching about Paul and Barnabas making a famine collection in Antioch and taking it up to the mother church in Jerusalem, not least because it was the source of many of their troubles, exporting conservatives who wanted the rapidly expanding, Gentile-dominated churches to adopt Jewish law, particularly circumcision. Paul was never comfortable in Jerusalem, but he nonetheless never flinched from doing his duty there and Barnabas, according to Luke's description of him (unique except for a similar description of Stephen, cf. Saint Stephen's Day) seems to have had the open temperament to keep Paul on an even keel. Here were the newly denominated Christians paying their respects and offering their gifts to Bishop James (cf. Saint Philip and Saint James's Day), regardless of their potential differences.

The Gospel echoes many of the themes in the story of Barnabas and Paul. It begins with the commendation of love, and the possibility of the ultimate sacrifice which Jesus was to make for his friends, and which Paul almost made with Barnabas during their first missionary journey. It then refers to the laying on of hands, which Paul and Barnabas underwent together before the mission to Cyprus, and which they were to perpetuate by appointing their successors. It concludes with encouragement that prayers to the Father will be answered, evidenced in the divine direction of Paul's mission.

Sadly, we only see Barnabas faintly, as a serene counterpart to Paul's restlessness, but that should prompt us to think of our attitude to mission. The Pauline way, goaded by the prospect of eschatological closure, is sharp and urgent, demoting such ordinary human activities as marriage to contingent status. This has been the way of most Evangelical revivals which have all had a millenarian tendency. They have attempted to foreshorten time, to urge a swift and radical response, which has not infrequently involved a turning to God with a sybaritic turning away from earthly things. Yet all such revivals have ultimately lost credibility, because the clock continues to tick, and life goes on. While this approach may be effective in some circumstances, there is surely room for the kind of approach one imagines that Barnabas might have taken. The message is no less urgent, but the time we live with it is necessarily long.

The witness Paul imagines is short and ends traumatically, whereas the witness of Barnabas, we might surmise, is less dramatic, symbolised by the probability that he was one of the few of his generation of leaders to die in his bed. Our Christian lives are not usually dramatic; they are lived over a long period, threatened not by physical violence but by indifference or low level hostility. From the time of confirmation to committal, we face a long haul, which requires Pauline adrenalin but also a steadier source of energy and perseverance.

If we are not careful, we tend to equate drama with commitment. Paul abandoned his career, went into enforced retirement and then suffered terribly before giving his life for Christ. Barnabas sold a piece of land, discerned the genius of Paul, and nurtured John Mark. For all Paul's heroism, Barnabas is the kind of figure to whom many might look for inspiration. We have not sold enough land, we have failed to discern, we have abandoned nurture for the quick fix, we hope to die in our own bed. There is also the danger that drama can become addictive, robbing us of the ability to be objective about our spirituality, externalising it, identifying it too closely with a Cross that becomes a logo rather than our Logos. Paul did not imagine this danger, because his sense of time was radically foreshortened, so we in turn must try to imagine what Paul could not, which is why we must always provide a contemplative counterbalance to his spiritual activism.

There is a sense in which we cannot spend the whole of our spiritual lives at the foot of the Cross. We may always live in its shadow, but we need both to see the light of Resurrection behind it, and to see the world illumined by it. Barnabas presents us with the model of a balanced spiritual life.

Saint John Baptist's Day
(June 24)

Collect   *Almighty God, by whose providence Thy servant*
                     John Baptist was wonderfully born, . . .
For The Epistle   Isaiah 40.1–11
Gospel   Luke 1.57–80

The opening passage of the Third Isaiah is one of the richest and most suggestive in the whole of the Old Testament. Many prophets were downright pessimistic, only slightly redeemed by more optimistic closing passages, some of which were added for effect by redactors, but the whole tenor of Isaiah 40–66 is hopeful. No wonder it caught the imagination of the Messianic-oriented Jews in the centuries before Jesus. All the Evangelists saw this passage as the key to the witness of John the Baptist and the arrival of Jesus (Matthew 3.3; Mark 1.3; Luke 3.4–6; John 1.23). The Synoptics quote the key passage but John puts it into the mouth of John the Baptist, explicitly affirming that he knows that he is the forerunner of the Messiah. The passage also contains the memorable metaphor of flesh as grass, which forms a powerful opening to 1 Peter, and the almost obligatory reference to prophets as shepherds.

In reading the Gospel, we must remember that at the point where John's story is taken up, Zechariah is dumb, as a rebuke for not believing he would be a father, and Elizabeth has just enjoyed a visit from Mary during which the two must have exchanged confidences about their recent, remarkable experiences. Elizabeth certainly knew the future of Mary's child, and it is difficult to imagine that Mary did not know about Elizabeth's, a future made specific by Zechariah's prophesy (which is referred to as the *Venite* Canticle in the Service of Matins).

Zechariah is specific. John is to be the forerunner of someone who will be greater; a realisation which John himself makes explicit (John 1.6–34; 5.36). John gathered disciples around him and began to preach a baptism of repentance for sin. He baptised Jesus (Matthew 3.13–17; Mark 1.9–11; Luke 3.21–22), but there was later rivalry between the two sets of followers (John 3.25–36), even though John was clear that his influence would wane as that of Jesus waxed (John 3.30). John was killed by Herod because he condemned Herod's unlawful marriage to his brother's wife (Matthew 14.6–12, Mark 6.17–29). The grisly account of his decapitation, ostensibly as the reward for a dance, is almost certainly allegorical. Some scholars believe that Jesus was actually a disciple of John until his death, when he took over the leadership of John's disciples.

John's distinctness as a prophet arises out of his specific mission to act as the forerunner of the Messiah. Whereas previous prophets claim to speak on behalf of God, and some of the later ones foreshadow the coming of a Messiah, John's link with the promised event is explicit in its antecedents, and lived out in his mission. Yet in spite of their closeness (Luke 2.36), there was always an element of tension, not least in the quite extraordinary account of John questioning whether indeed Jesus was the Messiah (Luke 7.18–23). Clearly, matters were not straightforward and John's influence far outlived him, being cited in Acts (1.5; 1.22; 10.37; 11.16; 13.24). Whatever the doubts about the details of the narratives about John's life, he was the unique combination of Jewish prophet and Christian martyr. He was the last, the strongest, and the shortest bridge between the Old and New Covenants, a status underlined in the construction of the *Venite*, whose first half refers to the beginning of the Jewish tradition, and whose second half promises a Messianic future heralded by John.

There are some who would relate the two readings by saying that Isaiah "foretold" the birth of Jesus, whereas others would say that the reality of the Messianic Incarnation grew out of prophetic soil, most markedly in the case of Isaiah. The difference is significant in our understanding of the nature of scripture, but it does not affect our belief in the seamless continuity of the Testaments and, paradoxically, the discontinuity of the incarnation.

John Baptist's status as a precursor should not obscure his radicalism. He was, in the line of his prophet predecessors, an anti-establishment figure who would certainly be viewed with great suspicion by the vast majority of churchwardens! His dress was scruffy and scanty, his diet outlandish, his language salty. Like all Nazarites, he never shaved or cut his hair. He challenged authority and told the religious leaders who came to see him that their practices fell short. It is easy to exaggerate comparisons between different ages, but the religious establishment John confronted was both comfortable in its authority, and deeply divided over some aspects of theology. John pointedly questioned the comfort, but seemed uninterested in theological niceties. Later Jesus quizzed the Pharisees about their scepticism over John's baptism (Matthew 21.23; Mark 11.28; Luke 20.2). It had clearly caused a stir, and created an atmosphere of self-criticism and debate helpful to Jesus' subsequent preaching. Yet perhaps John's overall message about repentance lacks the roundness and optimism of Jesus, who always tells people why they need to repent, and what will happen if they do. Perhaps these were not assertions that John felt himself able to make, which is in itself evidence of the relative status of the two. For all its limitations, John's role can still inspire us today. In an age of increasing uniformity, the lone voice of the radical prophet is invaluable, and the bravery of the "first mover" who risks articulating something still only half-formed may make it possible for those who follow to give form to a deeper truth. A truth that is a new way of starting and a new way of seeing, that changes the way we think of the world, ourselves and our relationship with God.

Saint Peter's Day
(June 29)

Collect	*O Almighty God, who . . . didst give to thy Apostle Saint Peter many excellent gifts . . .*
For The Epistle	Acts 12.1–11
Gospel	Matthew 16.13–19

Of all the Gospel texts which the devisers of the Lectionary could have chosen to represent St Peter, this passage from Matthew is the most unlikely, as it is the foundation upon which the Roman Papacy built its claim to authority. The probable explanation is that there was an even more pressing issue than Rome which the Reformist leaders had to face, and this was the very existence of bishops, which occupied a central place in Church controversy from the death of Henry VIII in 1547 to the Restoration after the Civil War of Charles II in 1660. On the monarchist side, this led to the maxim, "no bishops, no king". In other words, monarchs were only able to exercise effective authority over the Church of England through bishops appointed by them to the House of Lords. By contrast, the same monarchs after 1603 found it almost impossible to exercise control over the Presbyterian Church of Scotland. There is ample record in the sixteenth century of royal intervention in the preaching of doctrine, and one can therefore imagine the purpose behind the Collect, which calls both for right preaching and a right response which would certainly have repudiated any papal claim.

Peter's relationship with Jesus was close, admiring and impetuous and, as demonstrated here, he often takes the lead in affirming the reality of Jesus as Christ. On first impressions he could hardly be described as leadership material, but he is drawn in a Jewish tradition which never contemplated human perfection among its great leaders, except perhaps in the foundational figure of Abraham. Moses is harshly punished for the shortcomings of the people and forbidden entry into the Promised Land (Numbers 20.12), David commits adultery with Bathsheba and connives at the murder of Uriah the Hittite (2 Samuel 11.2–12:19), and Solomon, for all his wisdom, turns away from God late in his reign under the influence of idolatrous wives (1 Kings 11). Only the prophets escape at the hands of their faithful disciples and scribes, but, then, they were not leaders, but rebels.

None of the great figures of the Old Testament committed an act so serious as Peter's denial of Jesus (Matthew 26.69–74; Mark 14.66–72; Luke 16.54–62; John 18.25–28) and yet, so great is the power of the Holy Spirit in Acts, that from the time of the first Christian Pentecost, Peter becomes a decisive and fluent leader. This impression is only contradicted by a sour Pauline note (Galatians 2.14) accusing Peter of giving in to Jewish conservatives. In Acts 9–15 Peter and Paul alternate, only coming together at the Council of Jerusalem (Acts 15), when Peter pronounces against Gentile circumcision, and then disappears forever. Tradition has it that he went to Rome and wrote two Letters (1 and 2 Peter) just before his martyrdom in AD 66 under Nero, when he was crucified upside-down so as not to replicate precisely the death of Jesus.

Seeing Peter divorced from the Old Testament tradition of fallible leadership often leads to a caricature of him as the blunderer. He attempts to walk on water to greet Jesus, but, losing faith (Matthew 14.20), he makes a rash proposal at the Transfiguration (Matthew 17.4), and earns reproof from Jesus (Luke 22.31; John 13.336). Nowhere is he more harshly treated than in Matthew's Gospel which, significantly, is the "Gospel of the Church". It says a good deal for the way in which the early Church conducted itself that such an iconic figure could be subjected to so much negative criticism, sometimes bordering on ridicule.

Yet what emerges from all the narratives is a man who was prepared to stick his neck out and take risks for Christ (Matthew 16.16). Even in his most difficult period, between his denial and Pentecost, Peter never loses his spontaneity, running to the tomb (John 20.3–5) and leaping into the water (John 21.7). The one incident which is difficult to explain is the very last scene between Peter and Jesus (John 21.15–19a), when he is questioned three times about his love, and urged to tend the flock because whatever might have been in doubt, it could surely not have been his love. However, there is a possible note of rivalry between John and Peter in the concluding verses (John 21.19b–25). Once he took a firm grip on the emerging Church, Peter went on taking risks for which he was hauled before the Council (Acts 4.1–7, 5.27–40), and imprisoned at least once (Acts 5.18) before the incident described in today's reading. He risked conservative criticism (Paul's view is crude) by eating "unclean" food and mixing with Gentiles (Acts 10–11), and his was the decisive voice in favour of Paul, whatever their personal differences (Acts 15). Given later papal claims made on the basis of Peter's position, it is interesting that his first great theological pronouncement took place at a Council, giving due weight to what his colleagues advised.

The Church has always placed a very high value on Episcopal continuity, stretching right back to Peter (an issue which presented very difficult problems during the English Reformation), but the role of bishop has naturally changed through the centuries. Nonetheless, the twin role of the bishop as teacher and provider of oversight has never been lost. Today there are some who say that in view of improving transport and dwindling numbers, the Church of England has too many bishops, but there are others who say we have too few, most of whom are tied up in administration when we need a greater capacity to provide clerical oversight and promote mission. Whether we have too few or too many, we need more like Peter, but would he be appointed?

Saint James the Apostle
(July 25)

Collect	*Grant, O merciful God, that as thine Holy Apostle Saint James, leaving his father . . .*
For The Epistle	Acts 11.27–12.3[a]
Gospel	Matthew 20.20–28

St James the Apostle or "the Greater", not to be confused with James the son of Alphaeus (cf. Saint Philip and Saint James's Day), nor with James "the brother of the Lord", was probably the elder brother of John and son of Zebedee (Matthew 27.56; Mark 15.40). Called with his brother from their family fishing boat (Matthew 4.18–22; Mark 1.19; Luke 5.1–11), and confirmed in Apostleship (Matthew 10.1–4; Mark 3.13–19; Luke 6.12–16; Acts 1.13), he became one of the select group of four (with Peter, John and Andrew), and more often three (with Peter and John) who acted as Jesus' confidants. He was present at the revival of Jairus' daughter (Mark 5.37; Luke 8.51) and the Transfiguration (Matthew 17.1; Mark 9.1; Luke 9.28), and was close to Jesus in Gethsemane (Matthew 26.37; Mark 14.33). He is not mentioned in John, but some say this is accounted for by the humility of his Evangelist brother. The brothers were apparently fiery, which led to their nickname "Sons of Thunder" (Mark 3.17), exemplified by their castigation of a rival (Luke 9.49) and by their calling down fire on Samaritans (Luke 9.49–54).

In today's Gospel, James' mother, Salome, asks that the brothers should flank Christ in heaven, though this is put into their own mouths in Mark (10.35–45). On the surface this is a preposterous request for, as Jesus notes, the mother and brothers do not really know what they are asking. Yet they surely have a case. The family have made great sacrifices in following Jesus, as at least three of them have left home, and the brothers are, after Peter, Jesus' leading lieutenants (although where they propose to seat Peter in heaven is an interesting question). At the time of the question they are no doubt convinced of their own future loyalty. As matters turned out, James was the first Apostle to be martyred, by order of Herod Agrippa "with the sword" in AD 44 (Acts 12.1–2), having apparently been the first Bishop of Jerusalem (Galatians 1.10, 2.9). The account, so to speak, had been squared.

The question of the Zebedee family prompts us to ask what we are entitled to expect. On this point, Jesus is clear in dealing with the incident. He says that those who are considered least on earth will be greatest in heaven, and that service is the means of salvation. On other occasions, he makes the point more graphically. The rich will find it much more difficult to gain entry to heaven than the poor (Matthew 19.24), and, much worse, there is more than a hint that the virtuous will find entry more difficult than the sinful (Luke 5.31–32, 18.24). This is a particularly uncomfortable prognosis for those of us who are, in spite of our protestations, rich, compared with our predecessors and those who live in the developing world. It is also a warning to those of us who feel spiritually comfortable, set in our ways, strict in our observance and busy with church administration. What is it all for if we are to be balked at the last?

The first part of the answer is that how rich we are lies in our own hands. There is a strong argument for being prudential, for taking proper care of those for whom we are responsible, but that does not mean that we are entitled to build up wealth for the sole purpose of passing it on to our successors who might build further. The national aversion to inheritance tax is salutary. Further, the fact that the poor give a larger percentage of their income than the rich both to charity in general and the Church in particular, ought to prompt a much deeper self-examination.

The second part of the answer is that in trying to understand apparent sinfulness, we are apt to judge people on their conduct, on outcome. This kind of judgment is, technically, a prejudice, because it is made on the basis of ignorance. We do not know the trials God asks each of us to face, the resources each of us is granted and the motivation for the course of action we take. What Jesus is saying is that the obvious sinner—the stereotypical extortionist or prostitute—is much more likely to be conscious of falling short than the person who is subtle and self-deceptive. This is not simply an individual problem, as our society is much harsher on poor people who commit "blue collar" crime than rich "white collar" criminals. Worse still, perhaps, most of us are almost oblivious of the power we exercise individually and collectively, and equally oblivious of the powerlessness of the poor and oppressed.

All of us need periods of reflection to put ourselves into perspective, and a growing number of us are using our increasing affluence to enjoy religious tourism in such places as Compostela. It does not matter that there is no evidence that James ever went there. What seems to count is the accumulation of piety in a confined space; the thought that so many others have made pilgrimages to worship God and examine themselves. Unlike James, we are only leaving our jobs to follow Jesus for a few days, but that at least should help us to throw off the complacency that wealth and power almost inevitably bring. Hardly any of us are likely to be called upon to make the sacrifices which James made, but the sea shell should remind us that each of us has some sacrifice to make.

Saint Bartholemew the Apostle
(August 24)

Collect	*O Almighty and everlasting God, who didst give to Thy Apostle Bartholemew grace . . .*
For The Epistle	Acts 5.12–16
Gospel	Luke 22.24–30

Very little is known about St Bartholemew the Apostle except that he is listed in Matthew 10.3, Mark 3.18, Luke 6.14 and Acts 1.13. He is not mentioned in John, but he might be the same person as Nathaniel (John 1.45–51, 21.2), spanning the period from Jesus' initial call to his last post-Resurrection appearance. There are a wide variety of traditions about where he preached, none substantiated, and he is said to have been flayed before inverted crucifixion, which is why he is sometimes portrayed with his own skin in his hand!

Again (cf. Saint Thomas the Apostle), we are faced with the astounding sequence of events experienced by ordinary, moderately educated men who abandoned their normal occupations to follow Jesus, witnessed the climax of his ministry, fled at his arrest, were distant bystanders at the Crucifixion, were bewildered by the Resurrection, but were then inspired at Pentecost to preach, first in Judea and then in places far afield. The reading in Acts describes the quite extraordinary self-confidence and power of the Apostles after the coming of the Holy Spirit. Not only can Peter cure people, his very shadow is efficacious. This is so distant from the picture in the Gospel that is Luke's follow-on account of Matthew 20.20–28 (cf. Saint James the Apostle), which emphasises the importance of service and how it will be rewarded.

The account of discipleship from call to martyrdom represents the most extreme variety of contexts and emotions, which generally follow a "U" shape, with high optimism at the beginning of the mission and

again at the end. Bewilderment before the Crucifixion and after the Resurrection lie part way down, with the Good Friday events at the nadir. It
is a pattern that we should always bear in mind when we have temporarily lost that sense of inner assurance and are feeling bewilderment. We
might, worse still, sometimes experience a radical separation from God,
the spiritual equivalent of Good Friday. Good discipleship is not constituted in easy success and glowing testimonials, but in perseverance in
the knowledge that we will always be sustained by God no matter how
we feel. If we look at the lives of the Apostles, we can see that there is
such a conformity of pattern that it has a compelling logic. We may not
know how precisely many of them died, but the traditions are reassur-
ingly consistent. Those called by Jesus might have experienced doubt,
but they were ultimately filled with the Holy Spirit so that they might
bring the Good News and, ultimately, die as its glorious witnesses. We
are hardly likely to die for our faith, but our witness should be no less
glorious. We are asked, perhaps, to be steadfast rather than heroic, to
cheer the sick rather than to cure them, to give hope rather than inspiration to the weak, but we are still bringing the Good News.

Sometimes it is difficult to work out what is expected of us in a religious culture that seems equally to resent self-doubt and self-confidence.
On the first point, we are somehow supposed to maintain an even tenor
of faith, quite separate from our individual experience of God, of the
varying quality of our personal relationship. The imperative for a kind
of uniformity of response lies in the tendency to see God as a collection
of doctrines, an ontological package constructed from largely Greek
ideas, rather than thinking of God as a person with whom we have a
relationship—a dialogue process derived largely from the Old Testament experience of the Chosen People—which is subject to variations
for which we can not always adequately account. We describe the ontology and the dialogue as mysterious, which then makes self-confidence
look suspect. The way to handle this set of contradictions is to recognise
that one's doubt is ultimately not in God, but in oneself as a person coming to terms with the mysterious, whereas any confidence we have arises
from God's grace. That may appear to cast us in a "no win" situation,
but what it really does is to help us understand our creaturely position.
The problem of using the concept of mystery is that we are easily lulled
into using "God talk" in a very human way, and into using talk about
ourselves in a way that makes us more powerful than we are.

What we all dread is the nadir, the emptiness, the fear that the dialogue which has faltered and died, will never be resumed. Again, it is

easy to think ourselves into a "no win" situation whereby we are at fault because the dialogue has stopped and we are powerless to resume it. Yet again, the way to think about this is in terms of our role as creatures. For Bartholemew the matter was much more direct, much less theological, as the contrast between the Master and the disciple was sharp and real, whereas we have to rely upon the working of the Holy Spirit within us. His presence would naturally lead alternately to feelings of inferiority and admiration, of dialogue faltering and springing back into life, but it was a human drama, whereas ours is much more tentative. Yet we need not falter, but should take comfort from the passage from Acts, noting how the uncertainty of following even the concrete Jesus was replaced by utter conviction. Like Peter and his followers, teaching and healing, we are children of the Resurrection.

Saint Matthew the Apostle
(September 21)

Collect	*O Almighty God, who by Thy blessed Son didst call Matthew from the receipt of custom to be an Apostle and Evangelist . . .*
Epistle	2 Corinthians 4.1–6
Gospel	Matthew 9.9–113

St Matthew, traditionally identified with Levi (Mark 2.1–22; Luke 5.27–30) is, as the Collect notes, traditionally celebrated as both an Apostle and an Evangelist. Both traditions are almost certainly unfounded. The Gospel of Matthew was traditionally thought to have been written before AD 70, but it now seems more likely that it was written between 70 and 90. It was aimed at a Jewish audience, and the highly contentious style reflects the struggle by the early Church to make a clear distinction between new Christians and traditional Jews. That style, particularly in depicting the murderous role of the Jewish people in the Crucifixion, made it a primary anti-Semitic source text (cf. The Sunday Next before Easter). For centuries its authority as the most cited Gospel lay in the false belief that it was the source for, rather than the outgrowth of, Mark (cf. Saint Mark's Day). There are no established traditions with reference to Matthew the Apostle. Matthew is the "Gospel of the Church" and the only one to use the term *ekklesia* (16.18; 18.17).

The Epistle and Gospel seem uncomfortably at odds. Jesus, sitting at table in Matthew's house after he has been called away from his extortionate life, turns away a criticism of the Pharisees by saying that those who are well do not need a physician; that he has not come to call the righteous, but sinners. Paul, on the other hand, says that if the Gospel is hidden, it is hidden from those who are lost. This, however, turns out to be an example of Paul's clumsy wordplay, and the preceding sentence says that in preaching, Paul and his colleagues have given up any kind of underhandedness and preach the Gospel courageously, not timidly. Nonetheless, the assertion that the "God of this world" can so blind that it excludes the glory of God is a more forbidding prospect than that which Jesus allows. Further, for all his humility with respect to the origin of his personal gifts, one cannot imagine Paul sitting down with sinners for a meal. The drive of the convert clearly made it difficult for him simply to enjoy the time of day with those who might take comfort from his presence.

In spite of its liberal attitude to imprisonment, the contemporary Church shows few signs of a willingness to share time with sinners, and tends to take the Pauline view that people must either repent or be ostracised, which raises questions about our attitudes towards sin and sinners. The conventional wisdom is that we should hate the sin but love the sinner, but how often do we conflate the two, only seeing the sin in the sinner? Equally pertinent, how often do we judge the sin on the basis of an external act, without thinking about provocation and motive? Thirdly, how often do we slip into the easy bifurcation between ourselves on the one hand, and sinners on the other? There is certainly strong evidence that poor people are both more likely to commit crime and to be victims of it than rich people, but the answer is surely to reduce the poverty rather than simply condemning the crime. Over recent years, as rich and poor have moved further apart in the work places and into their exclusive housing ghettos, we are in danger of equating sin with poverty, stigmatising "feral" children and substance abusers, and taking an altogether more lenient line with "white collar" crime, no matter how outrageous.

On the other hand, it could be argued that the Church is taking a renewed interest in the unchurched—and ostensibly sinful—poor through its "Fresh Expressions" initiative, which raises the much more difficult issue of the relationship between Evangelisation and poverty. On the one hand, there are some who say that we should not "take advantage" of vulnerable people by preaching to them in their misery, or that indeed we cannot do so because misery closes minds. On the other hand, there are those who say that the poor are in particular need of the Good News. One way of looking at this dilemma is that the Good News which Jesus brings is not a doctrine of judgment and punishment, but a promise of social justice and so we might start there. We can prove our worth as ministers of the Word by being ministers of justice and compassion. In other words, the Good News in doctrinal form is not a substitute for social justice.

Because the Pauline view has largely prevailed, it is vital that we re-imagine our world through the eyes and actions of Jesus. Rowan Williams, in *Christ on Trial*, characterises Matthew's Gospel as the assertion of divine, dynamic wisdom against human, static nostrums. This is why there are so many passages attacking the Pharisees. Much of what passes for religious assertion, he says, is nearer to nostrum than wisdom. Looked at through the eyes of Jesus, the sinner is there to be saved because we are all to be saved. It will, in a catastrophic reversal of human nostrums, simply be more difficult for the rich and virtuous than for the poor and sinful. Perhaps in the rational twenty-first century where, in spite of post-modernist "playfulness", most people seem to be dogmatically sure of what they stand for, we need a generous presence of fools of the sort that accompanied kings and great statesmen in the Middle Ages. In his better moments Paul recognises this and, in being careful when he goes "off message", so must we.

Saint Michael and All Angels
(September 29)

Collect   *O everlasting God, who has ordained and*
                       constituted the services of angels . . .
For The Epistle   Revelation 12.7–12
The Gospel   Matthew 18.1–10

Angels occupy contested theological ground but, we might think of them in three ways. Firstly, there are angels like Michael who attend on God, and never leave the ethereal realm. Secondly, there are classic angels in the true sense of the word, messengers from God to man (cf. to Abraham Genesis 18; to Gideon Judges 6; to Tobit and to Mary Luke 1–2 inter alia). Thirdly, there are "guardian angels" personal to each of us. The second kind are most frequently cited and most obviously useful, and the third kind are somewhat contentious. The reality of the first kind relies primarily upon the highly wrought second half of Daniel, transposed into the high poetry of Revelation. Here, the battle scene almost certainly owes its origins to the Persian iconography partially absorbed by the Jews in exile (Daniel 10.13, 10.21, 12.1), reinforced in the Book of Enoch and elaborated in mediaeval iconography. Michael is regarded as the chief heavenly warrior, who became associated with St George in the late Middle Ages as a patron of chivalry (they jointly grace a UK order of chivalry).

The passage from Revelation has had a massive influence on Christian self-understanding. Without it, there would have been a far weaker sense of the battle between good and evil waged outside earthly bounds. In turn, this would have made the devil a much less powerful phenomenon. (The passage, incidentally, also conflates the serpent of wisdom in Genesis 3 with Persian iconography which depicts the serpent as the symbol of evil. Read without the later gloss, Genesis 3 is transformed.) In spite of the immense influence of Dante on Western Christendom, and the more specifically English influence of Milton, the main forces for promoting angels and demons were sculpture and painting. If we think of our own "view" of angels and demons, we will almost certainly settle on a mental picture from the fine arts. In this realm it is the symbolism, not the theology, that has the greater force. It is also readings such as these which have formed a mind set which makes heaven in some way concrete, quasi-Olympian; redolent not of the mystery of God but of earthly delights infinitely multiplied, with hell as the precise reverse.

They have also strongly influenced the tendency to think of the Creator in monarchical terms, a trope particularly favoured by sixteenth- and seventeenth-century monarchs claiming "Divine Right" of leadership. So entrenched are these images in popular culture, that concepts of heaven and hell have outlived basic knowledge of Christianity.

In spite of tentative ideas of life after death during the time of Jesus, there was clearly a notion of heaven, and the disciples wanted to take what they thought was their rightful place (cf. Saint James the Apostle). Jesus, somewhat severely, points out that those who will be most important in heaven are those who are least important on earth. In his time the infant mortality rate of approaching 80% was such that there was no sentimentality about children; they were only significant when they became economically productive. Jesus goes on to point out the penalties for subverting these innocent, unimportant creatures. Reaching heaven, he says in one of his sharpest teachings, is so important that any obstacle in ourselves must be destroyed. One reason for this, apart from the intrinsic value of behaving well, is that such children are being guarded and represented in heaven by angels. This is a key passage in the theology of guardian angels.

One of the most interesting discussions of angels is contained within 1 Hebrews, where it is argued that Jesus is "above" them in the divine hierarchy, but are they, in turn, "above" humans? On the one hand, we might argue that there can be nothing better than an existence totally devoted to God, rendering pure obedience. On the other hand, we could argue that because of their status, angels are simply glamorous servants who do as they are told, and that, in spite of the literary pyrotechnics, there is no way in which they could be defeated by evil forces. Looked at from these perspectives, they either have simply glorious or rather bland existences. Humans, on the other hand, have been specifically created by God in love to be able to choose to love God. Whether to be a choosing being is "higher" or "lower" than being a transparent servant of God is a fascinating question, which turns to some extent on our reading of Genesis 3. There is a strong tradition in Jewish theology which affirms the necessity of choice as the signifier of human dignity and worth. This has always been highly contested territory in Christianity, because the exercise of choice is expressed through actions. This was a critical issue at the Reformation, because of Luther's reading of the role of faith as opposed to "works". Some Protestants went further than Luther and denied that we have genuine operational choice because, regardless of what we do, we are either of the elect or not, depending on the strength of our faith in the saving death of Jesus.

It is difficult to trace the decline of angelic belief in the non-Catholic tradition, but it would be surprising if it did not relate in some way to a suspicion of almost all aspects of late mediaeval veneration, and the rejection of all kinds of intermediary devices including, at the extremes, the Church itself. In this sense, Protestantism, not the "enlightenment" was the source of contemporary theories of individualism, and it is therefore not insignificant that children are usually identified as "angels" when they are unquestioningly obedient!

Saint Luke the Evangelist
(October 18)

Collect	*Almighty God, who calledst Luke the physician . . .*
Epistle	2 Timothy 4.5–15
Gospel	Luke 10.1–7[a]

The Luke in 2 Timothy and Philemon is almost universally supposed to be the author of the Gospel in his name, and Acts which constitute two volumes of a single work, beginning before the birth of Jesus and ending just before the death of Paul, carrying the story of salvation from its traditional Jewish centre in Jerusalem to the Gentile centre of Rome. There is a tradition, as he was not an eyewitness of the ministry of Jesus, that he gained his information from Mary, but it is much more likely that his primary source was Paul, with whom, his text implies (Acts 16.10 onwards), he travelled on his later journeys. His style is cultivated, his narrative skills are unparalleled in the New Testament (cf. the Good Samaritan, Luke 10.30–37; the Prodigal Son, Luke 15.11–32; Rhoda, Acts 12.11–17), his philosophy is lucid (cf. Acts 17.22–33), and he demonstrates a unique sympathy with the figures in his narrative. Perhaps his greatest achievement is the first two chapters of his Gospel, which contain a unique narrative of the events before (the angelic appearance to Zechariah, the Annunciation, Mary's visit to Elizabeth, the Circumcision and Presentation of John) during (the Bethlehem stable, the shepherds) and after (the Circumcision of Jesus and his juvenile Temple visit) the birth of Jesus, including three of the great Canticles

(*Magnificat*, *Venite* and *Nunc Dimittis*) and the basic text of the *Hail Mary*. Perhaps more critically, without Luke we would have no account of the Church from the Ascension to the arrival of Paul in Rome, including the ground breaking "Council of Jerusalem" (Acts 15), which settled the Gentile question. Tradition says that he was a physician (a point heavily laboured in the Collect), and this may account for his particular sympathy for the poor and for women. As the Epistle points out, he was Paul's last companion before his martyrdom. Luke is supposed to have lived for more than twenty years after Paul, dying in Boeotia c. AD 84, which makes it difficult to understand why Acts ends so unsatisfactorily, not reporting the deaths of Peter and Paul. Perhaps he thought that these late events would spoil the balance of a two-part work which had the key events at its centre. Although his account largely agrees with Paul's own, it would be a mistake to think of Luke as an historian (there is, for example, no other contemporary reference to the Census in Luke 2.1). To his contemporaries, he would have been thought of as a biographer, but for us he is primarily a theologian. The closing passage of 2 Timothy (echoing Philemon 24), describes Luke, who only mentions himself incidentally, as being faithful to the end. Its main message is to commend evangelism to Timothy, while detailing its tribulations. In essence, Paul, about to die, is passing on the torch. The Gospel passage may have been chosen because there is an unsubstantiated tradition that Luke was one of the seventy who were sent out. Again, it speaks of hardship, of lambs being sent among wolves.

These passages are more relevant now than they were when they were chosen. At that time, there were disagreements about the precise nature of what different denominations believed, but basic belief in God was almost universal in Europe. Today, when the Church is deeply concerned with Evangelism, it is challenged to reach people who have been unchurched for so long that nothing can be assumed. The power of an affirming Church is counterbalanced by an increasing proportion of the population which does not know the basic elements of the Christian story, and as the gap widens, the task of mission becomes ever more difficult, forcing us to think how we can gain a foothold, now that so much of the Christian common frame of reference has collapsed. These passages are so important because the difficulty of the task, the necessary setbacks and sacrifices, can be easily obscured by "management speak" about "reach" and "targets", as if mission were a niche in marketing. We can also recognise Jesus' observation that the harvest is great but the labourers are few.

There is, however, a broader lesson to be drawn from Luke. He would never have cited the commonplace that religion and politics do not mix. He puts into the mouth of Mary (Luke 1.46–55 after 1 Samuel 2.1–10) the most radical Christian prayer and his rendering of the message of Jesus transforms Matthew's "Blessed are the poor in spirit" (5.3) to "Blessed are the poor" (6.20). For him the theology of creation and salvation are inextricably bound up with social justice. This has been a hard lesson for a church which abandoned its humble origins to become the established church of the Roman Empire under Constantine early in the forth century and has since possessed a high degree of wealth, power, and influence. Even today the Church of England is part of the establishment and is, in many places, almost exclusively a middle class phenomenon. A parallel tendency has been, against the tenor of Luke, for the Church to lecture poor people on their morality rather than standing alongside them in their struggle for justice. One of the small ironies of living out a flawed witness to Jesus is the frequency with which we say the *Magnificat*, but do so little about its fulfilment. It is now fashionable to remind ourselves that the Church is incarnational but, in the sense that Luke understands the term, our commitment is sporadic. Jesus took sides, but our fear of being accused of partisanship seems to hold us back. In this sense, although Luke appeals to contemporary sentiment, his is the most challenging of the Gospels.

Saint Simon and Saint Jude, Apostles
(October 28)

Collect	*O almighty God, who has built thy Church upon the foundation of the Apostles . . .*
Epistle	Jude 1
Gospel	John 15.17–27

Lists of the twelve Apostles (Matthew 10.2–4; Mark 3.16–19; Luke 6.14–16; Acts 1.13) place Simon "the Zealot" (or "Canaan") tenth and Judas (of James, Thaddaeus or Lebbaeus) eleventh. Simon is not mentioned otherwise by name in the New Testament. In order to establish a degree of consistency between the apostolic lists, and to render the number twelve real rather than symbolic, Jude has been conflated with Thaddaeus and Lebbaeus. Most scholars agree that he is not the author of the letter of his name nor is he "the brother of Jesus" (Mark 6.3; Matthew 13.55–57). Tradition says Simon and Jude were martyred together in Persia.

The Gospel, taken from Jesus' great discourse before his arrest, combines a restatement of the Trinity with a warning that those who bear witness to it will make worldly enemies and suffer for their faithfulness. The first chapter of Jude warns against infiltration into the Church by wicked people trying to undermine its message. They are likened to the wicked citizens of Sodom and Gomorrah, the heartless Pharaoh who treated the Chosen People cruelly, and to the rebellious angels (cf. Saint Michael and All Angels). This is balanced with a promise to those who are faithful. The early Church (cf. 1 Corinthians 12) was so overwhelmed with the power of the Spirit, manifested in such forms as the gift of tongues, that it must have been difficult to distinguish between the highly charismatic and the plain wicked. This is a warning against egotism and excess but, equally, we must take care that we do not exclude those with gifts that do not accord with prevailing fashions, our own preferences, or those which threaten the status quo. We are apt to be more suspicious of under-regulation than over-regulation. We are also in danger of relying on regulation and monitoring, rather than building, trust. The Gospel begins with the exhortation that we should love one another but, except in the case of children, it is not usual to manifest love through regulation.

We are reminded in the Collect of the need for sound doctrine and this in itself can lead to over-scrupulous disputes, but set in the context of an established Church with a state ordained legal framework, the danger is greater still. This is not to deny the importance of doctrine— the emphasis by Jesus on the roles of the different attributes in the Trinitarian economy is eloquent on the point—but we need to be able to distinguish between what is essential and what is a matter of individual conscience. Not unrelated is Jude's tendency—echoing Paul—to exclude rather than absorb sinners. In contrast with Jesus' injunction that our forgiveness should be unlimited (Matthew 18.21–22), the implication in later writing is that adherents will only have one or two chances. The issues of trust and sinfulness are closely related, because regulation and stricture are not respectively suitable. If we trust that God will favour the righteous then, out of love, we should trust each other, and as we are all sinners, depending on God for our salvation, we should have a better capacity to live alongside and communicate with the egregious sinner. In seeking to make distinctions for better order, we are forced to define those we can trust and those whose sins we can tolerate.

The commandment of love has not been abridged, and neither has the presence of the Holy Spirit been withdrawn from us. We might think that the kind of people Jude feared were rather obvious subverters and that we are well defended against them, but he thought his opponents were rather subtle, and so too are ours. In adopting secular methods to analyse our plight, and our strategy for dealing with it, we might be in danger of falling prey to those who threaten us. We know a murderer, an adulterer, and a blasphemer when we see one, but we are apt to be less suspicious of the bureaucrat, the regulator, and the tribunal. Sometimes our allegiance to secular liberalism lulls us into compromises we should not make. Christians have colluded with the secular state in framing a "just war" policy (for Constantine), perpetuating slavery (until the early nineteenth century), and sanctioning gross inequalities of income and wealth (more recently on the basis that these are less harmful than Marxism). Yet these are rather obvious shortcomings compared with the self-satisfied preservation of the status quo and the transfer to the secular state of our obligation to serve.

Although the reasons for it are obscure, St Jude is the patron of desperate causes, and he is our last intercessory resource. We might remember this when we consider the place of the Church in society. We do not exist to collude nor to congratulate. We are incarnational and prophetic, and that means living out our witness in a hostile world. Jesus pointed this out to his followers and we should not forget it now. In spite of gaps in our knowledge, we can safely conclude that most of those listening to Jesus on the last evening of his life gave their lives for him. We will almost certainly be asked to do much less, so we should not grudge what pain we are called upon to suffer for his sake, not least because we are assured that our suffering will not be in vain.

All Saints' Day
(November 1)

Collect   *O almighty God, who hast knit together Thine elect . . .*
For The Epistle Revelation 7.2–12
Gospel   Matthew 5.1–12

Saints are profoundly the same and profoundly different from each other. However different saints may be on earth, the picture of them consolidated, so to speak, in heaven, is the image that tends to stick, testimony yet again to the immense power of the imagery in Revelation (cf. Saint Michael and All Angels). This somewhat undifferentiated picture is helpful in the first instance because it emphasises that sainthood is not a Christian monopoly. The heaven of John the Divine is peopled with witnesses from the sacred history of Israel, twelve thousand for each tribe, and so the heaven of the New Testament is not, at the very least, monopoly Christian territory. There is an interesting theological quirk in this image, because the tribes of Israel are worshipping the Lamb, John's symbol for Jesus. Had this mystery of timelessness been better understood, we might have escaped from the terrible blight of Christian anti-Semitism (cf. Saint Matthew the Apostle). Even if in some obscure way the Chosen People were somehow responsible for the suffering and death of Jesus this was, according to Revelation, an aberration. One of the key themes of the book as a whole is the "war" between Israel and Babylon, which prefigured the war between Christian spirituality and Roman secular power.

Paul uses the endearing term "the Saints" to describe those who are living lives faithful to Christ. They are, in other words, living among us, and it is that sense of the presence of the Kingdom on Earth that we need to nurture if we ourselves are to aspire to sainthood. We must be aware of the danger of confusing the ultimate bliss of sanctity with its earthly prelude. When we say that a person is "a saint", we are generally thinking of those who live in a state of serenity, indifferent to circumstance, but that is not the way of saints on earth. Perhaps the quality that strikes us most when we read accurate (as opposed to panegyric) accounts of the Christian saints is how stubborn, or even bloody-minded, they were in the face of authoritarian or peer pressure. Such accounts also underline, as they should, that saints are not necessarily any better behaved than the rest of us. The story of St Augustine's early waywardness and repentance is tirelessly quoted, but this is to miss the point. Augustine may have gone through a grand transformation, but it did not stop him being a sinner. A saint is not a person who has had the good luck to make a deathbed repentance. In this respect, the Christian saints are much more in the direct line of the Old Testament prophets than priests.

The lives of many saints should be a warning to us all to be much more open to and respectful of non-conformity. The people who agree with everything that everyone says and does, and who meekly sit while the poor are oppressed, are not likely to be saints in the classical sense. While the saints of the generations before the mass media only had their rough edges knocked off by sculptors and glaziers, the saints of the twentieth century have been much more real to us in all their complexity. Within Christian circles those we most often think of are Dietrich Bonhoeffer, Martin Luther King, Nelson Mandela (though still alive), and Mother Theresa. You only have to go to a media archive to see how morally complex all their lives were, and how they were not always equal to the challenges that faced them. What marks them out, however, is fierce non-conformity, the refusal to accept oppression and exploitation, the need to stand up, at the risk of death, for the cause of freedom and justice. None of them died for the established Christian church as such, although Bonhoeffer's stand in the 1930s against the established Lutheran Church was a key component in his oppositional witness.

Such thoughts might lead us to examine the list of virtues which begins the Sermon on the Mount, which is chosen presumably to represent the virtues most often found in saints. To understand the connection we need to rid the key concepts of their contemporary overtones. Poor in spirit, meek, righteousness, merciful, and pure in heart are all terms which need an understanding of their meaning for the Evangelists and early modern translators. Perhaps the ideas we relate to most easily are peace-makers and those who are persecuted, as these are qualities that pertain to life and death. Yet Jesus is speaking to his new and humble disciples. They all merited sainthood in the last resort but nobody living with them could have known how things would turn out. Perhaps the people who least look like saints are the most likely candidates.

On this day which sums up our view of sanctity, it would be as well to clear up a sixteenth-century controversy which separated the Reformers from Catholics, and which still persists in the Church of England. If we believe that there are saints in a special relationship with God (or "in heaven") then they are fit intermediaries or intercessors between us and God, but this initial form of the meaning of "pray", to ask, must be distinguished from the narrower idea of "praying to" as a form of worship. Perhaps it is not inappropriate in this last commentary to note that this is yet one more example of a not very major controversy which has unnecessarily divided Anglicans from other Christians and from each other. The saints were not noted negotiators.

Bibliography

Allen, J.W.: *Political Thought in the 16th Century*, Methuen, 1941

ARCIC: *Mary: Grace and Hope in Christ*, Morehouse Publishing, 2005

Armstrong, Karen: *The Battle for God: Fundamentalism in Judaism, Christianity and Islam*, Harper Collins, 2001

Bolt, Robert: *A Man for All Seasons*, 1966

Bradshaw, Paul: *Eucharistic Origins*, SPCK, 2004

Burridge, Richard: *John: A Bible Commentary for Every Day*, Bible Reading Fellowship, 2007

Dawkins, Richard: *Unweaving the Rainbow*, Penguin, 2006

Eliot, T.S.: *Four Quartets*, Faber & Faber, 1952

King, Nicholas: *The New Testament*, Kevin Mayhew, 2004

Lash, Nicholas: *Holiness, Speech and Silence: Reflections on the Question of God*, Ashgate, 2004

Putnam, Robert: *Bowling Alone: the collapse and revival of American community*, Simon & Schuster, 2000

Radcliffe, Timothy OP: *What Is The Point of Being A Christian?* Burns & Oates/Continuum, 2005

Rahner, Karl: *Foundations of Christian Faith: An Introduction to the Idea of Christianity*, Crossroad Publishing Company, 2008

Rawls, John: *A Theory of Justice*, Harvard University Press, 1971

Schweitzer, Albert: *The Quest for the Historical Jesus*, Dover Publications, 2005 (first published 1906)

Shakespeare, Steven and Raiment-Pickard, Hugh: *The Inclusive God: Reclaiming Theology for an Inclusive Church*, Canterbury Press, 2006

Sontag, Susan: *Illness as Metaphor*, Picador, 2001

Vermes, Geza: *Jesus the Jew*, Collins, 1973

Vermes, Geza: *The Nativity: History and Legend*, Penguin, 2006

Vermes, Geza: *The Passion*, Penguin, 2005

Vulliamy, Ed: *Orchestral Manoeuvres*, Observer, 29th July 2007

Williams, Archbishop Rowan: *Christ on Trial: How the Gospel Unsettles Our Judgement*, Zondervan, 2000

Wolfe, Tom: *The Bonfire of the Vanities*, Picador, 1987

Wright, Tom: *Simply Christian*, SPCK, 2006

Thoughts for Reflection

The First Sunday in Advent

1. Imagine a world without gas or electricity; what difference does this make to the idea of darkness and light?

2. How does the doctrine of the incarnation of Jesus square with the condemnation of worldly pleasures?

3. How comfortable is the military metaphor of armour, in the Collect but clearly taken from Paul, within the context of Paul's emphasis on love?

4. How can we make the idea of the humble king relevant in a world where kingship is largely nominal, and humility confused with subservience?

5. How do we approach the waiting time of Advent when we are under so much pressure to make elaborate preparations for Christmas, and to celebrate long before the special day arrives?

The Second Sunday in Advent

1. How does New Testament concern with an imminent "Second Coming" affect the meaning of the texts for us?

2. Should the Church accommodate a variety of ways of understanding Scripture and, if so, how?

3. What is our understanding of hope?

4. Is Paul's use of the circumcision metaphor useful or confusing today?

5. Is astrology dangerous or just harmless fun?

The Third Sunday in Advent

1. How different were the cousins Jesus and John and the prophets John and Paul?

2. In what way are Ministers successors of John?

3. Where, under God, does authority lie in the Anglican Communion and Church of England?

4. What connections and contradictions are there in the concepts of justification by faith and earthly judgment of human conduct?

5. How important is social class in the writing of Shakespeare?

The Fourth Sunday in Advent

1. What was the different significance of Elijah and Isaiah to the Jewish contemporaries of Jesus?

2. Why was John baptising people and why would the religious authorities have taken notice of this?

3. How, in the next few hours or days, might we make straight the path for the arrival of Jesus?

4. What is peace?

5. In the context of the way we live today, what is the meaning of "moderation" and, in such an interconnected society, can we really "be careful for nothing"?

The Nativity of Our Lord

1. How far are these readings a corrective to contemporary sentiment?

2. How can the popular Christmas welcome be turned into Easter rejoicing?

3. Are angels a help or hindrance to the Christian message?

4. How do we explain the

absence of Mary?

5. Consider the symbolism of the Christmas tree and its decoration.

Saint Stephen's Day

1. How helpful was the distinction between those who prayed and those who waited at table in the early Church and how relevant is the division between priests and deacons today? Is the implied hierarchy divisive and disrespectful, or enabling and affirming?

2. Compare Stephen's court room declaration in Acts 6–7 with Peter's court room declaration in Acts 5.17–42.

3. Would we have thrown a stone at Stephen or, like Saul, held the cloaks?

4. What does the story of Stephen tell us about religious conservatism?

5. Why might forgiveness be so important on Boxing Day?

Saint John the Evangelist's Day

1. How much does it matter that one person may not have written the works attributed to "John"? How much does it matter that Chapter 21 of John was written much later than the rest of the Gospel?

2. What are the key differences and similarities between the Synoptics on the one hand and John on the other?

3. How would the Church be different without the Gospel of John?

4. Is the conversation between Jesus, John, and Peter significant or trivial?

5. From what he says of himself, what kind of person was the John of the Gospel?

The Innocents' Day

1. Compare the genealogies of Matthew and Luke, note the differences, and explain what they might mean.

2. Has our attitude to the children of untimely death changed because of the recent papal "abolition" of Limbo?

3. Explore the contemporary records of the life of Herod and compare it with Gospel accounts.

4. Does Revelation stretch the metaphor of Jesus as the Lamb of God too far?

5. How should the exile of Jesus inform our attitude towards exiles?

The Sunday after Christmas Day

1. How important is the distinction between a theology which says that humanity, although flawed, never ceased to be the children of God, and the theology of incarnational adoption?

2. Was Jesus born for all humanity or just some of us?

3. What do we mean when we say that doctrines are "provisional metaphors"?

4. How do you imagine Joseph?

5. If Jesus had brothers and sisters. . .

The Circumcision of Christ

1. Jesus was the last in a long line of unlikely babies.

2. What do the Gospels and Acts tell us about Mary?

3. Is there any significance in the name Our Saviour was given at His circumcision?

4. What are the similarities and differences between the Circumcision and

baptismal covenants?

5. How have the visual arts affected our reading of Scripture?

The Epiphany

1. What are the outstanding features of Matthew and Luke's Nativity accounts?

2. Does it matter whether Jesus' visitors were wise men or kings?

3. In his assertion of independence, how close was Paul to overstepping the mark?

4. Discuss the conflicting pressures facing Herod.

5. What three gifts would you bring today? Why?

The First Sunday after the Epiphany

1. Is it possible to read the Gospels with strict adherence to the Chalcedon doctrine?

2. What are the barriers to establishing a true sense of self?

3. Why is this story so important to Luke's narrative?

4. What were the elders and Jesus talking about in the Temple?

5. Contrast the dangers facing the obviously wicked with the obviously good.

The Second Sunday after the Epiphany

1. How would you reply to someone saying that the consumption of alcohol is wicked and/or maintains that they were drinking grape juice at Cana?

2. How would you conduct a skills audit of your Parish Electoral Roll?

3. Is reluctance to delegate charitable or uncharitable?

4. Is it significant that Jesus' first miracle was performed at a wedding and/or is it a prefigurement of the Eucharist?

5. Why is the Cana miracle remembered at the Epiphany in some Christian traditions?

The Third Sunday after the Epiphany

1. Compare the figure of the Centurion in Matthew and Luke and consider the typology of Centurions in the New Testament.

2. Contrast the dangers of centralised and dispersed power.

3. Are you the Centurion or the leper?

4. What are the strengths and dangers in Paul's pastoral qualification?

5. How might the Gospel be understood differently by people living in countries which are or have recently been occupied?

The Fourth Sunday after the Epiphany

1. How is Paul's theory of the ruler relevant to us today?

2. Think about the contemporary equivalent conditions to being "possessed by a devil".

3. What are the arguments for and against the disestablishment of the Church of England?

4. What is a Christian's political duty?

5. Do you agree that in social relations we should avoid discussing religion and politics?

The Fifth Sunday after the Epiphany

1. Is the parable of the wheat and tares too anthropocentric in the way it understands God's justice and mercy?

2. How helpful is it to think of divine judgment in terms of civil justice?

3. Does your church feel like a household or a club?

4. How do you know a tare when you see one?

5. How would you know for yourself whether you are more like wheat than a weed?

The Sixth Sunday after the Epiphany

1. What are the strengths and weaknesses of the 1 John and Matthew speculations on heaven?

2. Consider the role of theology as an exploration of uncertainty and mystery.

3. Is science any better than theology at achieving certainty?

4. Is the Church perpetuating the mistakes it made over the astronomical revolution?

5. Is the idea of consumerism as a false prophet a cliché?

The Sunday called Septuagesima

1. Imagine running a modern business on the lines of the vineyard.

2. How similar are bodily and spiritual discipline?

3. Where would you place yourself in the line between first and last and why?

4. How would our law and politics be different if we applied the "Veil of Ignorance" device?

5. Are there special obligations in respect of their personal lives on those who preach?

The Sunday called Sexagesima

1. Was Paul's failure to revisit Corinth an accident or the result of cowardice?

2. Modernise the parable of the sower.

3. Write a simple paraphrase of the Epistle.

4. What are the proper limits of dissent in the Church?

5. Write a character sketch of Paul.

The Sunday called Quinquagesima

1. Is Corinthians 13 a suitable wedding text? If not, what other readings would you suggest?

2. Why is loving so difficult?

3. Consider Romans 13 as a critique of the contemporary Church.

4. What childish things must we leave behind?

5. Compare Romans 13 with your favourite poem or song about love.

The First Day of Lent

1. Is the fusion of penitence and penance helpful?

2. What are the pros and cons of giving things up and taking things up?

3. If you could only give up or take up one thing, what would be the most difficult?

4. How do you account for the rather strange designation "commonly called Ash Wednesday"?

5. Design a special prayer regime for Lent.

The First Sunday in Lent

1. What are the three temptations you find it most difficult to resist?

2. What was your strategy for designing your Lenten observance?

3. Compare churches that observe an annual cycle and those which do not.

4. In Lent should we behave as we do when watching a play and deliberately put Easter out of our minds?

5. How do you explain "the devil" today?

The Second Sunday in Lent

1. Did Jesus make a mistake when he initially rejected the woman of Canaan?

2. How do you understand the concept of being inhabited by an evil spirit?

3. How do you reconcile our dependence on the mercy of God with the idea of God's vengeance?

4. Can you reconcile our belief that we were created to love with our biological disposition to compete?

5. Why are we so much more exercised about sexual rather than financial immorality?

The Third Sunday in Lent

1. Is the Anglican Communion a "house divided against itself"?

2. Why is Luke such a good storyteller?

3. Trace the steps to the gas chambers.

4. Why are holy people most in danger?

5. Design a short course on carefulness of speech.

The Fourth Sunday in Lent

1. Consider Paul's struggle with the Abraham legacy.

2. If Jesus was open to all, why have we made entrance rules?

3. Consider the problem of miracles and science.

4. How does John use miracles differently from the other Evangelists?

5. Do we pick up the fragments?

The Fifth Sunday in Lent

1. One morning, a young woman elbows the Vicar aside, climbs into the pulpit and proclaims herself to be the Fourth Person of the Godhead. . .

2. Why should the Jews have at least taken Jesus' claims seriously?

3. Is the language of animal sacrifice useful in understanding salvation?

4. Imagine a soteriology based entirely on faith or works.

5. Consider the many aspects of Abraham brought out in the Lenten Readings.

The Sunday next before Easter

1. Are the twinned practices of processing with palms and being anointed with ash medieval superstitions best abandoned?

2. How different would the Passion accounts be without Barabbas?

3. What is the difference between Shoah and Holocaust?

4. What does the Epistle have to say about our attitude to non-Christians?

5. Consider the influence of Isaiah and Jeremiah on the Passion narratives.

Monday before Easter

1. Does Mark have anything special to offer in his Passion narrative?

2. Does it matter where, when, and by

whom Jesus' feet were anointed?

3. There is a tradition that Mark's Gospel owes much to St Peter. How fair is he to his supposed source?

4. When Jesus admitted that he was the Christ, what options did his judges have?

5. Write the story in Mark 14 as the script for a soap opera.

Tuesday before Easter

1. Consider the different "faces" of Pilate in the four Gospels and other sources.

2. Why was Elijah so significant for Jesus' contemporaries?

3. What does Mark's account owe to Isaiah and Jeremiah?

4. Does Albert Schweitzer have a point?

5. Mark's Passion is stylistically simple but cinematically powerful.

Wednesday before Easter

1. Is there a conflict between being Eucharist-centred and a belief in penal substitution?

2. Consider a picture of Jesus, supported by an angel, sweating drops of blood.

3. How similar are Judas and Peter and how different are they from the other disciples?

4. What do the different accounts of the trial of Jesus tell us about the Evangelists and about him?

5. How responsible are we for the relationship between poverty and involvement in the criminal justice system?

Thursday before Easter

1. How significant are the different accounts of the

Institution of the Eucharist?

2. Are our celebrations of the Eucharist too formulaic and too focused on "people like us"?

3. Draw up the bitter and sweet accounts for what most Christian traditions call Maundy Thursday (including John 13–17)

4. Remind yourself of the Stations of the Cross.

5. Pick a character or group in Luke 22–23 and chart the changes in attitude and action.

Good Friday

1. Should we preach on Good Friday or let the Gospels speak for themselves?

2. How helpful is the imagery of animal ritual sacrifice in explaining the Crucifixion?

3. What do John's unique insights contribute to our understanding of the Passion?

4. Behold the Lamb of God.

5. Compare different paintings of the Crucifixion.

Easter Eve

1. Is there any significance in the role of the women in the Resurrection narratives?

2. How do we draw the line between religious devotion and fanaticism?

3. What are the arguments for and against reinstating the ancient Easter Vigil and rites of Initiation?

4. Discuss the Credal phrase "He descended into Hell".

5. Is Easter Day a better occasion than Ash Wednesday for making resolutions?

Easter Day

1. Tell the story of Easter morning from the point of view of one of the women or one of the Disciples.

2. Think of some alternative Easter greetings and responses to those customarily used.

3. Is the Resurrection integral or incidental to the atonement?

4. What significance is there in the difference between the Synoptic accounts of Easter Morning and that of John?

5. Is the idea that the Resurrection is the actual conquest of death rhetorical or real?

Monday in Easter Week

1. What theories might the Apostles have developed to explain the empty tomb?

2. How much does it matter if the Institution of the Eucharist included many followers including women?

3. What line of exegesis might Jesus have followed on the road to Emmaus?

4. Is the mention of food in Acts and the Gospel pointed or incidental?

5. Tell the Emmaus story from Cleopas' point of view.

Tuesday in Easter Week

1. Does it matter whether Jesus had a physical presence after his Resurrection?

2. Explain the Christian doctrine of the after life.

3. Compare Acts 10.34–43 (Monday in Easter) with Acts 13.26–41.

4. Distinguish physicality, sexuality, and lust.

5. If Jesus appeared again would you prefer a spirit or a body?

The First Sunday after Easter

1. How important is New Testament chronology to theology?

2. How strong is the link between water, blood, and the Spirit and the "persons" of the Trinity?

3. How serious are we about the power of the Church to forgive our sins?

4. Describe a principled relationship between Church and State.

5. Do we live in a world hostile to Christianity?

The Second Sunday after Easter

1. Discuss the advantages of the interlocking metaphors of shepherd/lamb and priest/victim.

2. Are there problems with the metaphor of Christians as sheep in respect of their individual and collective exercise of free will?

3. How important is the difference between the time perspective of the early Church and our extended time frame?

4. Does the contemporary role of the Bishop as an administrator detract from the role of shepherd?

5. Refashion the shepherd/sheep metaphor for a contemporary, urban congregation of children or adults.

The Third Sunday after Easter

1. How difficult is it to reconcile the doctrine of the humanity of Jesus with statements in the Gospels about his forthcoming death and Resurrection?

2. How different are the Gospel accounts of the trial and condemnation of Jesus compared with what we know about Jewish

and Roman criminal procedure and, on this basis, was Jesus' prediction of death justified?

3. How different is Peter's approach to Roman authority from Paul's or John's?

4. Consider the implications of Peter's statement that we must submit to authority even when it persecutes us.

5. Describe the trials of a contemporary pilgrim.

The Fourth Sunday after Easter

1. Consider change and uncertainty now and in the sixteenth century.

2. What connection is there between sin and suffering?

3. Discuss the purposes of the "Great Discourse" (John 13–17)

4. Was Jesus a theologian?

5. Draw up an inventory of your power and influence.

The Fifth Sunday after Easter

1. Is there a conflict between faith and good works?

2. Is philanthropy a form of prayer or can it become a source of pride?

3. Explore different senses of the word "good" and the concept of "the good"

4. What did Jesus mean by "I have overcome the world"?

5. Write a prayer which specifies the role of the intercessor, Jesus as the intermediary, and God as the recipient.

The Ascension Day

1. What extra dimensions do Luke's two accounts of the Ascension give to the story of Jesus?

2. How do the Ascension accounts contribute to Trinitarian theology?

3. Why might the disciples have been happy after the Ascension (Luke 24.50–52)?

4. Discuss contemporary views of John 22 and Mark 16.9–20.

5. Write a Creed for today.

Sunday after Ascension Day

1. How does food shortage change ideas about selfishness and justice?

2. Compare the moral challenges of martyrdom and indifference.

3. Has the ecological debate altered your sense of time?

4. Explain the mutuality of faith and good works in the economy of salvation.

5. Compare the requirements for a healthy body and a holy life.

Whitsunday

1. Draw the Holy Spirit.

2. Relate the Jewish First Fruits to the Christian first fruits of the life of Jesus.

3. How significant is gender assignment to the Holy Spirit?

4. What is the connection between the prompting of the Holy Spirit and our decisions and behaviour?

5. Is the Church the sacrament of Jesus or the Holy Spirit?

Monday in Whitsun Week

1. In what way is the Holy Spirit central to sacramentality?

2. Trace sacramental development in the New Testament.

3. Contrast the different attitudes to the relationship between the human and divine in paganism,

Judaism, and Christianity.

4. If Jesus was sent to love and not condemn, why do we find it so difficult to imitate him?

5. Is moral superiority adequate justification for aggression?

Tuesday in Whitsun Week

1. Trace the history of the rift between the Judeans and Samaritans.

2. What are the arguments for and against a consolidated or sequential initiation of Baptism, Eucharist, and Confirmation?

3. Is there any future for Confirmation if Christians receive their First Communion before it?

4. Is your Bishop like a shepherd?

5. How like a sheep are you?

Trinity Sunday

1. How do the readings relate to the Trinity?

2. How have the meanings of the words "person" and "economy" changed since they were used by early Councils of the Church?

3. Think of contemporary illustrations which would help us better to understand the mystery of the Trinity.

4. How would you face the charge that Christianity is not monotheistic?

5. Explore the links between physics and theology.

The First Sunday after Trinity

1. What is the relationship between the Creator and humanity from the perspective of each?

2. What might it mean to say that God's love is "perfected" in us?

3. To what extent does the force of a parable lie in its anthropology?

4. How helpful is the idea of hell?

5. Are you Dives or Lazarus?

The Second Sunday after Trinity

1. How viable is a society based solely on love?

2. Is fear a necessary or desirable deterrent?

3. Is taxation and voluntary donation an adequate response to human need?

4. Discuss the place of social class in the Church of England.

5. Make a list of common excuses for refusing to attend the banquet.

The Third Sunday after Trinity

1. Compare the stories of the shepherd and the housewife.

2. Tell contemporary stories conveying Luke's message.

3. Discuss the proposition that neither faith nor good works is the route to salvation.

4. How far has Christianity escaped from the Old Testament formalism of the Law to which Jesus and Paul so strongly objected?

5. Is human imperfection a necessary precondition for exercising our freedom to love?

The Fourth Sunday after Trinity

1. Compare Luke 6 with Matthew 5–7.

2. Explore the concept of the "liberty of the children of God".

3. How do you feel about the use of the metaphor about blindness in explaining moral positions?

4. Explore the relationship

between divine judgment, moral principles and civil justice.

5. Create some modern images to illustrate Luke's point about motes and beams.

The Fifth Sunday after Trinity

1. Does the way in which the Gospels are written distort or enhance our sense of their reality?

2. Discuss the relative merits of full time and part-time ministry.

3. Do we expect too much of our clergy and teachers?

4. What are the dangers of associating righteousness with suffering?

5. Have you experienced a similar event to the haul of fish?

The Sixth Sunday after Trinity

1. Consider the relationship between motive and outcome in civil justice.

2. Consider the contrast between Plato and Aristotle on the subject of perfection.

3. How do you react to the idea that imperfection is a necessary precondition for the exercise of free will?

4. Is there any sense in which the theological debate between atonement-centred and Resurrection-centred Christianity is useful?

5. Can you see a link between atonement-centred Christianity and original sin?

The Seventh Sunday after Trinity

1. How would you react to a stranger writing to you as Paul did to the Romans?

2. Are there any significant differences in the six accounts of mass feeding by Jesus?

3. What are the arguments for and against using the withholding of sacraments, and what is the theological basis for withholding oneself from sharing sacramental fellowship with others?

4. Discuss the continuities and discontinuities between manna, the mass feedings of Jesus, and the Institution of the Eucharist.

5. Tell the story of a mass feeding as if you had been there.

The Eighth Sunday after Trinity

1. How confident are you of judging people on the basis of an initial encounter?

2. Discuss the apparent conflict in Romans between Paul's pleas for unity and love and his plethora of moral proscriptions.

3. Compare the kinds of false prophets confronting Jesus and Matthew with the false prophets of today.

4. How should traditional Anglicanism react to particularist tendencies?

5. Is the idea that the meaning of the Bible is clear enough to justify authoritarian pronouncements a recursively self-referential proposition or the true foundation of a Scriptural Church?

The Ninth Sunday after Trinity

1. Explore the reasons why the Jews were kept in the wilderness for 40 years and why Moses was kept from the Promised Land.

2. How helpful is the story of the Jewish experience in the desert as a moral pointer?

3. What do you take to be the

point of the story of the master and steward, particularly the last verse of the passage?

4. How should we balance moral consistency with pastoral care?

5. Are moral decisions entirely personal?

The Tenth Sunday after Trinity

1. Consider the friction between priests and prophets in the Old Testament.

2. Is it fair to say that Jesus' cleansing of the Temple was an attack on materialism?

3. What are the criteria for establishing an appropriate balance between liberty and uniformity in a Church context?

4. Discuss the dangers of Biblical access without teaching.

5. Imagine a church where people care as much about the Bible as about their professions.

The Eleventh Sunday after Trinity

1. What are the strengths and weaknesses of parables and their use of caricature?

2. Compare Paul's account of the successive post-Resurrection appearances of Jesus with the Gospel evidence.

3. How well founded is Paul's claim to Apostleship?

4. What tools do we need for realistic self-assessment?

5. Is there room in an established Church for saints?

The Twelfth Sunday after Trinity

1. Is dependency on God and human responsibility a paradox?

2. Why did Jesus perform mighty acts?

3. Explore the idea of Moses pre-figuring Jesus as an intercessor.

4. What are the similarities and differences between being in love with another human being and being in love with God?

5. Let us consider the beauty of God. . .

The Thirteenth Sunday after Trinity

1. What do you think of the proposition that religion and politics should not mix?

2. What is the civic duty of a Christian?

3. Is it sustainable to love a Samaritan but hate Samaritans?

4. Who are you in the parable of the Good Samaritan?

5. Recount the essence of the parable in a modern setting.

The Fourteenth Sunday after Trinity

1. Do you think there is a credible link between poor manners and the development of immoral behaviour?

2. How well do Paul's two lists match up as pairs of opposites?

3. Are there better ways of describing what Paul calls "flesh" and "spirit"?

4. Think about unconditional worship and the Book of Job.

5. Tell the story of the cure from the point of view of one of the nine who went away and the one who came back to Jesus.

The Fifteenth Sunday after Trinity

1. Is Paul's characterisation of Jews and Christians unhelpfully crude?

2. Construct an argument for behaving in the twenty-first century like the lilies of the field,

or explain why the ideal of the lilies of the field is fanciful

3. Consider the conflict between spending on the family and spending on the poor.

4. Devise some basic rules about the ownership of income and wealth.

5. What are the root causes of anxiety?

The Sixteenth Sunday after Trinity

1. Can you reconcile the concepts of God's unconditional love and "divine retribution"?

2. Is the idea of thanks appropriate to an unconditional relationship?

3. What are the strengths and weaknesses of Luther's attack on prudential moralism in favour of Justification?

4. Can theology be undertaken without an individual commitment to belief in God?

5. Is equality simply a numerical concept?

The Seventeenth Sunday after Trinity

1. Discuss the strengths and weaknesses of socially stratified societies and contemporary individualism.

2. What is the underlying purpose of rituals governing eating, drinking, and social conduct?

3. Should we continue to campaign to restore the "traditional" Sunday?

4. Write a short essay in praise of self-restraint.

5. Does St Paul advocate Church unity at all costs?

The Eighteenth Sunday after Trinity

1. Describe the moral threats posed by "the world, the flesh and the devil".

2. Can moral acts be ranked and why would we want to rank them?

3. Is fear a legitimate motive for doing good?

4. Discuss the tensions between the teachings of Jesus and Paul in the way they view unethical behaviour.

5. Why is the response to the ecological crisis veering towards imposed rather than voluntary solutions?

The Nineteenth Sunday after Trinity

1. To what extent is the opening proposition in the Collect a paradox or a symbiosis?

2. What can we learn from divine love about human love and vice versa?

3. How far is the liturgy and practice of the Church systematic and/or accidental?

4. Is it true that religious believers behave better than non-believers and does this matter?

5. Tell the story of the healing from the perspective of the sick man.

The Twentieth Sunday after Trinity

1. Is it legitimate and/or helpful to rank texts such as parables as less or more important than each other?

2. What do you understand by the idea that the good and bad shall equally enter the Kingdom without any questions being asked?

3. Discuss the case of the diner who lacked a wedding garment.

4. Explain the concept of Christ's Kingdom in simple,

jargon-free language.

5. Discuss the merits and drawbacks of apocalyptic literature.

The Twenty-First Sunday after Trinity

1. How clear was the dichotomy between the early Christian and Roman moral and spiritual outlooks?

2. How has the Greek idea of Catharsis evolved into a contemporary psychological tool?

3. Is there a fundamental incompatibility between faith and medicine?

4. What is the purpose of Services of Healing?

5. Would you still fight for the military metaphor?

The Twenty-Second Sunday after Trinity

1. What is your reading of the parable of the master and servant?

2. How would you distinguish good works from duty?

3. To what extent does secular government make up for our collective and individual shortcomings?

4. What inspired Communism and why did it largely fail?

5. Why do most of us despise politicians and steer clear of active participation in politics?

The Twenty-Third Sunday after Trinity

1. What does Genesis mean when it says that God found creation to be "good"?

2. How do you account for the persistence of Gnostic tendencies within Christianity?

3. Is politics an honourable profession and, if not, how would you improve it?

4. What are the pros and cons of disestablishing the Church of England?

5. How do you understand the maxim "render unto Caesar" in the context of debates about ethical legislation?

The Twenty-Fourth Sunday after Trinity

1. Is sickness a useful metaphor for thinking of sin?

2. What is the case for allowing the Sacrament of Reconciliation to fall into disuse and the case for reviving it?

3. Is sin a way of encapsulating what we do or the consequences of what we do?

4. Consider a balance sheet and varying distance as two ways of thinking about sin.

5. Write a dialogue between the woman with the haemorrhage and the young girl after their cures.

The Twenty-Fifth Sunday after Trinity

1. Describe Jeremiah's turbulent relationship with the Judean monarchy.

2. How far is the feeding of the 5,000 an attempt to depict the Kingdom?

3. Has your journey from advent to the end of the Church year been different from previous years?

4. What events in Church and state have affected your view of salvation?

5. Has the Kingdom come or must we go to it after death?

Saint Andrew's Day

1. Trace the traditionally assigned journeys of Andrew.

2. Describe the life and letters of Polycarp and Ignatius of Antioch.

3. From a theological rather than a tactical standpoint, discuss the merits of direct speech and the softened formulae of diplomacy.

4. Discuss static and dynamic models of theology.

5. Should Scotland have a patron saint from Scotland?

Saint Thomas the Apostle

1. Set the doubts of Thomas in the context of the four Resurrection accounts.

2. What do we mean by simple faith?

3. Suggest ways of striking a balance between mystery and rationality, between Mythos and Logos.

4. Think of famous people who have been characterised (or caricatured) as the result of one alleged or actual miscalculation, error of judgment or misrepresentation.

5. How do we resolve the circularity that the Bible is the Word of God because it says so?

The Conversion of Saint Paul

1. Are there any significant differences between the three accounts of Paul's conversion?

2. Discuss the concept of Paul as the thirteenth Apostle.

3. Why do some Christians find Paul's theology more attractive than the teaching of Jesus?

4. To what extent is Christianity a Pauline creation?

5. Choose a letter of Paul and write

a letter to which it is the reply.

The Presentation of Christ in The Temple

1. Was the Reformation reaction to Mary justified?

2. How well do the themes of purification and presentation fit together?

3. How useful is Mary as a halfway house between God and humanity?

4. How relevant is Mary to the plight of contemporary lone parents?

5. Consider Mary as a feminist icon.

Saint Matthias's Day

1. Does Judas receive a fair deal from the Gospels?

2. Why are we so anxious to establish individual culpability for mismanagement and crime?

3. What is the link between our political behaviour and the life chances of individual people?

4. Recall an incident in your life which almost happened and which might have changed it forever.

5. As the metaphor of card games is somewhat crude, think of some other ways of explaining the uncertainty of life.

The Annunciation of The Blessed Virgin Mary

1. Is the virgin birth a necessary precursor to the incarnation?

2. In what way was Mary acting on behalf of humanity when she accepted God's commission?

3. Consider the accounts of the relationship between Mary and her son.

4. How important are the

doctrines of the Immaculate Conception and the Assumption of Our Lady into heaven?

5. Outline recent developments in Anglican/Roman Catholic dialogue about Mary through the ARCIC process.

Saint Mark's Day

1. Does it matter when and for whom Mark wrote his Gospel?

2. Why do you think Mark emphasised the secrecy of Jesus' mission?

3. Consider Mark's passion narrative (14–15) as a film script.

4. How useful is the metaphor of the vine in John 15 for a contemporary audience?

5. Does it matter if there is no strong connection between Mark and Venice?

Saint Philip and Saint James's Day

1. What are the salient features of the Epistle of James?

2. How would you explain the saying of Jesus that "in my Father's house there are many mansions"?

3. In what way is doctrine a question rather than an answer?

4. What is the proper relationship between experience and doctrine?

5. Elaborate on Jesus' saying that he is, "the way, the truth and the life".

Saint Barnabas the Apostle

1. Consider the incidents involving Paul and John Mark.

2. What did it mean to be a Christian in Antioch?

3. Describe the history of one of the great Evangelical revivals.

4. Can religion become addictive?

5. Imagine the autobiography of Barnabas.

Saint John Baptist's Day

1. Discuss the relationship between Jesus and John.

2. In what way did Isaiah "foretell" the coming of John and then Jesus?

3. Prepare a meditation on the *Venite.*

4. What characteristics did John share with his predecessor Prophets and with Jesus for whom he prepared the ground?

5. How would a person like John be received in today's church?

Saint Peter's Day

1. What is the Church of which Peter is the foundation?

2. Consider the relationship between Saint Peter and Saint Paul.

3. What is a bishop?

4. How different would the Church be if bishops saw themselves cast in Peter's mould?

5. Do we have too many or too few Bishops?

Saint James the Apostle

1. Given that they made sacrifices for Jesus that most of us would not make, how unreasonable was the request of the Zebedees to flank Jesus in heaven?

2. How can we work out what we should give to the poor?

3. What do you understand by Jesus' statement that sinners will find an easy passage to heaven?

4. In view of its pilgrimage status, does it matter that it is highly unlikely

that James ever travelled to Spain?

5. Explore the concept of pilgrimage.

Saint Bartholemew the Apostle

1. Bearing in mind the "U" shape from calling to martyrdom, can you graphically depict the spiritual life in any other ways?

2. Do the Bartholemew and Nathaniel stories fit together?

3. Consider different aspects of self-doubt and self-confidence.

4. Consider the idea of God as an ontology package and a dialogue process.

5. Think of your own spiritual nadir or that of one of the saints.

Saint Matthew the Apostle

1. Trace the history of anti-Semitism from Matthew to Hitler and beyond.

2. Describe changing views of the dating of the Gospels in the twentieth century.

3. In what ways is Matthew the "Gospel of the Church"?

4. What are the links between Old Testament Wisdom Literature and Jesus?

5. Reflect on the Fool in *King Lear*.

Saint Michael and All Angels

1. Trace the theology of angels.

2. What is the significance of the "war in heaven" and has it been misunderstood?

3. Explore Jewish and Christian interpretations of Genesis 3.

4. Is humanity "above" or "below" angels?

5. Make a prize collection of jokes about heaven.

Saint Luke the Evangelist

1. Discuss the unique historical contribution of Luke/Acts.

2. How unique is Luke's interest in the poor and in women?

3. Without Luke, what is left of the infant Jesus?

4. Without Luke, what do we know of the birth and early development of Christianity?

5. Should religion and politics mix?

Saint Simon and Saint Jude, Apostles

1. Consider the three antitheses in Jude between: the cities of the plain and Abraham's family, Pharaoh and Moses, and the good and wicked angels.

2. If we cannot imagine dying for a doctrine, why are we so tenacious in arguing about doctrine?

3. Is the Spirit's manifestation in the gift of tongues a special gift for a special time or should we be alive to it now?

4. What are the particular perils of being an established Church?

5. Is there any such thing as a lost cause?

All Saints' Day

1. Discuss the importance of the Book of Revelation as an animator of the Christian vision.

2. What is a saint and who qualifies for the designation?

3. Discuss ideas of morality and sanctity.

4. Who is your favourite saint and why?

5. Re-write the Beatitudes for today's Church.